# Beautiful Bad Girl

# The Vicki Morgan Story

## gordon basichis

Santa Barbara Press
1985

For Bugs.

ACKNOWLEDGEMENTS
My thanks to Marcia Basichis, Roy Brady,
Dorothy Thompson Balsis, Lois Shearer, and
Jonathan Beaty for all their assistance.
To Casey, Joe, Gavin, Marco, Harris, Jules,
Brian, Phillip, Susan, Marty, Ruth, and Robin
for all their support and understanding.
And special thanks to George, Jim, and Dorothy
for their courage and their impeccable taste.

ISBN: 0-915643-14-6

Cover design by Mary Schlesinger
Design by Jim Cook
Typography by Cook/Sundstrom Associates
SANTA BARBARA, CALIFORNIA

Library of Congress Cataloging-in-Publication Data

Basichis, Gordon Allen.
    Beautiful bad girl.

    1. Morgan, Victoria Lynn, 1953-1983.  2. Bloomingdale,
Alfred (Alfred S.), 1916-1982.  3. Mistresses--California
--Biography.  I. Title.
HQ806.B38  1985        306.7'36'0924 [B]        85-26155
ISBN 0-915643-14-6

Published by
SANTA BARBARA PRESS
1129 State Street
Santa Barbara, California 93101

BEAUTIFUL BAD GIRL

I KNEW VICKI MORGAN perhaps better than anyone else ever had. During the nine months prior to her death, we spent hours talking about her life, her relationship with Alfred Bloomingdale, what had happened, and why. It was as painful as it was funny, and often mesmerizing. For this was no tale of a bubble-headed cupcake and the lecherous old man who kept her. This was a story filled with power, intrigue and obsession.

As a young girl, Vicki Morgan was determined to escape the stifling boredom of her working class surroundings. She was a genuine romantic, a blue-jeaned rebel, a rock and roll tomboy who dropped out of high school to give birth to her illegitimate child. She was exceptionally pretty, shrewd, and had a high degree of native intelligence. She was imbued with a keen sense of wit and a special charm that attracted men and drove them crazy...rich and powerful men who pandered to her every whim and material desire, while leaving her emotionally stranded as they ordained the course of her early destruction. At one time Vicki was sure she had it all, but in the end she discovered she had nothing.

Vicki Morgan may be typical of many young girls who fall victim to the trap of greed and exploitation. She too is part of a terrible legacy, a tough and perplexing heritage of emotional servitude and class distinction. She, like too many others, lived beyond her years and died before her time. It's a pity that so few understand the causes and effects of this terrible syndrome.

Where others, like Dorothy Stratten, Colleen Applegate and Edie Sedgewick, had little insight into their troubled lives and became passive victims, Vicki lived her life to the fullest and managed to last for nearly thirty-one years, telling me before she died, her own true story.

From Vicki Morgan I learned a great deal. It was hard not to, since no other person I had ever met lived the way she had. Her life as a mistress was more than a job; it was a tremendous adventure, a passionate epic with raw perspective into the hearts and minds of international society, its corporate rulers and political leaders as told by the one outsider who, through an act of fate, got close enough to see it all. Consequently, she was deemed a threat to the established order that had tried to suppress her and continues to try to this day.

As the writer and survivor of what will soon be two full years of calamity and hell, I've spent a lot of time alone pondering this story. I think about Vicki, her murder, and what has since happened to me. Little did I know, when I first met Vicki in November of 1982, that her story would become my story as time slalomed through a volatile sequence of the oddest circumstances. Today, upon reflection, I am grateful for the experience.

# 1

VICKI MORGAN'S STORY is a classic American tragedy. She was the runaway rebel from middle-America who got in over her head with rich and powerful people. A tall, willowy, long-legged ashen-blond, she was basically a good kid who had the face of a beautiful model and the guts of a soldier of fortune. Yet, throughout her life, she struggled with insecurity, pushing hard against enveloping fears. She walked on the edge and searched for adventure, her troubled psyche delicately balanced on a tightrope of different personas. With the backing of Alfred Bloomingdale she could push it to the limit, live in grandeur and style. She came to think of herself as a conventional being, a Republican no less, beguiled by the irony of the dual roles she played.

Vicki was smart and she knew it, but she was inhibited by her lack of formal education, having dropped out of high school at the end of tenth grade. Vicki was a dreamer, a jaded romantic who, through much of her life, netted between a quarter- and a half-million dollars a year. It was easy come, easy go, and she spent her money lavishly and foolishly, an easy mark for friends and strangers. Vicki Morgan had lived in a fairy tale and died in a nightmare. When the end came, her money and friends were gone.

Vicki and I were first brought together by Michael Gruskoff, a mutual friend of ours, for whom I was writing a screenplay. Mike, a noted movie producer and former agent, had lived with Vicki for a year or two in the middle seventies, and she had called him requesting his help. She wanted to write a book to set the record straight. What was unknown to me was that he'd already given Vicki the names of other writers to get in touch with. She met with several, but apparently she wasn't satisfied, and Michael reluctantly suggested me.

"Gordon's the best of the writers I sent you," he had told his former girlfriend. "He can write in his sleep. But he's trouble, and I don't think the two of you would get along."

Comments like Michael's were like a red flag, a virtual challenge to Vicki Morgan. He knew it and she knew it. I was the only one who for months wasn't sure what was going on. I was ignorant of their rivalry, spawned from their disjointed romance, which had occurred nearly eight years before.

"Would you be interested in writing the book about Vicki Morgan?" he had asked rather casually one Sunday, when my wife Marcia and I had stopped by his house for a visit. It was a surprising suggestion coming from Gruskoff. Through MGM, he had optioned the film rights on my novel, *Constant Travellers,* and I'd been assigned to write the script. Michael feared I wouldn't take it seriously and tried his best to govern my time. He prodded and probed and insisted I wasn't working hard enough. Eventually we started to fight.

Now, despite a rather acerbic exchange of opinions just two weeks prior, Michael was turning me on to one of the greatest scandals of the decade. I didn't understand his motivations for putting us together. Was he doing this as a mutual favor, or as a means of getting me out of his way?

I had reasons to be dubious. For one thing, I was soured by all the gossip. Vicki and Alfred had been the talk of the town since early July, when she filed her palimony suit against Bloomingdale, retaining the notorious Marvin Mitchelson as her lawyer. Demanding some $5 million in damages, she had exposed the more tawdry aspects of their twelve-year relationship, including the sado-masochistic practices of this scion of American society and intimate advisor to Ronald Reagan. If there was any depth to Vicki Morgan's story, it would be difficult to prove, since few would ever bother to comprehend anything beyond the stereotypical explanations for the motives of Alfred and Vicki. After all, in a story like this there was no room for depth and complexity, not among those selected few, the true purveyors of the marketplace, whose special talent was turning subjects like this one into unmitigated trash.

"It has to be more than some cheap, sensationalistic story," I told Mike Gruskoff. "And she'd have to agree on no publicity. If it's anything at all, it'll be a long, hard process, and I'd want to get it done first, before it's announced in the Hollywood trades."

Gruskoff looked at me and fired his special kind of grin, like he knew something that I didn't.

"What is it?" I asked, hoping to entice him to give up what he was thinking, wondering what old, magnanimous Mike had his eye on, be it the film script, the book, or one more pleasant night with Vicki. He just shrugged and shook his full head of whitish-gray hair. I should have known by the look in his eye that things could go wrong in a hurry. Knowing Michael, he would love it when they did.

"I'll call her," said Michael, "and give her your number. Then she can get in touch with you." He paused, stared at me for effect. "I don't want to be in it. Keep my name clear."

"You don't want anything? Not even the film rights?"

"No. It's a gift. You and she can work out the arrangements."

So there I was on a clear November night, driving up Beverly Estates Drive, the winding road that led to Tower Grove Drive at the rim of Benedict Canyon. I was curious, but not optimistic, even though I had liked what I heard on the telephone. Vicki Morgan sounded like no dummy. She'd been direct and articulate when she'd spoken to me. I was intrigued, and felt sympathetic for what I discerned were her true affections for Alfred, but was afraid any vestige of those affections had probably been steamrolled by the press.It could be argued that she had asked for it, if not deserved it, by claiming to have "cured the Marquis de Sade Complex" of a member of Reagan's kitchen cabinet. What had made her do that? I wondered. What were the circumstances that made her come forth with such damning information on one of the most prominent men in the country? And why had his family and associates let her do it? Why hadn't she been paid off or shut up?

I stepped out of my car and thought it over before approaching the white stucco house, numbered 1611 Tower Grove Drive. Earlier in the evening I had considered the ramifications of going to Vicki's place, surveillance and such being what it is today. But what the hell? I was an ambitious fellow, street-wise and city bred. I was restless, and for sometime I had been looking for a challenging opportunity to which I could fully commit myself. And if this was it, despite all the furor and possible danger, I was cocky enough to think I could get away with it.

I looked up at the stars, the deep black sky, and the silhouettes of brush and houses perched on the rim of the canyon. But I'm a realist as well. I also looked for unmarked sedans. A minute passed before the door swung open and a woman appeared, separated from me by the expensive filigree on the wrought iron gate. It was Mary Sangre, who I would later learn had been Vicki's companion for the past year or so. She stared at me for an instant, and then looked away as she opened the gate.

"Vicki'll be out in a moment," she assured me before retreating down the hallway.

I stepped into the living room and looked around, hoping to glimpse Vicki's character through her taste in color and decoration. I looked into the steel and smoked glass wall unit, its lights spotting, among other things, a sculpture of a quartz crystal hand reaching outward from a greenish base. There were different plates, objets d'art and, oddly, Alfred Bloomingdale's boy scout medallion. His prestigious rank of Eagle Scout was preserved forever in its acrylic lucite casing.

I advanced to the windows, with their silver, vertical blinds half opened for a view of Los Angeles, the lighted grids of city blocks flickering in the distance below. The living room was arranged in predominant shades of black, white and gray, and the furniture was essentially modern. Essentially I thought, but not actually. The down, custom sofas, and the milky glass on the tulip floor lamps were more reminiscent of a Hollywood matron in quest of "hip" than they were of a younger person. The prodigious bric-a-brac, the knick-knacks and the overkill of coasters and ashtrays denoted to me a lonely old woman who passed the time reading *Architectural Digest*. Matriarchal modern was how the furnishings could best be described. I wondered, catching sight of the tall, stainless steel flamingo hiding among the potted plants, where was the deadly vamp?

When Vicki entered the living room, the first thing that struck me was her height. No one had ever called it to my attention. At five-foot-ten she was tall enough to look right into my face when she spoke to me. My being over six feet tall meant nothing to her in terms of intimidation. She stood erect, proud of her height and aware of its potential advantage, especially on shorter men. Despite her troubles, she still had the basic instincts for controlling a situation. It was part of her countenance, a reflection of money and power.

By the time she said, "Hello, I'm Vicki Morgan," I was beginning to get the picture. With a firm grip she shook my hand. Her almond green eyes flashed, scrutinizing mine for a negative reflex. This woman didn't get where she'd been on her looks alone. Something was happening behind those eyes. Maybe even a thing called "life." What a pleasant irony, I thought as I introduced myself. She gestured for me to sit down.

"On the phone you told me you believed I'd been in love with Alfred. No other writer ever said that before. Do you really believe it?"

I took my time before I answered, although I knew exactly what I'd say. Here she sat with her ash-blond hair falling straight past her shoulders, her face lightly touched with makeup, and a trace of freckles serving as flattering evidence of her Irish background. She was dressed in a cashmere sweater and a pair of faded blue jeans. Indian moccasins covered her feet. She seemed very young to me, more like a kid than I expected. This was not the arrogant, brittle beauty in the photograph of legend. She was fresh-faced, almost wholesome, more like the pretty girl from Main Street, America, than the tainted, painted strumpet she'd been made out to be. She had looks, guts, brains and the posture of a wholesome personality. What had gone wrong with such a fabulous composition that had caused her downfall?

I was surprised by the contrast between the going gossip and my first impressions of Vicki Morgan. If this woman was all that she was cracked up to be, the model *femme fatale*, a coven of one in the witchcraft of greed and debauchery, then there was no way a single, dying old man, or for that matter, a team of dying old men, would ever keep her from getting whatever she thought she wanted from life. Not when there were legions of live, healthy men who'd give anything for a girl like Vicki. By all rights, she shouldn't have to worry a day in her life. Unless of course, she had been in love with that one old man — Alfred Bloomingdale. It had happened before, I realized. Old movies are full of such noble ideas. I could see immediately where Vicki Morgan was susceptible to such concepts of classical romance. Could it be like they say at the end of the movie, "She blew it because of the guy"?

"I know you loved him," I said finally. "For one thing, I can tell by the way you used his name on the phone. You say Alfred, not Al, or any cute little nicknames. But it's not what you say, necessarily, it's the tone behind it. I hear the familiarity, the comfort it gives you."

"We were together for almost thirteen years," she blurted out. "He loved me and I loved him like no other man in my life. And it wasn't all seamy, believe it or not. I looked after him. I took care of him. My problem was that I forgot to look after myself."

I had paid special attention to her tone of voice, its cadence and inflection. The oddity was so apparent it was hard not to be curious. Despite her inherent sultriness, she spoke and gestured like an older woman. The way she shook her head, waved her arms around, and even laughed reminded me of my grandmother, or someone's widowed aunt. All we needed were some nifty floral slipcovers, lace doilies and a lavender sachet to give it that special flavor. What did the others think, the writers, strangers and friends who sat down to talk with her? Had they seen anything odd? What was it like to be a young girl living among geriatrics? You had to be a fool not to realize Bloomingdale's impact on Vicki Morgan. To be the child and the dowager at the same time, in the same body, is a difficult maneuver. Alfred, I could see, had made her into a lady—his lady—a coltish, sexy teenager, who was conversely embellished with old-world manners and charm. Having captured her when she was just a baby of seventeen, he'd taught her some of what he knew, but she took the rest of it from there. When alive, he lavished her with money and protection, but left her unprotected when he died nearly thirteen years later.

She talked and I talked, and the hours passed by unnoticed. I had not expected her to open up so readily, nor had I expected to remain so long in her company. I'd figured I'd spend only a couple hours listening to my share of the trials and tribulations of Vicki Morgan. But as the night passed, I began to understand her and see that special aura that makes legends out of certain people. I also understood that legends can be spawned from tragedy, and those who are part of it have little control of their fate.

As I spoke with Vicki that first night, I saw the wheels turning, her eyes burning with suspicion as she watched me for any signs of deception. Still, she rambled on, rummaging her way through her personal history like a hobo at the city dump. She had no idea where to begin her story, and stammered in a desperate search for form and continuity. She was frustrated and confused, frightened and vulnerable. She was determined to protect herself from additional emotional injury. Yet she was able to put her fears and doubts aside and bear down on her memories, adding life and character to the things she had to say.

Vicki's profession was conversation. She was used to talking in marathon sessions. She had mastered the technique of wearing people down by engaging them in lengthy dialogues, so words were repeated and subjects recycled until exhaustion took hold and any lies and ill intentions were finally revealed. Then she had them, ensnared by contradiction, fearful of her rejection. This, I suspected, was how she often got her way.

Vicki had once been a tomboy, and some elements still remained. It made her funny and sassy and more complex. She was aware of herself as the renegade and used such traits to her advantage. It helped her project herself as willful and strong. She had learned to act tough while still a baby, and years of practice had taught her to meld her tough kid's persona with her more worldly, feminine charms. She bobbed her head and rolled her shoulders, her boyishness accented by her height and slender frame. When she was less absorbed with being the lady, she'd speak earnestly, allowing the cigarette to dangle from her sensuous lips. She'd been the leader of the teenaged bad guys, a real wise-ass with standards for men to live up to. Too bad if you destroyed yourself trying to pass her test.

"To most people I'm the witch, the whore, someone to be afraid of. I intimidate the men and threaten the women. And yet so few have any idea what it's been like for me. Not as simple or as easy as it seems. Believe me, Gordon," she urged, her eyes widening, her head shaking as cigarette smoke curled from her mouth. "It's all kinda funny in a sad sorta way. I'm really somebody who nobody knows anything about."

# 2

FOR THE NEXT five days I didn't hear a thing from Vicki
Morgan. We had agreed we'd reached no conclusion at our
first meeting, except that writing this book would be a long
and arduous process, and not something to be taken lightly.
But I knew we had reached an understanding. It was too
apparent, the exchanges came too easily. The chemistry
was right; she was aware of my sympathies. I believed she
had been subjected to an injustice, having been openly
ridiculed and denied compensation. She deserved something, I believed, after a dozen years of companionship.

"There will be times when you'll hate me," she'd said that
night. "I'm not easy, especially with something like this. I
mean, I never dreamed I'd be telling my life story. Especially to a man, no less."

I'd agreed, in fact, that she had the potential to be a
genuine pain-in-the-ass. We both laughed at my observation.

"She's more than a full-time job," advised someone who
knew her.

I hadn't argued, not after meeting her, hearing her tell
me about the men in her life. Some were dead and the rest
were still recovering from their romantic experience. Perhaps there was an exception here and there. I didn't want to
think she was pitching a shutout, that she was as dangerous
as she first appeared. But I was now committed to the idea
of the book and even eager, regardless of the obvious potential for danger, be it from Vicki or those who feared what

she might have to say. In the meantime, I waited for her call.

After several days it came. Now that we were face to face she let me know the truth. "You shook me up the other night," she admitted, when we met at her house for the second time. On the telephone she had copped a plea when I'd asked why I hadn't heard from her. She said only that she'd been busy and unable to get in touch.

"I started thinking," she continued, "about all the things you were asking me. Why don't I have any money? What made me take Alfred's offer in the first place? I thought about what you said, that the only thing I did wrong was not to save any cash. That I was feeling guilty for what I did with my life. Somehow it all caught up to me. For three days I barely slept."

"So what did you come up with?"

"I want to write this book, but the thought of it just scares the hell outta me. It's so demanding...especially for me. I'm a high-school dropout. I read, mind you, but I've never written more than a letter."

"You're a talker, with a natural sense for story."

"You think it'll come pretty easily?"

I shook my head. "It'll never be easy. So if it's me you intend to write it with then you better be prepared for the work involved. It's harder than you can imagine."

"Gordon, I know how hard it is. People are scared of me. Or what would happen if they had anything to do with selling my book. I had some of the best agents in town get in touch with me. A couple even flew in from New York, just to meet over lunch. The William Morris Agency wanted to handle my entire package. There've been others. Then something frightens them, and they back off."

"All of them? You mean they don't like money?"

"It's not that. They know they can make a fortune off my story. It's Betsy and her friends that no one wants to go up against. They know everyone in power."

19

"I'll remember. Believe me."

"Gerald Ford supposedly called someone high up in the William Morris Agency and told him they'd better not sign me."

"How do you know that's true?"

"A friend, Marvin Pancoast, told me. He works there."

"You're telling me that people are trying to suppress this book, but at the same time you don't believe there's a threat to your life? You do remember what I asked you? When we first sat down to talk? Are we gonna get killed for this, or what?"

"Oh...it's nothing like that," she tried to assure me. I don't know any big secrets, just little ones here and there. They're not worth killing us over. Don't worry, at least half the people in Washington know what I know."

She smiled at me. "I guess I know some things about some people though. But if you want to know the truth," she went on, "I'm sorry I didn't pay closer attention. I'll have to think about who did what, and where they did it. There was a whole lot going on at the time."

Alfred wasn't around anymore, and Vicki still had trouble believing it. In conversation she'd forget herself and speak of him as if he was still alive. There was no pretense, no whimsical fantasy, she simply forgot that he was dead. She would talk about him with disturbing familiarity, providing me with a broad-based overview of the complexities of her story.

Vicki, I came to learn, was Alfred's creation. In many ways he was good for her and in others he was the cause of her downfall. While she was still a kid, he so shaped her perspective that she could never accept another point of view. Whenever she tried to change her lifestyle, he was there to distract her. He ruined her marriages and destroyed her relationships. He made her his mistress and trained her to sit by the phone and wait for his call. At night he was noticeably absent from her life, as he attended with his wife Betsy the social and political functions that a couple with their status was obligated to attend. On those restless nights, Vicki went out and often got into trouble. Eventually, she claimed, she realized she was trapped and being driven insane. But during the twelve years they spent together, they shared a relationship so unique and so complex it approaches the surreal. It was a love fraught with contradiction, provoking obsessions and pathological jealousies. Ultimately, it would kill them both.

When speaking to me about herself during those early sessions, her voice was filled with sadness and irony. "I'm one of the world's greatest shoppers," she declared. "I can tell you what's where, and what you have to pay to get it. I know Rodeo Drive and all the department stores like the back of my hand.

"I used to make U-turns in the middle of Rodeo Drive because I spotted something, no...thought I spotted something in a window. Even though I didn't need a damn thing more. I have clothes in my closets with the price tags still on them. Brand new. Never worn. Just something for me to do.

"It got so crazy that I used to call the stores and buy over the phone. I bought refrigerators, gas ranges sight unseen. I used to tell them to send me the most expensive one. No one had ever told me that the most expensive is not always the best. I figured...hell, if it's more money it has to be better quality. I'm really naive in many ways. It's like yesterday I was seventeen and woke up to find I was thirty years old."

Vicki took a deep breath as she stared inquisitively in my direction. "You want to know what I did for the last ten years? That's it. I went shopping with Alfred's money."

"And now you want to write a book," I interjected.

She flicked her ashes and smiled at me. "I can see it already. You're as tough and selfish as I am. But you're the one who understands me, who knows what I'm talking about. Wouldn't it figure it would come down to someone like you?"

"I'd never be as dumb to think of myself as your very first choice. What happened anyway? You would think you would have throngs of writers and agents driving up here in buses. All the silence and emptiness makes me wonder why I'm the only one here in the audience."

. She grew more serious as she hesitated and let me wait for her reply. "Gordon, I told you before...I have one helluva story to tell. I was the object, alright. Men used to fight over me. I was the prize, honey. I was a symbol of power and status. And I was Alfred's mistress. That's what kept me entertained. Kept Alfred on his toes. He knew not to push me too far."

"What about the other guys?"

She smiled and nodded, took a long drag on her cigarette before she answered me. Vicki was enjoying herself, feeling more loose. "Some of the other guys were serious about winning me over. And the rest were assholes who had no business getting in over their heads."

"Somehow I get the feeling that you may have talked a few into getting in over their heads."

"I suppose I did. I didn't say I wasn't neurotic. Pretty girls usually are neurotic. No one's more insecure than a pretty girl. You're always afraid of losing your looks."

Vicki was always considered a stunning beauty. When she was a child growing up in Montclair, California, a dusty rural suburb, an hour's drive to the east of Los Angeles, people would praise her looks. Constance Laney, Vicki's mother, was well aware of her pretty daughter and pushed her into modeling jobs. Vicki was hired occasionally for print-ads and catalogues. According to Vicki, she was quite a charmer, with myriad expressions and the ability to portray varying emotions. But there were sudden shifts in

Vicki's personality which caused her mother great consternation. Vicki was rebellious and restless, with little regard for the conservative standards her mother had hoped to instill in her. Her mother would attempt to discipline Vicki by restricting her, prohibiting friends from visiting. She bought a lock for the telephone to prevent her daughter from sneaking any calls. But Vicki turned fifteen in 1966, a year in which social upheaval was endemic to America, particularly in California.

"My mother suffered extremely bad luck with men," Vicki told me. My father, Delbert Morgan, had married her during the war when he was stationed in England. She was the daughter of the caretaker to the Royal Family's country home in Norwich, England. They moved to Colorado Springs, Colorado. That's where I was born, eight years after my older sister Barbara. My father was a bad boy and had left my mother for another woman while I was still in the womb."

Soon after the breakup, Constance moved herself and two children back to England. After two years there, she returned to America, to Colorado, where she married Ralph Laney, and bore two more children, sons Patrick and John. With the future looking brighter, the family moved to California, when Ralph, a tool-and-die maker, was offered a job as foreman in the plant near Montclair. However, several years after his relocation, Ralph Laney was struck by a heart attack in the back seat of the family car, as they were snacking at the local Tastee Freeze. He died several hours later. Unfortunately, his life insurance policy had expired the day before he did.

Early on, Vicki thought of herself as an outcast with a father who expressed his affection by sending a check in the mail. Vicki would lie to her classmates, claiming her father had bought the clothes she was wearing, when in reality, it was just his money and her own good taste. She felt pretty and she was accepted. She was proud to be chosen the best-dressed girl in her high school. Then she discovered she was pregnant, and her world began to fall apart.

Gary Haskell was Vicki's first love and one of the local bad boys. He was nineteen, rebellious and attractive, the perfect match for Vicki Morgan. He was the solitary thrill in a desolate city, and Vicki was in love with him.

"People who are in love, make love," Gary informed her after they had been kissing and petting for nearly two years. Vicki was just thirteen when they had started going steady, and now, at fifteen, she was given the big ultimatum. At first she wouldn't go for it, claiming she'd rather wait until they were married, or pretty close to it. Gary reacted to the news by breaking up with Vicki and taking up with someone else. A few months later he was back. She gave him hell for leaving. He passed it off as her sexual hangups. If she'd just give in and sleep with him, he proposed, then everything would be okay.

This time Vicki went for the deal. She'd had enough of the loneliness of the past few months. Vicki couldn't stand to be alone. If life in Montclair was bad for her, it was ten times worse without Gary. And in time, Vicki discovered that sex was not a dreaded sacrifice as her mother had claimed, but a wonderful venting for the deepest emotions. She was thrilled by the powers of sexual energy, the creative stimulation of everything happening at once. This was love at its best, everlasting and genuine, just like a rock-and-roll song.

Seven months later, Vicki discovered she was pregnant. For three months she ignored the fact that she hadn't had her period. It took a few good bouts with morning sickness to bring reality into focus. These things aren't supposed to happen, not when you're only fifteen and a half years old.

She told Gary one afternoon just after they finished making love. It was still, and the curtains fluttered in the faint breeze as shades of spring were already yielding to the dry heat of summer.

"Gary, we're going to have a baby," she said, and the second the words left her mouth she regretted it. In the stillness of the room, she watched Gary wrinkle his face and stiffen his arms. His body taut, he hovered above her and stared quizzically into her eyes.

"What are you going to do about it?" he wondered, detaching himself from the situation. He could see that she was stunned by his question. He could see the coldness envelop her as she studied him with her green almond eyes.

"What am I going to do about it? Is that what you're asking me after three years? What am I going to do? I'm gonna have to take the responsibility for the whole damn thing, because you want nothing at all to do with it. I can tell by the way you look at me, Gary. Vicki is on her own."

"What will I tell your father?" demanded Constance Laney after Vicki gave her the news. "You know I have to call him."

"I don't care what you tell him or anyone else."

A series of litanies and volumes of epithets garnished this priceless moment. Constance reminded her daughter of her frequent attempts to instill in her the proper discipline. She had turned out the lights in the house and waited half the night in the bushes for Vicki to return from a date...to prevent this very thing from happening. She had been too lenient. She should have paid heed to her instincts and been stricter with Vicki. Now, here she was, she complained, a modest employee stuck as the cashier in the high school cafeteria, divorced, widowed, with four children to support. And now an illegitimate grandchild would be arriving in December.

God had not smiled on Mrs. Laney. He had instilled religious convictions in her which forbade abortion on moral grounds. Vicki had considered abortion, but on that question mother and daughter couldn't begin to see eye to eye. Vicki was shipped off to St. Anne's, a charity home for unwed mothers.

It was 1968. St. Anne's was filled to capacity with pregnant teenagers, and more were on the waiting list. Big stomachs were everywhere in the dormitories, a sign of the times. There were victims of rape, victims of incest. There were girls who had one sexual experience and had gotten pregnant. But most of the girls were there for the same reason as Vicki...the consequence of a single, teenage love affair. In certain ways, if such a thing could be measured, these were the girls who had been hurt the most; they were the ones who were the most confused. For they had loved and been rejected. What had been affection was now neglect, as lovers and families cast them aside to pay for their sins, mainly in the company of nuns and other pregnant girls. It was a time of bitterness and for changing her priorities.

Each girl was assigned a guidance counselor and was required to attend a weekly meeting. Vicki's counselor was a man, a condescending bureaucrat who insisted, at her tender age, that she give up her child for adoption. It was for the best, he repeatedly assured her, citing his years of experience with helping the girls of St. Anne's. He stated his belief that, except on rare occasion, illegitimate children should be given up to a grateful and responsible couple.

"Yeah, sure...uh huh," Vicki would mutter, her eyes focused elsewhere. Not only did this asshole, as Vicki expressed it, fail to understand her personality, but he was sounding more and more like she had little choice in the matter. Well, Vicki decided, this was one time she'd make her own choice. She was tired of being told she was incapable, especially by an ignorant stiff in a worn-out suit, with his intimated threats and constant reminders of the fact that, after its birth, her child would be taken from her for thirty days, so that she could reach the "proper decision." She was unrelenting, determined to keep her child.

It was only after she had given birth to her baby that Vicki heard from her father in Texas. He didn't visit or call, he merely sent her a letter. In neat and legible script he urged her to give up the child for adoption and move to another town, so the disgrace wouldn't haunt her forever. Having read the letter, Vicki tore it to pieces. She cried for hours. The message was clear. She was alone in the world, left to her own devices. When her son Todd was born in December, they did in fact take him away for the thirty-day period. When they returned a month later to ask what she had finally decided, Vicki's answer was still the same. She would raise the boy herself, and not give him up for adoption.

"He's my son," she told them. "Mine. And no one's gonna take him away from me."

"What is the father's surname?" asked the nurse. "To be recorded on the birth certificate."

"Morgan," Vicki replied. "His name is Todd Morgan."

"No, you don't understand," the nurse started to explain. And then she looked at Vicki, the burning eyes, the defiant posture. "People don't. . ." she tried but was interrupted.

"People don't what?" Vicki demanded. "I told you his last name is Morgan, and that's what you write down."

Vicki and Todd returned together to her mother's house. Constance, who was embarrassed by her sixteen-year-old daughter's unwed status, laid down more stringent rules. These too would be ignored. Vicki was wary of the arrangements her mother made when it came to raising Todd. Constance wished to assume the everyday responsibility for his rearing. And when people didn't know otherwise, Mrs. Laney implied that it was her child and not Vicki's. Constance, in the domestic hierarchy, was to be referred to as Mom, and Vicki was to be called none other than Mommy. At best, the situation was untenable; at worst, it was the beginning of an all-out war.

With Constance taking control of the baby, Vicki stayed away from the house. She went out with the local boys. She dated openly, ignoring her mother's protests. She dealt drugs and fooled around. Hardened by her experiences, she became the leader of the pack, which still included Gary Haskell. She gave them direction. She challenged and she taunted. One time she instigated a collective run-away plan, and she and her friends, with guns, drugs, and whatever money they could lay their hands on, stole a car and made a dash for the California state line. Before they reached it, they were apprehended by the police, returned home, and sentenced to more drudgery in the town of Montclair.

Vicki was determined. It was time to make her escape. The creeping, gnawing fear of entrapment led Vicki finally to tell her mother she was moving to Los Angeles and would be sharing an apartment with her girlfriend Emmy.

Mrs. Laney had a fit. A terrible battle erupted between Mom and Mommy, as various challenges and familiar accusations were hurled back and forth inside the walls of Mrs. Laney's modest home.

"You lack responsibility," her mother ranted. "You hussy! You're running out on your son!"

"I have to build something for me and Todd. And I can't do it here. Don't you see that?"

Her mother would hear none of it. She threatened to file for custody and retain custody of Todd forever. But despite the threats, Vicki struck out for Los Angeles. She could no longer tolerate the stagnation. She felt like she was dying a slow death of discontent, working sporadically at menial labor while dreaming big dreams that she felt would never happen. Not here. Not like this. Sure they told her that this was the land of opportunity. But that was only part of the story. You had to be in the right place at the right time. Land of opportunity or not, fortune was where you found it. Success was how you made it. There were no true patterns or rigid standards...just as long as you got to the top. Nothing for something was a sucker's rate of exchange.

Vicki was tired of getting nothing. She was drained and exhausted, confronted by her worst fears. There was no denying it. She'd made a mistake and had been abandoned. She was alone, on her own, with nothing but her looks and wits to see her through. She'd find a way to make it. She knew she couldn't miss.

# 3

VICKI AND I had been meeting almost every night in November and now December was drawing near. Once again Vicki would have to move, because she could no longer afford the two thousand dollars a month she was paying for rent. With the help of her friend and live-in companion, Mary Sangre, she leased a condominium over the hill in North Hollywood, conveniently located across the street from Mary's new apartment. For a condo, it was decent, with three bedrooms, three baths, and a view of the concrete banks of the Los Angeles River. However, it was not up to the standards Vicki had grown accustomed to during the years of her relationship with Alfred Blooming-dale. This was a step down, and was for Vicki a grudging acknowledgement of retreat. It would be a spot from which to work and dream and plan for the day she'd once again be back on top. Meanwhile, since there was no adequate space for three dogs—she'd once owned five—Vicki was forced to give away the white German Shepherd and the aging Shih-Tzu. Katie, the burnished Doberman, was kept for company and protection.

"After all those years with Alfred, you'd think I would've finally bought a house," she lamented. "You know, I must've looked at thousands of places. Every major realtor on the west side of town knew me. They believed I was the daughter of a Texas millionaire." She laughed, her thoughts momentarily lost in the past. "I'm quite sure by now they all know the story. How could they miss it?"

She turned and looked me in the eyes, studied me carefully for signs of disapproval. I stared back and said nothing, waiting for her to go on. She sensed it and was embarrassed by my silence. She was self-conscious about being examined, or pressed for her deeper perspectives. But I was her last hope and she knew it. Earlier, as the light-hearted adventuress, she had volunteered the minimum needed to charm and to captivate. The rest she had kept inside, where, despite what she did to distract herself, her self-awareness had expanded chaotically and ultimately caused her emotional breakdown. Vicki couldn't live with what she had learned, and had done her best to keep the lid on. At one time it had meant taking fifteen to twenty Valiums a day.

"Anyway...I never did buy a house," Vicki went on, after putting her thoughts into focus. "I was like some wealthy gypsy, moving around the town. I rented one place after another, either in between marriages or whenever I got bored and wanted to try on a different lifestyle for size. Now I have to move again and it's killing me. To the Valley yet. I used to swear I'd never live in the Valley. Things like that were a matter of pride. Status. That's the word. Status. What was once all so goddamned important is now a visual blur. Things. So many things I've had. Different living room sets, bedroom sets, clothes, and automobiles. Now, none of this shit means a thing to me. I'd love to walk out and leave everything right where it is."

"You don't really mean it," I prodded.

Her eyes widened. "Don't I? I wish I had the guts."

Come December 7, Vicki moved for the final time in her life. Her half-brother Patrick leased a truck from somewhere and had recruited several of his friends. Marvin Pancoast was also there to assist, along with one of his pals and Mary Sangre. Mary, resenting me, kept to herself in an alcove to the rear of the house. I had called Gavin Murrell, a friend of mine and the general supervisor of a construction firm, and asked if there were any laborers who would work that Saturday.

"I'll see what I can do," he said.

He worked wonders. On moving day he came driving up Tower Grove Drive, followed by two carloads of construction laborers. Truly it was the cavalry to the rescue, and the prodigious groupings of Vicki's furniture, accessories, clothes and everything else were loaded and moved in record time. Unfortunately, as Vicki predicted, it wouldn't all fit in the smaller condominium. Things were left in boxes and then stacked and shoved into every available space. The expensive forest of potted plants were either given away or left outside where they eventually wilted and died. None of it seemed to bother Vicki. She handled it stoically, maintaining that this was her make-or-break situation and there was no sense in worrying over "a few dumb possessions." I had to give her credit for not dwelling on the inevitable.

"All the money that I have left is from selling my Mercedes," she said as if she were reading my thoughts. "It's a little less than seventeen thousand now. And I have to pay the closing costs on the telephone...the additional rent, Todd's private schooling." She shook her head in disbelief. "I'm not used to worrying about things like paying bills."

"Welcome to reality," I laughed, gesturing to the condominium. "It's tough making money from here."

She nodded and lit up a cigarette, exhaled deeply before raising her glass to her lips. I noticed this time it wasn't the usual Diet 7-Up. She was drinking white wine now, out of the magnum bottle. I was drinking scotch, from the inventory Vicki had brought with her from the house on Tower Grove Drive. There the wet bar had not been used in quite some time, judging by its layout and the dust on the various whiskey bottles stored in the gray, lacquered cabinets.

"You don't drink much?" I had asked after a couple of meetings.

"Hardly ever, anymore. I don't like the taste of alcohol, except for some dry white wine. I used to keep the cabinet stocked for guests, or mainly Alfred's friends. Alfred wasn't a drinker. He drank iced tea. Loved iced tea. But I used to arrange luncheons every now and then, and he wanted me to keep the liquor around for whenever he entertained."

"Who did he entertain?" I asked her.

Vicki hesitated, and answered only after giving attention to her choice of words. I smiled at the caution, the signs of the wayward kid who didn't want to blow it by revealing too much too early. She was frustrated, angered that it was taking so long to answer me. She knew I was watching as she struggled with her thoughts. Finally, calmly, she responded in total candor.

"Some were just friends of his, and some were his business associates. Some of them were part of Reagan's kitchen cabinet." She smiled. "They used to love me," she went on, confident and energetic. "They would talk openly about their wives and children. What they thought of this one... who was out of political favor... who was in.

"You see, Gordon, most of these men don't marry for companionship. They don't share, or really talk with their wives. They have no idea at all about what women are really like. What women think about... how they respond. It's a whole set up from day one. It's designed to—what is it?—perpetuate the family. The women shop, have charities and banquets and crap like that to keep them busy. The boys hang out with the boys and try their best to move the world around. Most of them see hookers or have girl friends. A few of the braver souls will keep a mistress, like Alfred did. Only Alfred gave me the kind of money the rest don't even dream of. I'm the last of the breed. Alfred saw to it. There's only four or five other women that I know of...that I even heard of...who get the kind of money that I got from Alfred."

"Vicki, how could you go through all that money?" I asked again, a ritual now since the night of our first meeting. I believed her, I truly did, when she lamented she was broke. But how in the hell...?

"Everybody asks me the same thing. You have to stop... you see that's why everything gets so confused...you have to see it from my perspective, my experience. When it starts at sixteen, the attention, the adulation, if for no other reason than you're a pretty girl, and from sixteen on it never ends, and when no one tells you, or explains it, what makes you think it's ever gonna stop? You see, it's not just Alfred, it's always been like that for me. When I was younger, a kid, I didn't know why. I thought it was because they liked me. I didn't realize certain men, men who move to conquer, need someone like me. Someone who's strong... who's loyal. Only trouble is that most men aren't strong enough for me. I overwhelm them after awhile. See, they don't know me, or care about what's going on inside. If I'm, say, with Alfred, and another man who's interested competes with Alfred, it's got nothing to do with me personally. I'm the prize, the trophy. One man, another man...hell most men, wealthy men, all my life they'd give me whatever I wanted. Except for love. Not love as I understand it. Except for Alfred. He was that fucking crazy."

It was Earle Lamm who first demonstrated to Vicki the tribute men would pay to a pretty girl. "The face that launched a thousand ships," Earle proclaimed throughout their relationship and for many years after. Earle was forty-eight when he married Vicki Morgan. She was sixteen. Like Gary, Earle was Jewish, but Earle was more sophisticated. He had divorced and moved to Los Angeles from Chicago. Earle was attractive in a swarthy fashion. He was a man of taste, if a touch flamboyant, with his silk shirts, his gold watch, and gold chains around his neck. He wore expensive, tailored slacks and walked in Gucci loafers. What Vicki didn't know until after they were married was that Earle wore a toupeé. She was flabbergasted the first time she stepped into their bathroom and found the hair piece perched on its styrofoam head.

Earle and Vicki were married in Las Vegas at one of the classic, all-night chapels, a tacky stucco cottage, complete with flashing, heart-shaped neon lights. It was the first of Vicki's three marriages to take place in Las Vegas. A somnambulistic refugee from the House of Wax performed the ceremony as his fat wife and two motley witnesses observed this sacred affair. Sparing no expense, Earle Lamm paid extra for the bouquet of flowers and the recorded music in the background. "We've Only Just Begun" complemented the entire five minute service.

Shortly after the newlyweds returned to their posh highrise condominium in the Sierra Towers, Vicki discovered what her married life foretold. She discovered new and different sides to her husband, many of which she definitely didn't appreciate. Earle was a freak and a degenerate gambler. And Vicki, the small-town girl, was not prepared for his excesses. While making love, Earle would pop amylnitrates and shout obscenities in Vicki's ears. He suggested repeatedly that they should have a threesome. He particularly wanted to see her make it with a black woman. She resisted at first, but eventually Earle had his way. She was easy prey to his assertions that she was just the country bumpkin and therefore out of touch with big-city standards. To keep a man, Vicki was led to believe, you had to do kinky stuff, lest he grow bored and leave for another woman. Abandonment was what Vicki feared the most.

Earle soon suggested they attend orgies, so he could watch Vicki with different men. Meanwhile, he leased her a new Cadillac Seville, and when she didn't like it he amenably traded it in for a Mercedes 280-SL. He gave her money and credit cards, and encouraged her to look nice. He was proud of her and wanted to show her off to his friends.

"At sixteen," said Vicki," I became the darling little showpiece. You should've seen me, with the jewelry and the cute little outfits. You wonder how I got this way. It started with Earle."

Earle, however, despite Vicki's arguments, did not want Todd around. It ruined the salacious Lolita image that Earle so treasured in Vicki. Todd's visits were restricted mainly to weekends. Vicki found this painful and confusing. Often she would drive to Montclair, pick up her son and drive back into Los Angeles, where they'd spend the day together before driving back to her mother's, where she'd face moralistic diatribes and charges that she was neglecting Todd. Additional money would often clear up the matter.

After awhile Vicki got bored with her marriage. Earle's age was starting to show. While he was content to stay home at night, drinking and watching television, Vicki craved activity. She had turned seventeen, and the domestic routine was already wearing thin. Restless and crazy with boredom, she increasingly spent the nights with her girl friends, cruising Los Angeles in her two-seat convertible. They would stop at the night spots or go for late-night snacks. While making the rounds Vicki started meeting people. She became acquainted with various celebrities, different actors, sports heroes, and movie producers. Theirs were glamorous professions, and in talking with them Vicki felt the attraction for that kind of lifestyle. She told them she was a model, and they agreed that she was indeed a "very pretty girl."

Earle and Vicki continued having problems. He grew suspicious and jealous and was less tolerant of her nightly excursions. "I don't like you being out so much," he told her.

"It's not like I'm doing anything wrong," she protested.

"I don't care. It's not right for you to be out every night with your friends."

Finally, after months of arguing, Earle registered his disapproval one night by beating up on his lovely, young wife as she emerged from The Candy Store, a now-defunct private club on Rodeo Drive. Hidden in the shadows, like Orson Welles in *The Third Man*, Earle waited nearly two hours until closing time for Vicki to exit the club. Finally she appeared with the rest of the crowd as they emptied onto the sidewalk. A girlfriend and a young actor accompanied Vicki as she walked the half block to her car. She and her friends were about to drive away when Earle squealed up in his Cadillac. Before Vicki could believe what was happening, Earle was reaching inside the Mercedes and dragging her from the car.

"You bitch!" he hissed as he slapped and cursed, smashing her head against the fender. A thin stream of blood ran down her forehead as Vicki struggled to escape from Earle. She cried for help, but the crowd simply watched it all with typical L.A. cool. As for the young actor, at the sight of Earle Lamm, he panicked and ran away.

After that night, things were never again right between Vicki and Earle. Strange as he was, she loved him, or at least she didn't wish to hurt his feelings, and therefore she forgave him for his actions. However, she was much too aware of Earle's insecurities, highlighted by his terrible fear of losing her, to ever again be the subordinate wife. The roles had been reversed, and now she was the dominant force and it was Earle who was the dependent one. She became the mother and he became the child. Sex, naturally, was no longer exciting, and as time passed, Earle Lamm understood their marriage was bound for disaster. Even so, he struggled to maintain it, since he was unequivocally in love with Vicki, obsessed and out of control. He grew increasingly embittered at the signs of the collapse of their marriage.

With all of his idiosyncrasies, Earle Lamm was and always would be there for Vicki Morgan. Long after their marriage had ended, he was loyal and supportive. He'd come to her aid wherever she was, whenever she asked. Truly he loved her, and for years he was intent on winning her back from Alfred Bloomingdale. But his obsession finally got the best of him. In order to make the kind of money he believed was necessary to compete with Vicki's lover, Earle became a smuggler, and for his efforts was arrested, convicted, and sentenced to two years in a Mexican prison. A couple years after his release, he died at fifty-three from a heart attack. He had loved and lost and gone down in despair. Earle Lamm had had it tough.

# 4

FROM THE DAY she first met Alfred Bloomingdale, Vicki's life would never again be the same. Young and impressionable, Vicki was introduced to the world as Alfred knew it. It was the world of money and power, that of Machiavellian strategies and corporate skullduggery, where scions of politics and economics joined hands for their own convenience. Alfred explained to the seventeen-year-old Vicki, life was for the living, what you wanted was for the taking, and the best way to achieve it was through the sophisticated use of coercion, manipulation, or anything else that worked.

"The best defense is a good offense," Alfred would say to her, reciting this time-worn cliché. But Alfred truly believed it, and was able to apply it with a special panache. He was a man who governed by example. What he wanted, he went after, and he was relentless when in pursuit.

"You should've seen him," Vicki once told me. "He'd get like...crazy. Forget taking no for an answer. This, to Alfred, was simply unheard of. Instead he'd just push and push and push until you finally had to say 'alright already.' He'd wear you down, until he got his way."

I never met Alfred Bloomingdale. In some ways I wish I had. He was an original, for good or bad, a genuine wild man with tastes and habits reminiscent of ancient Roman debauchery. He was the veritable charioteer, a Machiavellian warrior thrashing his way through society's rat race. Victory was never his, and never was he satisfied. But

Alfred enjoyed his power and kept himself amused. He covered plenty of ground with his myriad business ventures. Versatility was the cornerstone on which he built his career. Consequently, he often spread himself thin and was thought to be lacking in substance. He was often impatient and could be abrupt and obnoxious. And then there were times when he could be positively charming, finding humor in everything, a trait he passed on to his mistress. Alfred spoke rapidly, in a gruff staccato that was partially the result of a throat-cancer operation. Alfred said what was on his mind; skeptical, ironical, and often misguided he nevertheless was a man of responsibility, a trusted friend of Ronald Reagan. Alfred Bloomingdale, along with Holmes Tuttle, Henry Salvatori, Jack Wrather, Earle Jorgenson, and the late Justin Dart, were the President's friends, the inner circle. A fully catered kitchen cabinet, this group of very rich Californians not only helped put their friend in the White House, but returned their state's Republican contingent to its position of national domination.

Surprisingly, Alfred Bloomingdale had been in politics longer than Ronald Reagan or anyone else in his kitchen cabinet. He was only twenty-seven when he became Treasurer of New York City during the infamous era of corruption at Tammany Hall. This type of involvement he preferred to working in his grandfather's department store, where he had once been a clerk. However, Alfred grew bored with politics, and in the 1940s, he involved himself in show business and was responsible for the production of a number of Broadway shows and several Hollywood movies. In 1941 he married Barbara Brewster, a showgirl, but divorced her two years later. For a short period of time he managed Frank Sinatra. But again he grew bored, and with two partners he founded Diner's Club, the world's first major credit card service.

As the pioneer to the world of plastic money, Alfred discovered that one advantage was having access to customers' files. Previously confidential and potentially sensitive business and personal information could be very useful to an ambitious man; it also did wonders for our intelligence agencies, by helping them keep track of the eating, sleeping, and travel habits of America's leading executives. All sorts of notables were suddenly under clandestine scrutiny. Every Diner's Club receipt was a clue or story in itself. What a novel and relatively easy means of surveillance. Now, as computerized credit has grown more sophisticated, such methods are routine, as file after file, list after list is generally monitored by one agency or another. But Diner's Club was established in the 1950s, the era of the Cold War, with all its paranoia and men like Tailgunner Joe McCarthy, Secretary of State John Foster Dulles, and Dulles's brother Allen, founding director of the CIA, and Richard Nixon. This was the time of A-bomb spies and one Russian crisis after the next. And here was Alfred Bloomingdale, ready to do some favors.

Alfred was a product of the old society—bred of tweeds, protocol, and etiquette. He preferred to downplay his influence and resented the *nouveau* authorities, the power brokers who allowed subtlety and understatement to be stampeded by their material ostentation. He was disposed to old, black suits, thin, black ties, and white shirts, the traditional business uniform. He cared little for jewelry, wearing only an expensive watch. When it stopped running he bought a new one and threw the old in a drawer rather than have it repaired. In his money clip he carried a thousand dollars in crisp, new bills in various denominations. His experience with Diner's Club had convinced him it was better to pay in cash rather than be traced through the use of his own credit cards. Although at times he appeared to be careless, he was generally meticulous in covering his tracks. To say the least, he was a visceral man with rooted dilemmas that left him trapped between his personal interests and his inherent responsibilities. He expressed to Vicki the need to be free, and yet he remained a captive of his rank and ambitions. His eclectic interests stirred a constant need for diversity, and he was compelled to associate with leaders from virtually all walks of life. Magnates of industry, political heavyweights, and major underworld figures were considered his friends. And, as the years progressed, Alfred at times served as a liaison in bringing different people together. He was the natural go-between and a player on the team. Though aware of his power, few ever understood Alfred Bloomingdale, mainly because he appeared so obvious. It was his nature to be garrulous, a trait that he used in the extreme to desensitize and confuse. He projected different things to different people. He was often confused by himself. And the few who did know about Alfred Bloomingdale were careful never to tell tales out of school, at least not publicly, even long after Alfred had died.

Perhaps more significantly, Alfred Bloomingdale had one of the world's greatest sex drives. Sex was his major release from the pressures and the dangers he was forced to endure, and, throughout his life, he was continually distracted by its destructive obsession. It's said he couldn't imagine having to go without "it" for more than a couple of days. Rather than suffer this terrible fate, he neglected his business and left it to the care of associates. Consequently, he lost money by the ton. But Alfred didn't seem to care. There is evidence, according to Vicki, that he wanted it that way, that going broke was a secret ambition, a means of purging his guilt and frustrations. Deep down inside he wanted to be a regular guy. He wanted to sit at the counter at Duke's Tropicana, and talk football over his scrambled eggs. He longed to be earthy and not burdened with corporate intrigues. By the time he died, he had visited hookers and brothels all over the globe, spending a yearly average of a quarter-million dollars in pursuit of his sexual adventures. All told, including Vicki, Betsy, and a legion of prostitutes, it must have cost him over $2 million annually, just to brush his teeth.

Vicki Morgan and Alfred Bloomingdale met quite by accident during the summer of 1970 in The Old World Restaurant, a modest eatery in the heart of Sunset Strip. Vicki had arranged to join her girlfriend Emmy for lunch, but on this rare day Vicki was early, the first to arrive. Well dressed and in a good mood, she left her car and started walking from the parking lot through the narrow alleyway that led to the restaurant's entrance. Bloomingdale and a female companion were following behind. Vicki, who by now was used to men pursuing her, could feel the unmistakable presence of his eyes on her back and heard his mutterings to the other woman who struggled to match his stride.

Having turned the corner, Vicki glanced over her shoulder and saw that he had closed the distance. He was staring right at her, smiling as he acknowledged her glance. She was not afraid and not attracted. She was curious, however, to see how far he'd go. Quickly she entered the darkened restaurant, hoping Emmy would be waiting. She wasn't. Vicki stood and lit a cigarette feigning indifference as Alfred strode through the door, his companion trailing behind.

"Would you like to sit down with us?" Alfred invited. He was a big man, tall, overweight, with a large mouth, and a prominent nose displayed on his craggy face. His ashen hair, thick and wavy, was parted and swept from the front to the back of his head. Basically he was not a handsome man, certainly not a cultivated, silver gentlemen who spoke the Queen's English. Alfred was a great deal rougher than that, especially with that gravelly voice of his, and the herky-jerky, nervous motions he'd acquired from his years of taking amphetamine diet pills. On first impression he didn't appear to have any money, not the serious kind that ran into millions. But there was something about him that projected authority. He was much too charming and self-assured to be just a middle executive who was taking his secretary to an inexpensive lunch. He was a man, she realized, who was used to getting what he wanted. She knew the type, and considered this, above all else, the most appealing characteristic she could find in a man. For the man who had his way in life was the man who had money. Vicki had recognized that fact while still in her early teens.

So she sat down with Alfred and Samantha, the other woman, and sipped iced tea while making small talk. Vicki, the western, small-town girl, had no idea who Alfred was, had never heard of Bloomingdale's department store, had never been to New York. Besides, he wished to talk less about himself and hear more about her. In response to Alfred's questioning, Vicki said she was married, had a son, and was taking tennis lessons from a respected pro. Alfred responded by telling her that his daughter Lisa had just returned from tennis camp and was looking for someone to play with. He suggested Vicki write down her telephone number so that he could pass it on to his daughter who would invite her over for a friendly game on their private court.

"It would be lovely," Alfred said, "for the two of you to get together."

Vicki scribbled her number on a paper napkin and politely excused herself to join Emmy, who had just arrived.

"Who was that?" Emmy wondered after Vicki sat down at their table. "Do you know him?"

Vicki shrugged and glanced back in Alfred's direction. "His daughter plays tennis. He wants me to meet her."

As he left the restaurant, Alfred walked by her table and pressed something into Vicki's palm. She felt it, sensed it was folded paper, but didn't dare look until he'd departed. Only then did she cautiously open her palm and straighten the wrinkled paper. She was astonished to discover it was a check paid to cash, written for $8,000.

"It's probably bullshit," Vicki decided after discussing it with Emmy.

"But it could be real," Emmy ventured. "Who does a thing like this?"

"I don't care," answered Vicki. "I'm not impressed. Unless it clears."

An hour later Vicki was standing inside Earle's Westwood office, waiting impatiently for her husband to get off the phone. Rush Batwin, Earle's partner, was standing beside her, curious to see what would happen. Vicki had shown him the check, and he knew Vicki was intent on cashing it, provided, of course, it was good. Rush was equally certain Earle would try to prevent her, but to no avail. Vicki was much too headstrong, especially when it came to money. Besides, she was outgrowing Earle with increasing speed, and it was only a matter of time, Rush believed, before some wealthy gentleman took her away from her husband.

"Earle, there's something I gotta show you," Vicki announced the moment Earle was off the phone. He had come around from his desk, all smiles and platitudes, and was preparing to kiss her when Vicki showed him the check. His eyes widened as he took note of the figure and the name on the check. Once again there was someone after his wife.

"What the hell is this?" Earle demanded. He was suspicious and angry. His forehead was creased and his eyes were narrowed as he waited for Vicki's reply.

"He just gave you this?" he asked after Vicki had told him her story. "Just like that...for nothing...he hands you a check for $8,000?"

"It's weird isn't it?" Vicki acknowledged. "Who is Alfred Bloomingdale, anyway?"

"You want to tell her, or should I?" Rush Batwin interjected. "He's one of the richest men in this country," he said before Earle had a chance to respond. "He's a very powerful man."

"It's a shitty move, if you ask me," Earle grumbled, his head sagging as he returned the check to Vicki. Yes, it was true. Another man was after his wife. Earle sighed and recalled the time that rich, old Huntington Hartford had spotted Vicki in a Hollywood parking lot and took down her license-plate number. A few days later there was a telephone call, from their good friend Huntington, no less, inviting them to a special party he was giving at his hotel in Pasadena. Earle, of course, had refused to go, but Vicki had talked him into it. Once there, he felt even more the fool as he stood alone with a drink in his hand, while Vicki talked and danced with the aging romantic. From then on Earle was easily demoralized, susceptible to even greater tension and jealousy.

Sensing Earle's chagrin, Vicki grew childish and playful. First she nudged her husband once or twice, hoping to tease him away from his misery. Gently she rubbed his shoulders, blew in his ear, and kissed him lightly on the neck. Her efforts seemed to leave him only more depressed. "C'mon, Earle," she cooed, while looking to Rush for added support, "let's go down to the bank and see if his check's any good."

Earle stiffened and glared at his wife. "Vicki, I won't let you cash it."

In the end, she got her way. Years later, during their last conversation, just weeks before he died of a heart attack, Earle admitted to Vicki that it was the worst mistake he'd ever made. His fear of losing her had overwhelmed his better judgment, and consequently, Vicki had lost her respect for him. More important, Alfred Bloomingdale had gained the advantage. For his modest investment he had Earle on the run and Vicki caught up in the game. It was only a matter of time, before Alfred would undermine their troubled marriage and have Vicki all to himself.

The following day Alfred began his telephone blitz. He started early in the morning. "I've got to see you again," he told her. "You're so beautiful. I've never felt this way about anyone before."

"Leave me alone," Vicki pleaded. "I'm married, for Christ's sake. I've got a child."

Alfred was in no mood for rejection. What did he care that he was making an ass out of himself? So what if he called her twenty times a day? He was no Adonis, and to win her over he'd have to play for the long run. He would charm, flatter, threaten, and promise. He would persist and connive, as he had learned to do so well. For this was no fly-by-nighter, no joker with a hard-on and a couple of hours to kill. He wasn't about to ring her up once or twice and, if nothing happened, say "forget it" and then let it go. This was a man who had found the highway and couldn't wait to take the ride. Whatever the cost, it didn't matter. At fifty-three, Alfred had fallen in love.

# 5

A PENSIVE VICKI MORGAN would sit alone in her bedroom, chain-smoking cigarettes and thinking of dozens of reasons for quelling Alfred's advances. Weeks before, she had told him she couldn't stand it anymore, that his relentless pursuit was making her irritable and nervous. She had threatened to tell Earle. She threatened to change her telephone number, especially if Alfred kept phoning her in the morning before Earle had left for work. Wisely, Alfred compromised and agreed not to call when Earle was home. Vicki felt better, as if things were going her way.

"Meet me for lunch," Alfred pleaded and, after several weeks of debate and deliberation, Vicki finally agreed. They rendezvoused at The Old World Restaurant. He argued his case throughout the entire meal. He'd never acted like this before, he claimed, had never seen a girl as beautiful as Vicki. He wanted her for his own, and he wouldn't take no for an answer. So what if she was married and had a child? Who was Earle Lamm, anyway?

Vicki listened and argued with Alfred. She was mesmerized by his ardent appeal, couldn't believe that a man his age, with his status, was behaving this way. What did she have that was so great that other girls didn't? "Besides, Alfred," she countered, "you're much too old for me. You're even older than Earle."

Before lunch was over Vicki knew she was simply outgunned. Here was a man, a virtual baron of high society, a manic, fuel-burning sonofabitch up against a rural-suburban flower child, a dropout with a lisp, an illegitimate child and a husband who'd confessed to her that every so often he'd slept with other men. She had just turned eighteen and lacked direction. She had no chance against this man. Even when she voiced an opinion that she sincerely believed, Alfred would turn it around and play such havoc with Vicki's insecurities that she would begin to doubt herself. Worse still, Alfred knew the truth about her: that she was bored out of her mind and increasingly restless, that she wanted to experience life and not just endure the tedium found in her daily routine, that she wanted to travel.

After lunch was over, she had decided that if he loved her that much, then let him prove it. Let Alfred, with all his supposed devotion, show her the top of the world.

At her third meeting with Alfred Bloomingdale, Vicki got more than she bargained for. Another week had passed, days of siege when he had bombarded her with telephone calls. Alfred was really bearing down, pleading, bargaining, hoping at last that she believed his sincerity. Vicki, more curious than physically attracted, agreed to meet him in front of Schwab's Drugstore, the now-extinct West Hollywood legend. All day it had been raining, and now there was a steady downpour. Nevertheless, Alfred, clutching an umbrella, was waiting on the sidewalk. Samantha, the woman from their first meeting, was standing nearby. Vicki pulled alongside the curb and lowered her window as Alfred bent over to give her instructions.

"We're going to meet at a friend's house, on Sunset Plaza Drive," he explained. "This young lady will show you the way."

Before Vicki had a chance to respond, Alfred was off to retrieve his car and Samantha was sitting beside her. She gave directions matter-of-factly, and then said nothing as Vicki and she headed west on Sunset Boulevard and then turned right up Sunset Plaza Drive. Vicki drove in silence up the steep and winding thoroughfare, puzzled, curious and slightly frightened.

"Did Alfred tell you what he wanted?" asked Samantha, adding to Vicki's fears.

"What do you mean...wanted?"

"I didn't think he told you," Samantha noted, realizing Vicki was in for a big surprise. "He likes to see several women at a time, if you know what I mean. He ties you up and whips you with his belt. It's all right, though. He never really hurts you."

Vicki was incredulous. Her eyes widened as she stared through the rain beading on her windshield. Out of the corner of her eye she glanced at Samantha, looking for signs of a practical joke. She studied the hard face, the overdone makeup, the tailored clothes and tacky jewelry and realized Samantha, who was a good ten years older than Vicki, wasn't the type who joked about such matters.

"It's disgusting," said Vicki. "I can't believe he really does all that."

"Twice a week, at least. Look, I know you're just a kid. You don't know what this kind of thing will do to you. Once you start, you'll never break out of it. So, if you want, you can drop me off and drive away. I'll give him a story."

Vicki was a nervous wreck. Her heart was pounding, her legs shaking and her usually sweaty palms were soaking wet. She shivered as she pulled her Mercedes into the driveway and, without so much as looking at Samantha, got out of the car. She stood in the rain and out of nervousness she smoothed out her skirt and tugged at the sleeves of her blouse. She glanced at her watch, smoothed her hair and followed Samantha up the walkway and through the door.

Kay, a bleached, platinum blonde was standing inside, waiting to greet them. She had big breasts and a full, round ass stuffed inside her slacks and blouse. She wore gaudy jewelry and her eyebrows were pencilled and arched. Vicki said hello and walked into the living room. She advanced to the large, picture window and, from high on the hillside, stared at the rain pouring down on L.A. Alfred emerged from the bathroom and spoke in hushed tones to the two strange women. Vicki watched at a distance and reviewed her decision to stick it out. She wondered if she was making a serious mistake, if she should pass on the curiosity and make a break for the door. Suddenly, leaving didn't seem like such a bad idea. But just then, Alfred called her name and beckoned for her to join him on the sofa. The other women, Vicki noted, retreated upstairs, leaving her and Alfred alone.

"Vicki, please sit down," Alfred gestured. He patted the sofa for added effect and then waited patiently for her to get comfortable.

Vicki looked him in the eye and asked him what he wanted. She was tired of the games, angry about the phone calls. What she didn't tell him was the fascination he held for her. How could a man his age persist and cajole and then lead her into something like this? She wanted to know more about him, about his whole fucking scene. Here was this man, this mighty pillar of society. Was he really doing this? Vicki still couldn't believe it, not even after hearing it from Samantha. She couldn't conceive that Alfred Bloomingdale, who appeared to have it all, was reduced to finding satisfaction in a lurid scene like this. Then what in the hell was going on here? What was the need, the attraction?

Alfred was going on about personal freedom, claiming what two people decided to do with each other was a matter of choice. "There's nothing ever wrong with what happens when two people agree," he was saying.

"Two people?" she interjected. It made her laugh. "Alfred, I count four! And God knows what else you might have upstairs."

Alfred leaned forward and squeezed her hand. "Vicki, you're the one who's special. There's something about you.

51

Any man can see it, but I'm the one to bring it out. Vicki, do you know what a mistress is?"

"Sorta. But why don't you give me your version?"

Patiently, Alfred defined the role of a mistress. He explained she was like a second wife to a man, and that she was always taken care of. There was security and longevity, for often the relationship between a man and his mistress lasted longer than his marriage. There was passion and caring, a home away from home.

"Alfred, I'm married. I can't be your mistress."

"Forget about your husband," shouted Alfred. "That's over!" Sensing her fear, Alfred lowered his voice and regained his gentle, patient tone of conversation. "Vicki," he said. "I'll take care of all of your needs. There's nothing you can't have. You can get what you need, whenever you need it. I'm that rich."

Vicki turned her head and stared at him from the corners of her eyes. She was suspicious and weary and just eighteen. "Men are always such big talkers. And you, Alfred, you don't even know who I am."

"Besides my wife, I know you better than any other woman. And I've known many."

Laughter slipped from her mouth as Vicki gestured to the two women who were waiting upstairs. "I can believe that about you. The rest is a little too much. What do you mean when you say you want to take care of me?"

"That you have nothing to worry about for the rest of your life. Vicki, I want to make love to you. If there's anything you don't like, just tell me and I promise you, it won't happen. This is me, Vicki, and this is what I do for pleasure."

Incredulous, she shook her head while allowing a smile to evolve at the corners of her mouth. This man, she thought to herself, is in a world all his own...on a long, strange trip. What a trip! She'd have to see it to believe it.

"C'mon," she smiled, standing and taking his hand. Together they climbed the staircase.

Upstairs in the master bedroom, Kay and Samantha were waiting for Alfred and Vicki. The women were naked and growing impatient. Kay sat and smoked on the edge of the bed, while the dark-haired Samantha stretched out on the mattress. Sullen and businesslike, they glanced up matter-of-factly when Alfred and Vicki appeared in the doorway. Vicki tensed when she caught sight of the two naked women and looked to Alfred for reassurance. He was smiling, his hand squeezing hers. The glint in his eyes, the stiffening muscles throughout his body indicated the pleasure he derived from the anticipation. He studied the women and then looked at Vicki.

"Remember, he said, "anything you don't like, won't happen. Would you please take your clothes off?"

Vicki was stunned and embarrassed. It suddenly dawned on her that she wasn't used to having strangers watch while she undressed. She'd always been self-conscious. She considered herself too skinny, with long, thin legs and breasts she wished were larger. Her face she knew was exceptionally pretty, most alluring and sensual. Only now she didn't feel very pretty, only ugly and cheap as she extended her arms and carefully removed her watch and the bracelets from her wrists. She shivered and blushed. As she stripped off her clothes she cast a furtive glance in Alfred's direction. He was observing her, a jubilant little boy grinning at the sound of the jingling bracelets.

"You're very beautiful," he marvelled. He was clad only in his socks and plain, white boxer shorts. White hairs coiled upon his barrel chest. He turned to the hookers in search of confirmation. "Isn't she beautiful?" he demanded.

The women nodded. "She sure is, Alfred," Kay agreed. "You certainly know how to pick 'em."

Vicki tried to calm herself as she struggled with her

clothing. Her palms were soaked, her heart was pounding. She had one leg raised, the other balanced precariously on a thin, high heel. She wobbled and nearly tripped while stepping out of her dress. Soon she was naked and she looked at herself, as if seeing for the first time her lanky frame with its narrow hips, long, slender legs covered by skin that was golden and downy. Her hair curled around her shoulder blades. She was nauseous and chilled as reality and fantasy grappled for control over her senses and clawed at her guts. Earlier, this had all seemed like a joke to her, a stupid, little game, a sordid one perhaps, but a game nevertheless. Now she was in for a rude awakening. This was no game for Alfred Bloomingdale. This was a serious occupation.

Alfred was reaching out, taking hold of her upper arm. He drew her close and kissed her, as Vicki reached down and began rubbing the hair on his belly. Kay, as if on cue, dropped to her knees and peeled off Alfred's white boxer shorts.

"Let me tie you up," he offered, and beamed like a happy child when Vicki consented. Using soft nylon cord he tied her hands behind her back and laid her face down across the bedspread. Again he kissed her, before turning his attention to Samantha and Kay. They didn't have it as easy as Vicki. He bound their wrists over their heads and then drew the cord up and over the top of the closet door and tied it to the knob on the opposite side in order to secure their outstretched bodies. The women had to stand on their toes in order to keep from dangling. He grunted in satisfaction before retrieving his belt. He started beating the women. Pausing for breath between strokes, he repeatedly brought the leather down across their asses. Kay gritted her teeth but she didn't cry out. But Samantha made a terrible mistake; she broke a cardinal rule by yelling and screaming, faking it, pretending he was really laying it on.

"You don't do that to me," Alfred bellowed, the sweat dripping off his brow. He whipped Samantha repeatedly until welts formed on her ass. Her legs were shaking and she was sweating profusely. Her cries now were genuine and convincing. Abruptly, Alfred stopped hitting her. He was panting, gasping for air.

Vicki thought she was lost in the Twilight Zone, or cast as a whore in an X-rated movie; it was the kind of thing her husband Earle had encouraged her to watch with him for its educational value. If only he could see her now, immersed in this squalid reality. What would he do? she wondered, but quickly the thought left her mind. She was too frightened to concentrate. Too curious. This man, this crazy man was certainly the main attraction, having by now contradicted everything Vicki had been raised to believe. He was something else, all right...a trip...a strange and curious trip. He was frustrated, out of place, and trying to cope with the demands of his rank and status. A man like this would give her no room for objective distance, no chance to lead a normal lifestyle. He was too demanding, wanting to draw sustenance from her youth and, in exchange, show her the world and supply her with money. Some offer to a precocious, teenaged girl.

"Look at her!" Alfred was booming. He was waving his belt in one hand while pointing a finger in Vicki's direction. "Isn't she incredible?"

The women agreed, knowing on which side their bread was buttered. Unfortunately they hadn't displayed enough enthusiasm and he subjected them to a series of lashes. "Answer me! Goddamnit! Isn't she incredible? She has a child, you know? She isn't cheap. She's someone special."

With that said, he stood over Vicki, who was still bound and laying on her stomach, and started spanking her ass. "I promise not to hurt you," he assured her. "I'm only using my hand."

Kay and Samantha, tied at the wrists and hanging from the closet door, watched in breathless silence as Alfred started making love to Vicki. His eyes were open wide, he was grimacing as his body strained for an orgasm. It came soon enough, and right after Alfred rolled over and caught his breath. He was looking at her, a weary smile etched on his face. She could tell he was exhausted, but satisfied, returning to what she deemed as his "normal self." Gradually, he regained control of himself. He stood up, walked to the closet door and untied Kay and Samantha.

"Ladies, you can go now," he instructed. He was cold and businesslike; his guttural voice was devoid of any emotion. All this must have cost him at least a thousand dollars, but he hardly noticed the hookers as they grabbed their clothes and departed.

Vicki was awed by the sudden change. He had turned it on and off so easily. It was amazing. Still, she hadn't liked it and was freaked out by his dementia. To be fascinated was one thing, to find it appealing was something else again. She disliked what he had done to her, and she hated herself for having done it. Yet, down deep she was satisfied. She had been flattered and thrilled and made to feel special.

"I have to be going soon," she explained, hoping she had read him correctly and that her intended departure wouldn't provoke him. "My husband and I have dinner plans."

Alfred smiled his kindly smile and helped her to her feet. "C'mon," he whispered. "Let's go take a shower."


I don't think that, until the day she died, Vicki fully understood what made her stay that afternoon on Sunset Plaza Drive. At least, that's what I concluded as I dragged out of her, in bits and pieces, at the oddest hours and strangest times, the most embarrassing aspects of her love affair with Alfred Bloomingdale. Understandably, it was not her favorite topic of discussion. However, in her better moods she would laugh ironically, quipping about the social hypocrisies and the mind-blowing public reaction. She could never believe it had raised that great a stink, the "updated version of *The Scarlet Letter*," as she liked to call it. And when she thought of the reasons for her sudden notoriety, an unanticipated debut after years of arcane living, Vicki was always reminded of the man she despised, the man she believed was a coward and self-serving traitor. She really had it in for Marvin Mitchelson.

"I never wanted to do it that way," she told me. "I wanted to settle it quietly." The sensationalism she blamed on her attorney Marvin Mitchelson. Renowned for the Marvin *vs.* Marvin palimony suit, he had urged her to lay it on thick. He assured her that the opposition, Betsy and Alfred Bloomingdale, would never dare allow her deposition to fall into the public domain, that they would insist it be sealed and remain under court order so that the lascivious details would be kept confidential.

"What a turnaround I got on that one. Betsy, or I should say Hillel Chodos, Betsy's lawyer, is real sharp. Sharp enough that I wish he represented me. Here I am, going on and on about Alfred drooling...I mean things he never did...just pouring it on...believing Mitchelson, thinking they'd settle, that they wouldn't dare risk this getting out to the public. Especially not with Reagan in the White House.

"But they did let it out. All over the world. Someone told me they saw it in the headlines of the Indonesian news-paper. Fucking headhunters probably know my name, have my picture pinned on the walls of their huts.

"I got it in spades," laughed Vicki. "All the wrong publicity. Enough to blow any chance of winning the case. Y'know, I was told that when they heard it was Marvin Mitchelson handling it, they breathed a sigh of relief. 'Mitchelson,' they said. 'Oh, then we have nothing to worry about.' Marvin, the champion of women's rights. Well, bullshit! He was only out for himself.

"He used to tell me what a great team we'd make, with me on the stand and him asking the questions. He thought he'd have them eating out of his hand. I think he always needed the money.

"I was that stupid, Gordon. No, I take that back. I wasn't stupid. I was naive. Lawyers! What did I know from lawyers? Alfred always took care of it."

In the months we spent together I got used to her castigations of Marvin Mitchelson. Mitchelson, according to Vicki, sold off her private photographs, with which she had entrusted him. Among other things, Vicki claimed, the famous attorney had solicited a number of agencies regarding the sale of his prospective book about her life. She claimed he never informed Vicki about his efforts to sell her story, nor did he receive her approval. For this and for a number of other things, she felt betrayed. She felt insecure and stupid for allowing these things to happen. I remember how she'd berate herself for not paying better attention.

But Mitchelson, the scandal, and her infamous financial mismanagement were essentially the results of her meeting with Alfred nearly thirteen years earlier. It was that star-crossed tryst on the affluent slopes of West Hollywood that created her destiny. Everything else, nearly everyone else, were incidental anecdotes, whistle stops aligning fate's charted course. No matter how you view it, or how hard you try to change the outcome, women like Vicki are bound for a tragic demise. Though some tried to stop it, no one could. It's almost like there's a certain metaphysical pattern, a destructive composition of spiritual dialectics that can never be synthesized. Choose to live a certain way and you choose to die by it as well. Maybe, for all of us, it's as simple as that. So in the end, only one question remains to be answered. Was it worth it?

# 6

INITIALLY IT WAS boredom that drove Vicki toward Alfred Bloomingdale. She was inquisitive, energetic, and a believer in classical romance. She yearned for adventure, the kind of stuff she'd see at the movies. Hollywood mythologies and offbeat fairy tales influenced Vicki from the very beginning. Much of her trouble came from extending herself, trying to live up to the romantic standards established in rock-and-roll ballads. There had to be more to life than a dull routine, than another good day of shopping. It wasn't enough anymore for her to be stuck at home or cruising the streets, her mind crammed with turbulent fantasies. She needed more, needed a man like Alfred who in his better moments was a fascinating man, a father figure with strange proclivities—and, like Vicki, a victim of impulses spawned from his troubled childhood.

"He was a trip, Gordon," Vicki would say about Alfred Bloomingdale. "When it came to men, he was a whole different story. He drew me in with his insanity. I couldn't believe a man that rich, that powerful, with his old-world status could even do the things he did, let alone so blatantly. Alfred, you see, never seemed to care. He didn't know about subtlety, and forget discretion altogether. He was like this big Baby Huey. If he tried to whisper you could hear him halfway across the room.

"I would say to him, Alfred, people will hear you. 'Let 'em,' he'd say real fast and guttural. 'There's nothing wrong with my talking this way. They can all go to hell, if they don't like it.'

"When he wanted something, he didn't ask, he demanded. Nicely, of course. At first. Unless whomever he was asking was slow on the uptake. Then Alfred would get a little louder, a little more forceful. You see Gordon, he knew he had the power, the money to do whatever he damned well pleased. When you have the name, like Bloomingdale, with the influence and upbringing, then you know the last thing people will do is try to get in your way. You can do almost anything, and unless you're real obvious nothing will happen; that is, if you have that power, and the money that goes along with it. Let's face it, I was attracted to that kind of power. I find it intoxicating.

"You see, that's my problem now," Vicki continued, referring to her diminished state in the world of finance. "Alfred taught me how to impose and get my way. With money. He never said anything about doing it when you're broke."

"What else made you stay that first time?" I asked. At times she was annoyed by my repeated questioning, preferring to turn up the fire in those green-almond eyes. She'd stare at me in silence, waiting for enough time to pass that it wouldn't seem awkward for her to change the subject. Vicki was quite adept at these transitions, having learned from years of avoiding embarrassing questions regarding the source of her apparent wealth. She believed it was to her advantage that no one ever knew everything. From Alfred she learned to avoid being pinpointed. From her own experience she thought too much explanation was senseless, since she'd never be fully understood. So to protect herself, Vicki kept many things secret, and omitted portions of others so that what she did reveal was imparted through selected vignettes. These varied, and were chosen according to the interests of the person she was speaking to and Vicki's mood of the moment. By the time I met her, this was a difficult habit for Vicki to break. But after awhile, she knew I'd keep prodding, searching for more than her patented explanations. It disturbed her and excited her at the same time. Vicki enjoyed the challenge of our dialogue. Clearly, she wanted to tell the truth about herself. She had an urgent need to express the perspective she'd gained from all those years in the combat zone. For only now was she starting to open up, confronting herself with the pain of being used. After Alfred's illness and finally his death, the realization of what she had done with herself was sometimes more than she could bear. Vicki would shake, and she began lapsing into drinking binges and heavy despair. She'd fight it, joke, get playful or spend hours looking up words in the dictionary. But all those years were haunting her, as the chronicle of her life unfolded. She'd ask me to lighten up, and for days she refused to discuss more than surface information. I pushed for more, which sometimes made her angry. She'd grow defensive, shouting at me and threatening to do the same to me one day.

"See how you'd like it," laughed Vicki. "With me asking you all these weird, personal questions. Taking pictures, snapping strobe lights in your face." She looked up, smiling ironically. "All I wanted was to get my money. I never expected any of this."

I shook my head and told her how smart I was, that I wouldn't get caught in a switch like hers. No public exposure for me, thank you. "Just answer me one thing," I added. "There was something else that made you stay that first time with Alfred and company," I insisted. "Something you're not telling me. What was it?"

"I had a son," she muttered after downing more wine. She spoke so softly that I could barely hear her. Her expression changed, she poured more wine and smoked another cigarette. Her hand was shaking. "I knew it was ending with Earle. It was only a matter of time. And I had a son and a mother who threatened to file for custody if I didn't send any money. I felt bad enough...the word is guilty, I suppose...for leaving him with her. You've met her. You know what she's like. And you just see the better side of her. She wouldn't dare let you see the other part, the strict Victorian morality that she used to enforce with a strap. Until she hit me once too often and I threw an ashtray at her. She turned and it only glanced off the side of her head, thank God. Otherwise, I would've been up for murder at twelve.

"But with Todd, my mother couldn't be sweet enough. She would treat him like a prince. It made me sick to watch her spoon feed him. He was already two or three years old. It made me crazy to think about losing my son, in a custody battle with my mother no less. I used to stay up all night and cry about it while Earle snored on the other side of the mattress. Like I said, Earle didn't want him around. He liked Todd, but my having a son would spoil the image. I found that most men couldn't handle my having a child. And being naive and immature, I started believing there was something wrong with it. Can you imagine? The men in my life, not all of them, fortunately, always made me feel embarrassed about having a child. All because they wanted just the image of me, the young, carefree and pretty girl. Sick isn't it?

"So what made me stay, you asked? I had promised Todd that I would always take care of him. He'd never go wanting. If I left Earle, I didn't know what would happen. Not that I was all that worried. At that age I had plenty of guts. But still....And then Alfred came along." Granted, there were other motivations—her vanity, greed and self-indulgence, and eventually, her genuine love for Blooming-dale. She could accept the consequences of her actions with a mixture of irony and disdain. It was in dealing with her son that Vicki believed she had no choice. It was her moral obligation, not just to provide extensively for his material comforts, but to elevate his station, assuring him the opportunities that she never had. She would do anything to accomplish this. And to accomplish this, she would always be forced to rely upon men.

To assure her financial security, she put up with lovers and husbands with whom life had gone stale. These men, with all their demands and shenanigans, were to be endured and manipulated long after the insensitivity of their demands had destroyed any hope of romance. Time and again she had approached them on faith and withdrew disappointed. In between she took what she wanted from whomever she wanted. It was her way of breaking even. Her good looks, her wit and her charm were the tools of her trade. Vicki firmly believed she had nothing else. Aside from the wild times, her son and the men who desired her, she had no identity. Even if she had tried to find one, she wouldn't have known where to begin.

So at eighteen, with a bad marriage, no education, and an illegitimate child to support, Vicki took the deal offered by Alfred Bloomingdale. Her mistake was in thinking she had driven a hard bargain for the false security and the trinkets and clothes she was given in exchange for devoting her life to his whims and fancies. She allowed him to shape her into any image he saw fit. He dressed her, paid her, and did his best to make her a lady. She was cast on the surface as a staid young beauty, a Republican no less, endowed with traditional etiquette and the diction of the ruling class. In the end, the baubles were sold off or missing, and the vast inventory of designer clothing was left hanging in the closets. Almost every day during the time I had spent with her, with thousands of dollars in clothes spilling out of virtually every drawer and closet, she walked around in sweaters and jeans.

At thirty, when I came to know her, she was in no mood to be charming and dazzling. She no longer had any use for dubious romances, nor for another marriage to the kind of men she felt had used her. For years she had been locked into a pattern of guilty compromise, a dishonorable truce between money and conscience. It was time, she believed, to forget about compromise, to get bold and funky and make it on her own. Clearly, for her, it was a matter of pride.

But back then, Alfred had said the magic words. "You can get what you need, whenever you need it. I'm that rich," Alfred had told her, setting it all into motion. It was storybook magic and adventure forever, that the man was putting up for grabs. He was strong and reassuring, appealing to the best of her fantasies and the worst of her fears. Whatever it was that attracted her to Alfred Bloomingdale also scared her half to death.

As the days came and went, lost in the drone of Indian Summer, Vicki sat alone in her bedroom with her chin propped on her knees and contemplated the pros and cons of Alfred's offer. She had no frame of reference and no one to talk to. She sat smoking and watching TV, allowing her thoughts to intermingle with the soap operas, as she struggled to determine her best course of action. She recalled most of what Alfred had told her that first day on Sunset Plaza Drive. She remembered what he had said about a mistress being a longtime tradition. He had called it respectable and explained that even his father had kept a woman for many, many years.

Vicki still wasn't convinced that taking up with Alfred was the smartest of moves. Alfred had frightened her and left her in a very weird state of mind. She shivered at the thought of his sex practices, his ties, his belts, his dildos—and that certain look in his eye. Vividly, she pictured him sweating; the perspiration dripped from his brow as he hollered and lashed these women with his premiere selection of men's leather belts. She considered his guttural theatrics and wondered if during those sessions he actually lost control of himself. What in the world had been the source of his demons? Where did it stem from, this driving obsession? She could see it pulling, pushing, tearing him apart. Did his friends know about it? What about his wife? Was she that far removed from her husband that she wasn't aware of his penchant for whipping bound prostitutes high in the Hollywood Hills? Maybe she just didn't care. Vicki wanted to know. The questions intrigued her. The answers had to be in a class all their own. It shocked her, that a man of his stature could behave this way. Earle was bad enough, with his multiple acts, his hookers and his sleeping with boys. But this? It was all too much, beyond the reaches of her understanding. Not even the soap operas, with their steamy string of infidelities, ever dared venture into this forbidden zone. Earle was harmless, but about this man she wasn't sure. Vicki shook her head and reflected on the intractable powers of fate. Leave it to her to cross paths with a man like Alfred Bloomingdale. In the ensuing trips up to Sunset Plaza Drive Vicki became more immersed in Alfred's scenario. She encountered a variety of women who, along with Kay, served as objects for Alfred's abuses. Before and after, with few exceptions, Alfred treated these women like dirt. He gloated, or turned cold and aloof when, at the end of a session, they accepted his money in exchange for thirty minutes' worth of theatrical misogyny and a dose of humiliation. In contrast, Alfred treated Vicki with the utmost respect, asking for her approval before trying anything new. With a patriarch's mien he consulted her and asked for her advice regarding who deserved a beating or what should be done to these women. Vicki found herself responding, giving her opinions, enjoying the power Alfred had placed in her hands. As time wore on Alfred, the "Master," dubbed Vicki his "Mistress" and ordered the women to do her bidding or face the consequences. When they failed to respond in the proper fashion, Vicki was commanded to crack their asses with gusto.

Bloomingdale made it very clear how Vicki should relate to these women. "They're nothing," he'd tell her. "You're the one who's special." He exhorted her to whip them harder, to let them know she was the boss and they were merely vassals, cultivated to service those with power and money. He made sure Vicki was present when it was time to pay them. He winked at her as he joked and bargained with the hookers. "All in the spirit of the game," he explained. "Everything in life is like that. You have to be aggressive. You have to be tough."

Alfred was tough, but not all the time. Early on, it became apparent to Vicki that Alfred could not stand up to Betsy. He feared her and dreaded any confrontation, preferring to duck her questions and dodge her accusations. She was tough with him, strict and maternal. He loved her for it, for serving as his icon, the embodiment of that superior female he had hated yet worshipped ever since he was a child. In the convoluted recesses of Alfred's innermost thoughts, he knew he would always believe in women before he believed in men. He would trust their powers, their ability to survive and prevail, long before he'd ever put much faith in the hollow comforts of masculine rhetoric. Women, he believed, would always win out in the end and, though trusting them, he despised them for their virtuosity. As a child he had experienced defeat through identification with his father, who had been abandoned by Alfred's mother, or the woman they claimed was Alfred's mother. Alfred was never sure who his mother was. What he was sure of, was his father's emotional destruction. He was haunted by the childhood image of Hiram Bloomingdale seated in his rocker, swaying back and forth in a trance-like state. For this and for other traumas garnered along the way, Alfred was obsessed with doling out punishment. He was determined to make them all pay.

Betsy, however, was determined to make Alfred pay for his frequent transgressions against the sanctity of their marriage. Apparently she had his number and knew how to use it to her best advantage. Periodically, when his running around became too much for her, or when she feared repercussions from her anointed social clique, she would confront Alfred, bringing her wrath down upon his twitching head, while forcing him to account for his latest series of indiscretions. Why couldn't he control himself, or at least keep it quiet? Not that she heard anything definite, just the whispers and the well-timed innuendoes. She reminded him of the embarrassment, the potential ruin of their business involvements and family standing. She warned him that she would never allow his foolishness and unfathomable desires to undermine her rising status. When cornered, Alfred appeased her by offering sums of money—which Betsy usually accepted—in exchange for dropping the issue. She'd take off on shopping sprees or go for long vacations, while he returned to his hookers, going on a rampage to make up for lost time.

Vicki detected the mixture of emotions whenever Alfred spoke of his wife. His ambivalence was revealed to her in his eyes and tone of voice. If nothing else, Betsy reminded him of who he was supposed to be in this world. A dentist's daughter, a native of Beverly Hills, the former Betty Lee Newling was proud and ambitious, penetrating all the right circles as she aspired to an even greater dominance in society. She wasn't about to allow a fine old name like Bloomingdale, a veritable fulcrum for social expansion, to be compromised by her husband's indiscriminate carousing. She knew better and, in spite of himself, Alfred did too.

Vicki would listen to his tales of domestic woe, including his loathing of wife and society. Repeatedly, he promised to divorce Betsy Bloomingdale so he could marry her. She knew he would never break away. Still, she tried her best to deny this stark reality, hiding the fact that this was life as it was, with many demands and few guarantees.

So Vicki, an unschooled teenager, and Alfred, a baron of the ruling class, made their pact. Each maintained that somehow, some way, their relationship would work out fine. They met at least three times a week, often having lunch together prior to the sessions up on Sunset Plaza Drive. When they were alone, Vicki loved to sit and talk with him. She felt secure and strongly attracted to Alfred and was grateful for his attention. He was a different man then, a charming and noble patron, not the wild beast that scared but excited her. He made it a point not to fawn all over her as other men did, but to win her over with old-boy romantics. She could see that he was happy to be in her company. He stressed to her how important the time they spent together was to him, and how it helped him overcome the pressures of his business. She believed him at first—with reservations, extreme reservations. But as time wore on, Vicki increasingly took Alfred at his word.

Alfred and Vicki first began their relationship when Alfred instituted the final break in Vicki's marriage to Earle Lamm. A little more than a month after they met, he asked her to accompany him on a business trip to Ft. Lauderdale, where he and his partner, Bill McCommas, a developer and investor from Topeka, Kansas, were building a hotel and resort facility. The Marina Bay Club, as it would later be known, was designed for the utmost in comfort and luxury. It featured its own marina and a series of "floating hotel rooms" with exterior boat slips, an ideal form of privacy enabling resident guests and potential smugglers to park their yachts just outside their doors.

Vicki argued that plans for such a trip were ill-conceived and premature. She was afraid Earle would catch on and cause a stir, something that, at the moment, she couldn't bear to face. "He's not stupid," she said. "He's already suspicious. He keeps asking me questions. I'm not sure what I should tell him."

Alfred countered by urging her to tell Earle she was going away on a modeling job. Alfred would give her money in order to make it convincing to Earle. She'd have $10,000 and additional money for shopping and playing. She would have a marvelous time lying on the beach all day with nothing to do. While Alfred conducted his business, she could think about getting away from Earle. She would feel better for the experience. And what's more, she'd be returning home with a gorgeous tan.

# 7

VICKI WOULD RETURN from Florida prepared to dissolve her marriage. With Alfred's permission, she had stayed extra days, visiting the Bahamas, where she sat in the sun and, between sips of *piña coladas*, nervously contemplating how she would break it to Earle. Vicki hated such moments, and even when it was her choice, feared the final, decisive separation. She was struck with a feeling of abandonment; she was the one who would ultimately be left alone. But with Earle, it had finally reached a point where there was no other choice. Vicki knew she couldn't go on any longer with all the faking and lying.

Earle had gotten the message, quite literally, after he had called her room at the Holiday Inn. When there was no answer, he had been mistakenly transferred to a startled Bill McCommas. Bill who occupied the room on one side of Vicki's, with Alfred on the other, had no chance to be flattered by what the desk clerk and the switchboard operator had mistakenly taken for granted. Earle was on the line, acting rude and asking uncomfortable questions. McCommas tried his best, but not for a moment was Earle appeased by the poor man's impromptu stammerings. Earle was abrupt and threatening as he said what was on his mind. When he finished with his caustic remarks, Lamm slammed down the phone, giving McCommas the chance to call Alfred and relate what had happened. Bloomingdale didn't seem at all disturbed.

"Leave it to you to get stuck with it," Bloomingdale roared, laughing with Vicki as they sat with Bill at dinner that evening.

"It's typical," sighed McCommas, lamenting his great misfortune that he was accused of being Vicki's secret lover, while reaping absolutely none of the carnal rewards. He watched Alfred and Vicki kiss and hold hands, while making plans for the time they would spend together. Bill had already noted the sums of money Alfred was spending on Vicki, and had commented on the now apparent hell-bent-for-leather approach with which Alfred proceeded in life. On one hand, it was amusing, as well as distinctive, to be partners with a man of Alfred's status. On the other, on the sobering level of business priorities, Bill could already see the potential for destruction created mainly through Alfred's pathological need for romantic distractions.

In the years to come, Bill, the reliable one, would often have to go to the front for his rather idiosyncratic partner. It would be McCommas who would have to explain why Bloomingdale, the supposedly mighty mega-millionaire, was always short of investment capital. Apparently, for McCommas, the inconveniences were worth the various trials and tribulations. He scrambled for the money that Bloomingdale's squandering necessitated, and he remained the loyal business partner, enhancing his own status and access to power while covering for Bloomingdale until the day Alfred died.

When Vicki returned to Los Angeles she went directly home and waited for Earle to arrive. Thankfully, Earle wasn't home yet, which gave her time to shower, change, and prepare herself for the final conflict. She could have never imagined what would ultimately happen. That evening, after Earle came home from work, they began the discussion, that started the argument, that turned into bitterness, leading to oaths, threats and a heap of accusations.

This was later followed by tears, amenities, and Earle's appeals for reconciliation.

"Men like Bloomingdale get bored with you," Earle ranted. "You're one more pretty girl, that's all. They get tired of one pretty girl and they trade them in for another."

"Earle, I'm not just pretty, I'm beautiful," Vicki argued. She was adamant, and quite annoyed with his pleading. She wanted this over with, simply, without all the grief and hassle. After all, this was not a borderline situation, a romantic dispute or fit of self-doubting. To Vicki, her marriage had long been gone, though neither had dared take that first step away. Earle had snuck off and done his thing, and she had done hers, having dated a rock musician or two that she had met while hanging out at the Record Plant recording studio.

"But this is different," Vicki explained to Earle. "This," she declared, "is pretty heavy. I'm falling in love with the man."

With that to ponder, Earle sat up all night, refilling his tumbler of whiskey, while Vicki escaped to the bedroom, smoked a joint and eventually drifted off to sleep. However, bright and early the following morning the telephone rang.

"It's Alfred," Vicki announced, having answered. She gazed into Earle's bloodshot eyes, noting his quizzical face surrounded by his ragged stubble, his open shirt and wrinkled trousers, and the up-all-night aroma that exuded from his body. She handed him the phone. "He wants to talk to you," she said, and then retreated back inside the bedroom where she could listen in on the showdown between Earle Lamm and Alfred Bloomingdale. She heard Earle rambling on and on about Alfred being an animal—an evil, disgusting sonofabitch who thought he could buy Vicki.

Alfred, however, was impervious to Earle's insults. "What'll it take to get you out of the picture?" was all he wanted to know.

"I'd never take money for the woman I love."

Vicki could only listen in for a couple of minutes before her nervousness and nausea compelled her to hang up the phone. She was caught up in a bartering system between two men who were not arguing as much for her rights and needs as they were for their own. She grew tearful, as an ineffable melancholy washed over her. She was sorry she had eavesdropped. She was sorry for a lot of things. What made it worse was the disturbing recognition that there was no going back and there was no standing still. Her fate was now essentially in the hands of Alfred Bloomingdale.

With a defeated Earle Lamm, none the richer but "out of the picture" nevertheless, Alfred wasted no time in transplanting his mistress to better surroundings. He leased Vicki the first of a number of houses, this one above Sunset Strip in fashionable West Hollywood. He bought her clothes and furniture and provided her with a cook and a full-time housekeeper. He gave her money and urged her to spend it. He wanted her to look good during the time they spent together. He insisted that she learn the proper social habits so that she could be poised and impressive when in the company of his business associates. She was now officially his mistress, and as such there was a major change in priorities. Vicki, like it or not, was part of the system, the very system that for a time she believed she was rebelling against. And as part of this system, and more important, as Alfred's mistress, she was forced to live within its boundaries, obey its protocol and demonstrate proper manners. Alfred was adamant. She must learn to be a lady.

In the coming months Vicki would discover that Alfred's idea of happiness was an odd combination of utility and idolatry. He coerced and manipulated, and then worshipped her. Vicki's monthly allowance steadily increased, with her knowing that, if she ran out of cash in the middle of the month, Alfred was usually good for another thousand or two. She learned how to bargain with him. If she wanted two, she would ask for three and then settle with him somewhere in the middle of the difference. In addition to the checks he wrote, Alfred—who had a penchant for crisp, new money, which his secretary furnished by making daily trips to the bank—gave his discarded currency to Vicki. Frowning, as if they carried disease, he'd pass her the old and wilted bills. To Alfred they were little more than trash. Upon reflection, Vicki remembered Alfred's throwaways amounting to as much as $500 a month.

"You sure know how to spend it," Alfred would tease her. "You and Betsy, you don't just like money...you need it."

"Just like a drug," Vicki laughed, accepting his checks and discarded currency. "Besides, you said you've got it, darling. You said to spend it. There's not a whole lot else for me to do."

"I call you every day."

"You call me twenty times a day. You drive me crazy sometimes with all your phone calls."

"That's part of the deal, isn't it?" Alfred chortled.

Vicki nodded and swallowed. "Yeah, that's part of the deal."

The part of the deal that wasn't wearing so well with Vicki was the frequent trips to Kay's on Sunset Plaza Drive. Alfred, who had promised the group scenario would taper off as time wore on, was actually pressing harder. Three times a week, on an average, Vicki would journey into the Hollywood Hills to meet Alfred for a little intimate gathering featuring Kay and some of her friends. These sessions were beginning to creep up on the defenses within Vicki's psyche. She was feeling guilty and ugly. She accused Alfred of being a sick man, of playing warped games with her mind. It was hard for Vicki to reconcile Alfred's insistence that she become a lady with his passion for bondage and beating, his commands that she involve herself with other women. Here he was, having an absolute ball, paying a fortune to climb on the backs of ululating prostitutes. Then he would turn around and lecture Vicki on the imperatives of proper etiquette or scold her for being lavish or buying too many clothes. To make it all a little more palatable, Vicki started drinking wine—only at lunch at first, but eventually, when she was alone at night, for the numbing and pleasurable high that would finally allow her to drift off into a long, deep sleep. Drugs, especially Valiums and assorted downers, were helping her get through the day. They blunted the senses, serving as a barricade against the dilemmas and questions that were beginning to plague her.

Vicki, from the outset, had refused to have call girls visiting her house, whether Alfred was paying the rent or not. Now she was objecting increasingly to Bloomingdale's frequent rendezvous at Kay's. After protracted arguments, Alfred finally acquiesced. They would lease, he decided, a special hideaway, a second apartment where they could have their own whores over for the evening, and not be so dependent on Kay. Maybe Vicki had friends, he wondered, women she could call?

This was not at all what Vicki had in mind. But, despite her threats and assorted protests, she capitulated, and, within a month, Alfred leased a two-bedroom apartment in the fashionable West Side Towers, a high-rise building on La Cienega Boulevard in West Hollywood. This, their conjugal meeting ground, was well stocked with alcohol and food. It had come furnished, but little knick-knacks and accessories were needed for the personal touch. Shopping for them gave Vicki something to do.

Alfred claimed the new apartment would at least assure Vicki's anonymity. Vicki wasn't convinced. She was already sensing among her friends and around town little things that made her uncomfortable. To combat these whispers, Vicki chose conceit and a haughty posture as her defense. She made it clear to everyone who challenged her that she was superior, special and beautiful in the eyes of wealthy men. Meanwhile, she grew increasingly concerned.

"These women are professionals," Alfred maintained when Vicki provoked him by suggesting the hookers were spreading the word. "They don't talk."

But they did talk. As did her friends, not necessarily the close ones, but those dull, pretty girls, the occasional Hollywood acquaintances Vicki kept around for company. Starlets, models and ladies just on the make, these women were attractive novelties who, with Vicki's assistance, Alfred could summon to his custom-built theater of cruelty. Such women usually needed money for the niceties in life, or just to pay the rent. And with these non-professionals, he was especially generous, doling out as much as $2,500 apiece for the privilege of smacking their asses.

Vicki did the calling. Not at first. But as time passed, the repetition and the weirdness of these sexual conclaves took on the complexion of another day's routine. Alfred picked out the hookers from his little black book and read the telephone numbers to Vicki, who would call the girls on Alfred's behalf. Sometimes, with Alfred's prompting, she'd bargain with them for better prices. It made Vicki uncomfortable. Her stomach fluttered, her palms sweated. Nevertheless, she overcame her anxieties and maintained control of the given situation. Her voice, with its quality of dusky assertiveness, exacted respect, and she gloated with satisfaction when the hookers acquiesced and she was able to bargain them down.

Later, Alfred persuaded Vicki to make the selections. Just eighteen, unwittingly and gradually, she became Alfred's procurer, choosing girls from his coveted directory. Eventually he had her calling her friends and acquaintances, usually during the evenings, when Alfred cried out for variety and when Betsy was out of town. Women often rejected the offer, but many didn't. Vicki told them how much cash Alfred was willing to part with and assured them that they wouldn't get hurt. Back then, to her it was all a game. She assumed it was a simple matter of "Hey, call up some friends, they'll make some money, we'll have some fun and I'll supply the champagne." Only years later, when I prompted her, did Vicki view it with different perspective, realizing she was serving as Alfred's pimp. What Vicki did understand was someone at last had delegated responsibility to her. He had entrusted her with power. She was the authority. Fate had presented her with opportunity. "It wasn't that bad," she had told herself. "Only a few hours out of a week." Besides, it made Alfred happy to see her make those calls.

For his birthday that year Vicki presented Alfred with fifteen naked hookers. On Vicki's command, and for $100 apiece, the ladies cried "Surprise!" in unison before emerging bare-assed from the master bedroom. Even for Alfred it was overkill. His mouth open, his head shaking, Alfred observed them in puzzled silence, as if the women were residual apparitions from a turbulent dream. He couldn't get over it, nor could the hookers, a ragged lineup of giggling young women who stood naked and uncertain, glancing furtively at one another for a sign of what to do. Vicki was growing uncomfortable. Alfred was feeling vaguely threatened. She had overwhelmed him, unwittingly confronted him with what was more than he could handle. Signs of mortality were inscribed in his pensive expression. Her stomach tightened when he turned and stared at his mistress.

Alfred's eyes widened, his head jerked back, and a smile spread out across his long and angular face. He was glowing now like a delighted little boy. Suddenly, in thunderous waves, he was roaring with laughter.

"Leave it to you, Vic!" he cried, raspy and coughing. He shook his head and with his tongue he traced the outline of his mouth as he regained control of himself. "Beats the hell out of another briefcase, or a goddamned shirt and tie."

Vicki shrugged and smiled, her widening mouth, hanging head and laconic, shuffling gait expressing the demeanor of a childish and wistful clown. She moved closer to Alfred, embraced and kissed him, tenderly pressing her face against his copious, barrel chest. She remained still, allowing him to stroke her hair. Soon he was breathing heavily. She kissed him, imprinting lipstick on his shirt.

"Happy Birthday!" she whispered, gesturing to the murmuring, onlooking hookers. "I paid for them myself."

# 8

TOWARD THE END of the first year with Alfred, Vicki had established a pattern to her life. A daily routine, a day of shopping, with its illusory sense of direction, made her feel secure, as if she belonged in Alfred's world. She convinced herself she was making arrangements for the days ahead when she and Alfred would grow even closer and she would participate in his business, rather than watch from the sidelines. In addition to Bill McCommas, Vicki by now had met some of Alfred's other friends: Sammy Colt, the grandson of the historically reputed arms manufacturer; Tuck Trainer, the tire manufacturer; and Justin Dart, the aging head of Dart Industries. She was an instant sensation as she captivated them with her poise, her aptitude for conversation. She possessed a reserve, a certain gentility which she would punctuate with mischievous innuendo. Charming, smiling, laughing at their jokes, Vicki listened intently while these rich, self-made cronies, who rarely got this close to such a pretty young girl, related cherished anecdotes drawn from the stories of their lives. It drove them crazy that she was able to touch in them something personal, provoking an intimate sense of themselves.

Alfred and Vicki began to travel more frequently. Occasionally, they would go to New York or Europe, but more often than not they would drive down the coast to the Rancho La Costa Country Club near San Diego, or fly east to the now-established Marina Bay Club in Fort Lauderdale.

The lovers seemed to have shared an affinity for the sunny hot weather.

Vicki enjoyed her stays at the Marina Bay Club, for she had the run of the place. And, with Alfred off doing business, she had a wonderful time by herself. Now and then she would play around, finding young men with whom she could share her leisure. Alfred either didn't notice or never mentioned it, although, when she cast her eyes toward the formidable types, the men who were possibly in Alfred's league, she was often cautioned.

"They're trouble," he would say when she teased him about their sex appeal. "Some of them are smugglers."

"So what?" Vicki pressed him. "Maybe I can score some really good dope," she giggled.

"No," he replied, exasperated and sighing. "You get mixed up with them and we could both have a problem. Someone might think it's attempted extortion."

Vicki was incredulous. "Alfred, what are you talking about?"

"Some years ago, before I met you, I had some trouble with the FBI. I don't need anymore heat from them. They thought I was using ladies to put the squeeze on some people."

"Were you?" Vicki asked.

Alfred shook his head. "Sometimes you gotta do things for your friends."

Vicki, at the time, was more amused than concerned. The full weight of Alfred's involvement, as well as her own, hadn't yet had its impact. She was young and agile, able to bounce back easily. Shopping, and not the lurking spectre of consequence, occupied the front row seat in her brain. Perfectly coiffed, with the latest of fashion gracing her willowy frame, wearing bracelets, necklaces and diamond earrings, she was a vision of sheer elegance, the translucent enigma from the dark side of luxury. Depending on mood shifts, she was either strident and cocky, or afraid she was unable to acclimate to this new pace in her life. But she wanted respect and she wanted recognition. She wanted to be amused and enlightened. She wanted to advance to a better station in life, to be more like Betsy and her esteemed coterie, the most prominent women in Los Angeles society. With Alfred's help, she believed she could make it and eventually find herself among the more glamorous of these closely knit and influential women, whom Alfred, during periodic sessions of "compare and contrast," would praise.

Vicki would never make it. For one thing, Alfred offered little assistance, preferring instead to keep Vicki childlike and innocent, more appealing for the things he liked the best. And Vicki on her own wasn't as fervently ambitious, or as willing to utilize her man's status as was necessary to gain personal access to power. She was a man's woman, of the old, old school, preferring to back her lover, encourage his success, rather than strike out in directions of her own. She would watch and comprehend, but, like a kid with her nose pressed against the glass, she was on the outside looking in, never fully prepared for the Machiavellian warfare employed by the ambitious matrons, who, through the social network, aspired to the highest levels of authority and influence. Instead, she would be forced to settle for the material trappings, the accouterments of wealth and position, with no identity, other than that of Alfred's mistress.

Ultimately she was a patsy, the gullible girl with bottomless charge cards, buying counterfeit tickets to the promised land. By eleven o'clock every weekday morning Vicki was out the door and on her way to Beverly Hills. She was a girl on a mission, buying everything in sight. They knew her in all the "right" stores and loved her as one of their better customers. She bought dresses and jewelry and things for the house. She bought dozens of wine glasses for the parties she and Alfred would someday throw. She bought silverware, flatware, crystal and china. She nearly cornered the market on linens, had stacks of napkins that catering

81

services would envy. She bought the best of wines, expensive samplings that were graciously handpicked by eager merchants. Grocery staples and household supplies were purchased in massive quantities, although Vicki, spoiled and twenty, never dreamed of bargaining for the appropriate discount prices.

In the middle of the day, in a street clogged with traffic, Vicki would swing a rapid U-turn, having spotted something in a window that she couldn't live without. The shopping and buying got her high, kept her going, and prevented her from thinking about the long nights ahead when she would be alone, getting stoned in her bedroom, fighting off that desperate sense of isolation that encroached upon her. Inebriants, the proximity of the live-in servants, and the friends she kept around for company did little to quell her fear of being alone. She explored her mind for a philosophical foundation, a system of belief with which she felt secure. She wanted answers to questions she couldn't articulate, and when no answers came, she found herself feeling guilty and constrained. Despair intruded, shadowed by grievous forebodings of what her future held in store. She would lapse into sessions of fervent self-pity, crying for hours on end, or make late-night, emotional phone calls to either bored or patient friends. Here she was, she'd say, looking great and going nowhere, preparing herself for nothing more than another day of shopping and the punctuality of Bloomingdale's nine A.M. call.

Other men, more or less, were out of the question. She refused dates for fear of having to explain who she was and where she was getting her money. Any encounters, if they happened at all, were short, sweet and superficial, devoid of any chance for emotional satisfaction. Intrusive questions could never be asked. Personal revelations were nearly always forsaken. Conditions of time and Alfred's ubiquity threatened to undermine any potential relationship. Vicki became expert at covering her tracks, weaving tapestries of camouflage which, at the same time, eluded and satisfied the male curiosity. Eventually her entire life became a series of multiple episodes carved from the truth and designed with amplified details until the perfect illusion was constructed. With its magnetic divulgences and surfeit elaborations, which were carefully monitored for permissible details, Vicki enjoyed the role of storyteller. She could play up the smallest of facts to her greatest advantage. She could go on talking for hours. She was captivating, witty, and pretty too. She revealed bits of herself while exposing nothing at all.

Dating, therefore, was more of a chore than a pleasure. Now and then she encountered infrequent exceptions, men who were in possession of charm and self-confidence, who could hold Vicki's attention, at least until their conversations started to repeat themselves. And, among them, few could stand Vicki's constant testing. She considered most men weak and insensitive. The majority were boring, and nearly all lacked original thought. In periodic flurries of optimism, she dated men or enjoyed a brief affair. And then she'd end it, retreating back inside her sanctuary, with her fantasies and servants. The servants cooked and ran the house while Vicki lay in solitude, contemplating life from the bedroom. Most nights she'd be asleep by the end of Johnny Carson's monologue. She'd dream romantic adventures and wondered if she should start going out again. But she couldn't avoid comparing other men to Alfred. Despite the boasting about their successes, and their half-hearted macho bullshit, none could ever be as challenging or as obsessed with her as Alfred Bloomingdale. Rather than face it time after time, Vicki drew deeper inside herself, disguising her uncertainties with luxury and bravado. She was a mystery to one and all, a beautiful and versatile emanation who, fraught with despair and frustration, became increasingly ripe for shallow escapisms, brief sojourns in the company of imperfect strangers.

The more I listened to Vicki, the more I was struck by how entrapped she was by the powers of fate and circumstance. Free will and self-determination didn't stand a chance, especially with someone like Vicki Morgan, someone homesteading in destiny's force-field. She loved to tempt fate and she loved to get away with it. And when things didn't turn out so well, she accepted the subsequent penalties with an ascetic's relish, bearing the consequences as battle scars in her quest for human experience.

"It comes with the territory," shrugged Vicki. "You feel locked in...but your mind...your mind is hyperactive. I was constantly struggling to suppress all those thoughts, those weird and disturbing questions that were subconsciously taking hold of me.

"Look, I was nineteen, twenty at the most, and I was trapped inside this certain lifestyle. I had money...things. I had more than most can ever dream of having. And I'm supposed to be happy. Only I'm not happy. I'm confused as all hell, and I'm so neurotic I don't even know if I'm all that confused. I mean, it's me, right? I'm the one who's living this way. I'm the mistress. I'm shopping, I'm seeing Alfred. I'm the one running wild in the streets with his money. I thought I had it all by the balls! But when I think back on it, I realize I had no idea what I was doing or what was even happening to me. And, thanks to Alfred, and my own thing with money, I was hooked, addicted to that way of life!"

I watched Vicki drift off in silent recollection. She rolled her eyes and shook her head. A nearly imperceptible smile ascended from the corners of her mouth.

"You get me thinking," she said. "You really do." In a moment she was laughing, allowing the irony to color her voice. "You know, about life in the good old days.

"I remember having all this red wine I had bought and stored for whatever occasion. I don't know. But I had three cases of this supposedly rare vintage that I knew absolutely nothing about, except that it was scarce and expensive. I

kept them for months. They were just sitting there. So...
one night I figured, 'Screw this,' and I opened one bottle and
then another, until, after a few weeks, maybe a month, all
the wine was gone. Sometimes friends would come over, but
mainly it was me sitting alone, having my personal wine-
tasting parties."

Vicki hesitated, smiled at me. "And this is one of the
more constructive things I did with my time," she admitted,
turning serious as she lit a cigarette and focused on additional thoughts. "When I say that I was trapped, I mean,
locked in. Up here, in the mind, where early on...from my
father...I was programmed into believing that a man
showed his love through money, the things that he gave you.
I mean, my father wanted no part of me. But...he sent me
money. And that, I convinced myself, was his sign of love for
me. Of course he loves me...he sends me a check. More
money than any of my girlfriends ever got from their
parents. Probably more money than any teenage kid should
have to spend on their own. And I'd take the money and buy
clothes with it, pretending it was my father who actually
picked them out for me.

"He and almost every man after that were judged by the
money they were spending on Vicki. That's how insecure I
was."

"What about Alfred?"

"Naturally, with Alfred...."

A bemused and smirking Vicki Morgan narrowed her
eyes, cocked her head to the side and stared at me, inhaling
deeply from her cigarette as she waited for me to continue
my probing. I could see her getting defensive. She was
attentive and curious, anticipating my thoughts. She was
the goalie, poised for the shot on her delicate consciousness.
Vicki enjoyed these moments. Even when they were painful, they would make her come alive. She was grateful for
the stimulation, the novel challenge of energetic debate.
Vicki well understood the value of an argument. Through

its heated exchange, she could probe and instigate, investigate the dynamics of my thinking, my motivations, the very basis of my logic, and compare it to hers. She demanded specifics, seemingly pointless details, and from these she determined sincerity. She wanted to trust me. She wanted to understand me. It was part of our growing friendship.

"So you used Alfred's money to convince yourself of his great love for you. If money was love then you could justify becoming his mistress. You could live without direction because you were living for Alfred's love. You weren't stuck in the rut, you were just waiting for things to change, that's all. Of course he loved you, he was obsessed with you, he called you twenty times a day. But you knew, no matter what you say, that he would never marry you. Not really. He was much too afraid of Betsy to make a move like that. But...he did give you money. Lots of fucking money. Which he'd give forever, as long as you were there. Waiting for his call."

Vicki just stared at me. She fought back the tears that welled in her eyes. She was thinking, retracing my words while considering possible answers. I watched and waited for her to shout and get crazy, accuse and hurl epithets regarding my cynicism and lack of understanding. But she retained her composure, and when she spoke, she spoke slowly and carefully as she measured every word.

"For twelve years," she acknowledged, "Alfred and I went on and off like that. For twelve years. Sure, some of it was the money. I'd be a fool to say it wasn't. But like I said, money had always come to Vicki. If it wasn't Alfred's money, there was always someone else. But there was no other man who had Alfred's energy. When he was with me, he was like a big, loveable kid, enthusiastic, doing everything fast! I loved that energy. He needed me, and I loved that too. We were so many things to each other. All these different...roles. Friend, lover, parent, child, and damn near everything else in between.

"Gordon, I'm not saying it wasn't crazy. We were classical obsessives, wanting everything, in spite of obstacles and consequences. Of course it was crazy. I suffered from at least one nervous breakdown. I mean, five months in a mental hospital is not a swell vacation. And Alfred, with his sick trip...we know what that was all about. But here I was, in love with the man, and yet, because of guilt and insecurity, I had this terrible need to be free of him. I could never accept the fact that I was just the mistress. That's right...just the mistress! Not until Alfred lay dying in the hospital, did I ever really understand what the story was. So to escape from Alfred, I married two men and lived with a couple of others. I dated out of impulse and married out of desperation. But I always went back to Alfred. Because of that energy, his sense of adventure, that other men, no matter what their ages, just didn't have. So I kept going back to him. And he kept me dependent. And I sat back and let him do it."

"You may have loved him, and he might've taught you proper etiquette and the rudiments of stylish living, but you got fucked. Let's face it. In all those years, he never helped you to expand and mature. He ruined all your other relationships so that no matter who or what else came into your life, you remained dependent on him. But when he was sick, you were the only one there, probably the only one who gave a damn. And when he died, he left you with nothing but shame and despair. Can you tell me this was worth it? I'm sorry, but some may not conceive of this as an enviable romance."

She frowned like a child and turned away from me, looking tired and melancholy as she reviewed her past. Reclining deeply into the cushions of her white, goose down sofa, her legs hanging over its arm, she pressed the back of her wrist against her forehead and stared at the cottage cheese ceiling. She was reminiscing. Time passed. She hardly moved. Occasionally, she'd pause to stub out her cigarette and light another, inserting with it a fresh piece of gum, the tiniest sliver of cinnamon sugarless, which Vicki chewed to kill the tobacco odor. Something that Alfred taught her. A nice gesture perhaps, but he could have forsaken such pointers and taught her how to survive instead. He could have provided in death what he had in life. He could have established something solid, like an insurance policy with Vicki as beneficiary, instead of leaving her with two wobbly contracts and a lifetime supply of broken promises.

I had heard Vicki's explanations as to why he hadn't provided for her, including her description of Alfred's fear of death and his denial of his own mortality. I had listened to her describe his weakened state, just prior to his demise, when he became enfeebled and could no longer function and was persuaded to render power of attorney to Betsy, who promptly cut off the funds. I listened, and much of it even made sense to me. Still, I didn't buy it. Whether he loved her or not—and I believe he did, deep down inside—Alfred really, I mean really, had it in for women. With Vicki, and with Betsy, perhaps in a different way, he had created and foisted certain dependencies and then left them stranded.

Vicki was almost ready to talk again. She sat up, lit another cigarette, and sipped from her glass of white wine. I sat quietly, wondering what she'd been thinking about. Whatever it was, I could tell she didn't wish to discuss it, yet I didn't push the issue by asking any questions, knowing this would only lead to an argument. In her own time Vicki would tell me what she'd been thinking, either later that evening or in a couple of days, after she had a chance to absorb the hurt and disappointment. Now I waited patiently, not wanting to upset her any more than was necessary to get at the truth, or whatever semblance of truth there was that she and I could ultimately agree on.

"What?" I asked casually, after a few moments had

passed in an awkward silence. This, she mistakenly assumed was my impatience.

"You're insensitive," she declared, exhaling her words in a column of smoke. "You're really a sonofabitch."

"So they tell me. Just be straight with me, that's all, and you'll make us both happy."

"I'm trying to. But I get so damn nervous when you get impatient with me. Then I try too hard, out comes the lisp and I lose my train of thought. Remember, a lot of this...I haven't thought about in years."

"If you ever thought about it at all. It amazes me, sometimes, what you can block from your mind. You just ran blindly through life without looking back."

"I'm the bad girl, remember? I'm not supposed to have regrets."

"But you do, right?"

"Do what?" she asked, her voice instilled with ice and sarcasm.

"You were playing hardball," I reminded her. "When you screw up in hardball, you lose."

"When you trust in men, you get used and you suffer."

"You were used?"

"Damn right, I was used!"

"By Alfred?"

She blinked her eyes and took a breath. "Yes. Even by Alfred."

It was time, I decided, to pour myself another drink. I stood and advanced to the wet bar, that ever-present condo amenity made of formica and stainless steel. I could feel Vicki staring, her eyes on my back, observing my gestures. I had pushed her before, but never as hard as this. Things were rapidly changing. I felt like a viewer who was projecting himself into the story only to find out I was already there. I felt light-headed. I poured scotch over ice cubes into a forty-dollar Tiffany glass. She had a few left from the salad days, thin, heavy-based tumblers, a simple design that delighted the hands that held them. I found myself in a soulful mood, touched by the quiet passion that, for weeks, had been drawing us together. I knew what she was thinking, and I knew what I was feeling. But why was I so surprised that I was feeling this way? I turned and faced Vicki, who was watching me, amused and disturbed by my expression, trying to read my thoughts.

"Is something the matter?" she asked me. She was concerned with my mood shift, alarmed by my silence. She studied my eyes for hostility. Apprehension lined her face. I began to feel uncomfortable. I was reluctant to start in with lengthy explanations. It was all very simple, just difficult to express.

I shook my head, tossed down my scotch and returned to my chair at the dining room table. "No," I finally answered her, "just thinking, that's all."

"About what?" she wanted to know. There was a light in her eyes, as if she had already sensed my thoughts and was just doing this to provoke me. "What is it?"

"It's been what? Seven weeks, maybe, since we started this trip down memory lane, talking for hours on the Vicki and Gordon show. I'm beginning to feel like I've known you for ages. Like we're two retired old cockers from Atlantic City, hashing out life from chairs on the boardwalk."

Vicki was smiling, playing with her wine glass. When she saw me react to her fidgeting, she sat the glass down and calmly folded her hands on the table. She was the lady now, poised and erudite, relishing the tension. "What are you trying to say to me?" she asked, advancing her questions like pieces on a chessboard.

"What am I trying to say to you?" I mimicked. "Like it's a mystery or something. You know exactly what's on my mind."

Her eyes were flashing. She was smiling triumphantly,

flicking ashes from her cigarette as she considered her response. "You mean...we have a problem here?"

"Yeah, a definite problem."

"What is our problem?" she smiled, putting the burden on me.

I sighed and finished the rest of my scotch. Our cat-and-mouse game had begun to annoy me. I was in no mood to continue with schoolboys' subterfuge. It would only work to her advantage and make me feel like a fool. Besides, what were we actually hiding? Something that had been inevitable from the beginning—the metamorphosis of our curiosity and ambition to that of attraction and desire. How nice! What perfect timing! Any day now, my wife was due at the hospital to bear our first and only child. I loved Marcia, my wife, and the idea of being a father. We had enjoyed nearly twelve years of love and companionship, to say nothing of having survived the periodic conflicts, the cyclic points of disjunction, from which either new perspectives are gained or the marriage is destroyed. We had endured the changes, critical disputes and threats of separation. We had resolved much of the turmoil stemming from our divergent interests. Since Marcia first learned that she was pregnant, my rowdiness had gone into remission, my inherent restlessness had been under control. We had been at peace with each other, at peace and optimistic, waiting impatiently for our son to arrive.

And now here I was, getting down to it, with Vicki Morgan yet, the candidate least likely to be voted the girl-next-door. The formalities were over. Pretense and etiquette had run their course. We could no longer deny the underlying tensions, the heightened emotions that, for weeks, we had ignored or somehow avoided. We had become absorbed with each other, curious and infatuated. We were the midnight debating society, two renegades laughing, feeling it out in marathon sessions until the pewter sky of the approaching dawn left us standing awkwardly in the doorway, reluctant to say goodbye. It was a time of late night phone calls and obscure sensations. Clearly, something serious was happening here. She was either the inspiration for my change and transcendence, or God's poetic justice for the things I'd done wrong in the past.

"What is our problem?" I said, finally prepared to answer her question. "We've fallen in love with each other. It's gonna fuck up a lot of things. You know it, I know it. . .but that's the way it goes.

"You look puzzled," I added. "Why's that?"

"Oh, I'm not puzzled," she assured me. She shook her head and stubbed out her cigarette. A smile was on her face. "I didn't think you would put it so. . .bluntly."

What the hell? There was no getting around it, no escape other than self-denial and total deprivation. And that wasn't about to happen. We had spent too much time together in intimate situations, conversing intensely about deeply personal subjects. We were not strangers who, though attracted and flirting, lacked the time and opportunity to begin to understand each other. Vicki and I knew each other, perhaps all too well. We were kindred spirits, instinctive rebels, who in our weeks together had laid the groundwork for our mutual attraction. And finally, when all was said and done, we shared the excitement of playing with fire.

# 9

WOMEN SEQUESTERED, fated to live in solitude, often develop a peculiar allure. They are possessed of a certain urgency brought on by a fear of isolation, of getting lost forever without hope of recognition. They are ambitious, but without direction. They are refined and magnetic, capable of blending subtlety with candor to gain the maximum effect on their listeners. Like mythical sirens, they learn to draw voyagers into their own world, where circumstance is manipulated to their greatest advantage. Elements of romance are aesthetically magnified, extended in time, exaggerating the significance of every nuance and detail. Every act is of historic importance, to be examined for its special meaning. Off-handed comments are subjected to careful scrutiny. Their lives are sparked and sometimes motivated by jolts of paranoia. Nothing is taken for granted. These are women like Vicki, who live within themselves. Psychologically speaking, they are all dressed up with no place to go.

Romance with Vicki was not to be taken for granted. It was a great debate from the starting gates, a satirical battle of wits. It was a game of push and pull for which the contestants, with all their logical discourses, their energetic and meticulous deliberations, should have been awarded honorary degrees in law. I was direct and forceful in my arguments, convinced in my mind that our involvement was a *fait accompli*. Vicki preferred to be coy and ambivalent, but sometimes she would dig in her heels, protesting vigorously, brandishing thirty years of psychic scars for me to examine, as she painfully and carefully defined the exploitation, betrayal and abandonment she had suffered in prior relationships. She pointed out that I was married and that, after Alfred, she had had enough of married men. She reminded me that for more than two years she had been celibate. "At least," she said, "I haven't slept with a man." She said the abstinence had left her asexual and afraid to start in again. She accused me of being selfish and insensitive. She claimed I was too much like her and, because of our similarities, we could never be compatible.

At this point, naturally, I was unwilling to admit how any of this could possibly have an adverse effect on our lives. I agreed, sure, there were obstacles and risks; that in fact, there was a multitude of possible consequences, but somehow they were less formidable than our missing out on what was commonly known as "a once in a lifetime opportunity." I projected comic vignettes of my eternal despair if we failed to make love before the apocalypse. Vicki admitted that I had a point. But what about our professional relationship? Would our being lovers only complicate matters, or draw us closer? she wondered. She didn't want to blow our relationship. Friendship was lasting, she said, but love affairs create obstacles and differences.

Of course, these concerns weren't so obvious when we began our romance. Instead, this was the hot and happy time as I reflected on visions of our making love in the natural light of the late afternoon. I remembered the clear, cold nights up on Tower Grove Drive when we looked out from her windows at the flickering lights of the city below. I reflected with some concern on a jealous and woeful Mary Sangre, Vicki's former lover and roommate, who early one morning tearfully departed, claiming she had an appointment to keep as she hastily retreated from the house. I thought of my friends and considered the ways to dispel their curiosities.

I thought of my wife, the pain of her labor and my presence at the recent birth of my son. I had not attended a single La Maze class, but having glimpsed the manual and being armed with a profusion of advice from my experienced buddies, I had persuaded a liberal-minded doctor to let me assist with the childbirth. To him I will always be grateful, for this was my greatest experience, one unsurpassed for its intimate sense of history and cultural timelessness, of being at one with all of humanity. I had marvelled at Marcia's courage and watched with awe as Casey came into this world. In less than twenty minutes from the time of his birth, I held my son in my arms. I recalled how his eyes attempted to focus on me as he studied my face with a curious silence.

Vicki was calling me at the hospital, making sure that everything was all right with mother and child. She asked if I was happy, and when I said yes, she reminded me again that above all, a father was responsible for the formative years of his son. A boy required love and understanding, direction from a masculine point of view. She couldn't say enough about the need for a father to spend productive time with his son. Without a strong model, Vicki claimed, a boy was destined for personal turmoil. It was her strongest belief, and she preached it with religious conviction. She was convinced her own failure to provide a father for her boy was the primary source of her troubles.

"Your son," she said, "is your ultimate responsibility. He comes before anything else in life."

Months later, this did, in fact, became my major concern in deciding the future of our relationship. But months later was virtually a lifetime away. This was just the beginning, the moment when lovers relish the intrigue, the mystery of passion and the struggle for mutual harmony. It is a time for getting lost in each other until the past and present fade away.

In keeping with the general confusion of our lives, Vicki's bedroom was usually a mess. Unlike the downstairs, which she kept clean and orderly, the upstairs was something else again. She would sponge the countertops, the sink, the shower and toilet, all with great diligence, but forget about her putting things away! Assorted expensive jackets, sweaters, underwear, and blue jeans lay in heaps about the room. Black-lacquered nightstands were cluttered with address books and empty wine glasses, empty pill bottles, packs of cigarettes and chewing gum. A television and a VCR recording unit were mounted atop the black, highboy dresser whose drawers were stuffed and overflowing. Hundreds, if not thousands, of dollars of beauty supplies and cosmetics were stacked precariously in the dressing area on the large formica counter just opposite the bathroom. For serious makeup sessions, which Vicki by now had pretty much eschewed, there was a crafted, lucite bench. There was an alpaca throw rug patterned like a tigerskin, which Katie, the Doberman Pinscher would later rip to shreds. Five-hundred-dollar monogrammed Pratesi sheets were covering the bed. There were two closets, stuffed with blouses, dresses, scarves, and belts. She had enough pairs of shoes and sneakers to outfit a centipede. She had a tremendous collection of handbags, and had set one inside the other wherever possible in order to conserve space.

There was a large, sliding glass window with a view of the driveway and the tan, stucco backs of the opposite row of condominiums. Noise from outside reverberated between the walls and then filtered into the bedroom. Voices, slamming car doors and the tinkling of glasses, plates and silverware were familiar sounds, reminiscent of my Philadelphia childhood when I used to sit inside my row house wishing I was somewhere else. I had hated it then, and found it even less appealing now. I would close the window in order to keep out most of the noise.

Vicki would open it. She claimed she did it for the air, but I was convinced she wanted to suffer to remind herself of her fall from grace. Like me, these noises represented her lower middle class background, the every day world where people went to work, came home and built things with power tools in their open garages. The commotion outside made it difficult for her to fall asleep. She would lie awake in silent apprehension, wondering if she'd ever regain the money and the chances she'd lost.

"That sonofabitch," she proclaimed one night. Her eyes were opened wide, her voice soft and wistful. I knew right away that she was referring to Alfred. "Look how he left me," she continued, as she climbed out of bed and, dressed in a tee-shirt and panties, started pacing the room. "I mean look at this," she said, picking up speed, waving her hands for emphasis. "All those years, and all that money, and I don't have a house to live in or a cent to call my own. And it's my fault. That's what kills me. It's my own goddamned fault. I used to be so...fussy," she acknowledged, after pausing to search for the word.

"What do you mean, fussy?" I asked.

"What do I mean?" she repeated, growing nervous and impatient with me. "I could never make up my mind. In the beginning Alfred tried to encourage me. He wanted me to buy something and then, in time, have it renovated, you know...done the way I wanted. But I was young, and coming from Montclair, you don't hear much about architecture and interior design. I didn't understand that you could take something and completely change it over. I thought Alfred was lying to me, or trying to get off cheap. Gordon, you should've seen what I thought of as cheap. Dumps, I'd call houses that today are worth...maybe as much as a million dollars."

"Sounds like Alfred was being real oppressive. How

much were these houses back then, in the good old days, before the great Los Angeles real-estate boom?"

"I don't know, maybe a hundred thousand to a quarter-million dollars."

"That's all?"

"Yes. Can you believe it? And I'm acting like he's forcing me to live in a rundown shanty. Oh, I don't know, maybe I couldn't commit myself. Although I can honestly tell you, I wanted a house. You see, a house was my voucher of credibility. It was a chance for security. I don't know why I felt that way, but I did.

"Yes, I do know why," she added after a moment's consideration. "Remember, money alone didn't mean that much to me. Money I could get from anywhere, especially at that age. But a house...that was something else. It was the difference between being treated like a wife, or being treated like a mistress. Money was only money, but a house was Alfred's commitment to me, a declaration of his love."

Vicki looked everywhere for her dream house. At eighteen the quest began, and it never ended as she searched in vain for the perfect house. Alone, or with a girlfriend in tow, she reconnoitered the best parts of the city. She had the top down and the radio blasting. She cruised the sidestreets and thoroughfares, drove up and down the winding, narrow canyon roads. For nearly ten years she drove around, looking for the house most befitting her lifestyle. It had to be just so, chic and funky, modern, but with a sense of age, and most importantly, the proper reflection of what she considered her storybook romance.

When she came upon something she liked, Vicki summoned Alfred, who obligingly, during his free afternoons, went along for the ride. Vicki relished these moments when they were off by themselves enjoying the intimacy and sunshine. In the confines of her two-seater Mercedes, Alfred was hers alone. Usually he was relaxed and jovial, his attention focused solely on Vicki. He would talk freely about some of his work and the people he knew. Apparently, he knew quite a few, but he hadn't liked many. He explained to Vicki that his world was cold and devoid of emotion, save for the baser drives such as greed, lust, and vengeance. He admitted he was part of that world, and said that she, Vicki Morgan, was his only uplifting experience. He reminded her how much he needed her, and he renewed his promise to keep her in style for as long as they both shall live.

However, as time wore on, Alfred grew impatient with Vicki and her fastidious taste in houses. He had grown bored with listening to the realtor's sales pitch and of being forced to pass himself off as dear old Mr. Morgan, Vicki's mythical father. And with the progression of time and their growing frustration, the couple began to argue. Long, bitter feuds ensued, coupled with assorted threats and insults. Alfred claimed Vicki was spoiled and much too demanding. Vicki, in turn, thought Alfred was hedging his bets. Meanwhile, puzzled realtors would stand mute and embarrassed, their arms akimbo, while the May-December romantics went at it tooth and nail.

No dispute over houses could keep the lovers apart. Tempers abated with the passage of time, and within a few days the couple was reunited. Vicki wasn't much for bearing grudges, once she'd made her point, and Alfred knew he'd live a lot longer without the extra aggravation. He enjoyed teasing and annoying her. He delighted in making her angry. But he couldn't stand it when she ignored him, refused to take his calls. He'd become exhausted and frustrated, distracted from his work. He would try repeatedly to get through to her on the telephone, but Vicki, when angry, either left him to the fate of the answering service or, worse still, left the receiver off the hook. Alfred hated it. He didn't even have the service to hear his demands and complaints. He would have to drive over to Vicki's and pound on the door. Sometimes she wouldn't answer, and sometimes she would let him in. With her legs crossed, her hands folded in her lap, Vicki would sit in formal rectitude, listening attentively while Alfred pleaded his case. She heard him assure, cajole and promise her a better tomorrow. And then she would forgive him. Until the next time around.

It took Betsy Bloomingdale to rattle the romance. Betsy, who had heard all the gossip, was angry and nervous. Her husband, once again, was making a fool of himself, at great risk to their social position. It was one thing for a man of his status to screw around on the side. It was another to do it in public. Even Betsy's dear friend and future First Lady, Nancy Reagan, had observed Alfred and Vicki embracing openly in the streets of Beverly Hills. Others in her clique had also seen them. It was becoming a source of excited gossip, like the sighting of Bigfoot. Now Betsy, quite by accident, had witnessed it for herself. She and her daughter Lisa had been standing across the street from the Ménage à Trois, a trendy hair salon on Camden Drive, when Alfred's Mercedes sedan pulled up to the opposite curb. They watched in amazement as a tall, slender, hipless young woman, similar in build to Betsy, climbed out of the car and, before entering the hair salon, kissed Alfred passionately on the mouth. It was clear that this was no hooker, no little sweet thing whom Alfred paid and then disposed of. This, indeed, was a menace. Vigilance was called for here.

Early the following morning, a loud and stammering Alfred Bloomingdale was calling Vicki from a pay phone, relating the news of his domestic crisis. She could hear the traffic passing in the background as Alfred informed her that Betsy and Lisa had seen them together, outside the Ménage à Trois. There would be no joy in Mudville, at least not in the immediate future. Betsy had changed all the telephone numbers at his office as well as the house. Only the main line remained the same.

"But don't call it, Vic," Alfred implored her. Please don't

call it! I'll have to lay low for awhile, at least until things cool down at home."

"Alfred, what am I gonna do?" Vicki demanded. He filled up her life with nannys, cooks, and servants, and now he was ducking out on her. She had all these expenses and no money with which to pay them. Her checking account was already overdrawn. Rent and utilities were coming due.

"Alfred...?"

"It'll work out," he tried to assure her. "I just need some time. I love you, Vic, I really do."

"Alfred....Dammit!"

"Vic, I gotta get out of here," he grumbled like a man on the lam. "People are waiting to use the phone." He promised he'd be in touch with her. And then he was gone.

Vicki sat in a dumbfounded stupor. It had happened so suddenly; a sweet dream had folded into a nightmare. She hung up the telephone and stared at it for a good twenty minutes, hoping that Alfred would call her back. Usually he phoned her ten, fifteen, twenty times a day. But on this day her phone remained silent. Tears filled her eyes, and that old familiar fear of abandonment played havoc on her nerves. Her palms sweated copiously and nausea clawed at her stomach. She opened her wallet and counted the cash. She didn't dare review her checkbook. There was little she could do until Alfred decided to call again. And there was always the distinct possibility that Alfred never would. It was time to take sleeping pills and get a few days' rest.

Days passed and Alfred didn't call. But by now, Vicki had regained her will and composure. Her fear had begun to dissipate, replaced by the anger of a woman scorned. Somehow, she would work it out, figure a way to pay the backlog of bills and the servants. She would get a hold of some money. She would stick it to Alfred. He'd stepped way out of line, and he'd be sorry. Vicki didn't like to be messed with.

Alfred was shocked when, one sunny morning, Vicki burst into his Century City office. Marilee Rabb, Alfred's secretary, had done her best to restrain Vicki, but to no avail. With her friend Emmy's assistance, Vicki pushed open the door and confronted Alfred. She found him sitting behind his desk, trying to smile. Angered, Vicki snatched a paperweight from a nearby table and prepared to throw it at Alfred. A wide-eyed Bloomingdale hit the floor and crawled underneath his desk.

"Vic," he was imploring from the safety of his knee hole bunker. "Let's work it out. We can talk about it peacefully and logically, like two adults."

She realized it made more sense than hitting him in the face with a paperweight. "Alfred, dammit!" she exclaimed, setting it back on the table. Already she was taking pity, feeling sorry for the poor, pathetic creature who was curled up under his desk.

Sensing the danger was over, Alfred got up off the floor. He was trembling, wiping saliva from his reddening face. He smiled at Vicki as he glanced at his chair, uncertain whether he should advance and kiss her or remain behind his desk.

"What are you trying to do to me?" Vicki wanted to know. "I don't hear from you. You don't send me any money. I've got payments up the wazoo!"

"Vic, I've been suffering too. I've been going out of my mind. I can't live without you. It's as simple as that."

"No, Alfred, it's not as simple as that. One minute you tell me you love me, and the next minute you cut me out of your life. Earlier this year you made me pregnant, and you told me you wanted me to have your child. And then you changed your mind and told me to get an abortion."

"You were the one who said you didn't want the baby."

"And if I'd had it? And you cut me off? That's why I didn't want it. There's no stability. What kind of life do I have with you?

"If you don't want to see me...fine. For whatever stupid reasons you have...they're your stupid reasons. But I need money to pay my expenses."

"How much were you thinking of?"

"A hundred thousand," Vicki answered without even batting an eye.

Alfred immediately launched into his reasons why he couldn't give her that great a sum. Mainly, he told her, Betsy had examined all the bank books, the checking accounts and any other place he had cash flow. She had counted it up and now monitored every dime.

"You have obligations to me," Vicki reminded him. "Remember, you told me you were rich. Think of all the times you came over to my house with a suitcase full of cash."

Suddenly Alfred started laughing. He picked up the phone and handed it to Vicki. "If you want money, then talk to Betsy. But be firm. She drives a harder bargain than I do."

By the second ring, Vicki had given the phone back to Alfred. She insisted he was crazy, although she was amused by his action. Still, he wasn't getting off the hook so easily. Not with all the bills she had to pay. Besides, he had insulted Vicki, had made a mockery of their relationship while revealing to her his terrible fear of Betsy. Fine! She'd walk out of his life, but with a check in her hand, a check that better be good!

An hour later Vicki left with a check made out for $20,000. The check was made out to Alan, Emmy's entrepreneurial husband, who agreed to serve as the beard so Betsy wouldn't discover for what purpose the check was written. The following day Vicki paid all her bills and prepared to depart for Europe. Her furniture was moved into storage, sold, or simply given away. Penny, the petite Oriental who had served for years as Vicki's personal housekeeper, was farmed out to friends, along with Vicki's five dogs.

Vicki couldn't wait to return to England, her mother's place of birth, where Vicki had lived during a couple years of her childhood. In England, she could think things out and plan for a new beginning. She was fortunate to have been invited there by Leslie and Bernie. They had offered her comfort and solitude, and a room in Bernie's London townhouse. It was a great place to make a clean break from Alfred. She looked forward to some peace and quiet.

# 10

VICKI FIRST MET Bernie Cornfeld when he was in a decline from the peak of his career. His innovative brainchild, the International Overseas Services, which he had founded in the 1950s as a corporate conglomerate, had been one of the world's richest entities. Structured as a "mutual fund for the common person," the IOS had accumulated funds of all denominations, in all currencies, from persons in the United States and Western Europe. Small amounts were pooled into large amounts, which in theory collectively gave the multitude of investors a far greater buying advantage for purchases of stocks and securities and, therefore, a greater percentage of the profits.

However, disaster had struck in 1970 when stock prices dropped and a man named Robert Vesco wrested control of the IOS from Cornfeld. Vesco is believed to have absconded to Costa Rica with anywhere from a quarter-billion to a billion dollars, leaving Bernie knotted up in the trick bag, facing charges in Switzerland and denigration in the rest of Western Europe. Ultimately, he would spend eleven months in St. Antoine's, a Swiss monastery that had been converted to a prison, before charges of fraud were dropped for lack of evidence.

Although he had become a legend throughout the world's financial capitals and was respected for his business savvy, Bernie was often criticized for his rather flamboyant life-style. An enigmatic character, intense and soft-spoken,

105

bearded, balding, and portly, he was a proverbial mother-lode for the attentions of the media. Bernie didn't in the least mind controversy. He thrived on the exposure and helped to cultivate his own notoriety. He was a public creature who enjoyed the pleasures of life and shared them with the people with whom he surrounded himself. He kept attractive young ladies at his palatial mansion, always a few at a time, and gave extravagant parties. Bernie was an excellent host and a generous man, regarded as a "soft touch" by a number of the down-on-their-luck celebrities who came to his house for dinner. For Robert Vesco, Bernie was an easy scapegoat.

Bernie maintained a house in London, a flat in Paris, and a French château, located just a few miles from the border with Switzerland, near Geneva, in addition to Grayhall, the thirty-five-room mansion in Beverly Hills, once owned by Douglas Fairbanks, Sr. He travelled often, accompanied by his girlfriend, Leslie Chern, and his closest business associates. He had seen the world and been with many women, but somehow, for some reason, he had been taken immediately when he first met Vicki Morgan.

Leslie and Vicki had been friends for a number of years and they had always remained in touch. While globe trotting with Bernie, Leslie made frequent long distance telephone calls to Vicki and wrote letters describing their business itinerary and a variety of Cornfeld's transactions. By talking with Leslie and by reading her letters, Vicki had gleaned more than a casual notion, and used to her advantage the information regarding what made Bernie tick.

She had visited Grayhall on different occasions as a guest of Leslie. On one occasion when she was invited to lunch, she was escorted by Alfred, whom Bernie had known since Bloomingdale's reign at the Diner's Club. Bernie was charming, the perfect gentleman, who served all the right food with all the right gestures. After lunch, he guided the couple through a tour of his much-publicized mansion, with its high, vaulted ceilings, its granite walls and marble floors. The interior decor looked as if the artisans of the Renaissance had mated with the opulent stylists of Beverly Hills. Burgundy velvet drapes covered the windows. Tapestries and oil paintings adorned the walls. The wooden furniture was thick and heavy. Covering the floor were oriental carpets, statuary, and large velvet chairs and sofas. Trees and shrubbery, accented with fountains, sprawled throughout the grounds. There was a swimming pool and tennis court, and a hot tub adorned with a fading mural of naked women. And finally, there was a special apartment built within the mansion to house Bernie's mother. He cherished his mother, and grieved deeply over her loss when she passed away at the age of ninety-one.

Now, with her clothes and jewelry crammed inside her Louis Vuitton bags, Vicki boldly departed for London. She was met by limousine and driven to Cornfeld's house in the city's prestigious Belgravia section. Leslie was delighted to see her, and Bernie was gracious and reassuring. He, the understanding patriarch, invited Vicki to stay as his guest for as long as she desired. That night the trio went out to dinner, and the following morning Bernie took the women shopping.

Vicki could easily perceive what Cornfeld was building up to. She had been around enough wealthy men to know their ploys, their tricks for getting their way. She was determined to teach Bernie a lesson. By the end of their quaint little shopping tour Vicki had come away with more than $30,000 in jewelry, clothing, furs, and accessories. She was everywhere at once, in and out of dressing rooms, commanding the sales help to bring still more of their very best selections. Was she ever enjoying herself! She taunted his libido and exploited his guise of generosity. What she bought, Cornfeld paid for, and with each new article Vicki could see he erroneously believed he was that much closer to climbing into her pants. Like ocean tides responding to the moon, she could almost hear the ebb and flow of Bernie's sexual juices.

He was in for a rude awakening. It was only a matter of time before he realized that Vicki was a tough one to bag. She had made plans for him after the previous night, when he sneaked into her room and slipped into bed, refusing to leave until Vicki's ardent protests and the sound of Leslie's tearful anxieties coming from the adjacent room, forced Bernie to retreat for the moment. Even now, as they traipsed about London, Leslie was showing signs of apprehension. Perhaps bringing Vicki to London was not such a good idea after all.

Leslie, who was short, dark, and pixie cute, envied Vicki. As much as she liked her, her feelings toward Vicki, like most of Vicki's friends, were always shaded by jealousy. Things came too easily for Vicki, they felt. Men like Bernie were hard to retain when Vicki was around. That aura of classic femininity, those magnetic good looks and charismatic intensity, struck men to the core and turned their heads as women cringed with fear and envy. What made it worse was Vicki made it seem so effortless.

The second morning of Vicki's stay, Earle Lamm announced himself at Bernie Cornfeld's London townhouse. It was a surprise for everyone...everyone but Vicki. The day before she had called Earle, who was still technically her husband, and begged him to come to her rescue by serving as her shield against Bernie. She delighted in the expression on Bernie's face when Earle stepped up to shake his hand. It was justice, she thought, for his betrayal the night before when he had tried to fuck her—mainly because she was Alfred Bloomingdale's mistress. Well, the hell with that! He was merely one more man who lusted after her. If they could only learn to deal straight with her, to demonstrate courtesy and understanding, then perhaps she could be different with them. For a man who was secure enough to be honest would win her heart and mind. But if men insisted on being assholes, then Vicki would treat them like "business as usual." In other words, she would take them for what she could.

That night Earle escorted Vicki back to Los Angeles. Alfred was delighted when he learned that Vicki had returned. From the moment she'd left he had been frantic, calling Vicki's friends, pleading for information as to her whereabouts. In lengthy monologues, with anyone who would listen, he'd speak of his love for Vicki, claiming how sick he was without her, how different he'd be if she ever came back to him.

Vicki's friend, Sally Talbert, could have cared less for Alfred's troubles. Sally had not liked Alfred from the beginning, and his loss was Vicki's gain as far as she was concerned. Friends like Janis Cozzi and Rebecca Knowlty, who were living and working at Bernie's, also demurred when questioned by Alfred. They claimed ignorance, made up excuses and basically told Alfred to sit tight, until possibly, Vicki was ready to speak with him.

Alfred couldn't wait for Vicki to call him. He contacted his friends, presidents of telephone companies, and implored them to provide Vicki's number. When their efforts came to no avail, he started driving by the Record Plant recording studio and other such haunts that had been favored by Vicki. She was nowhere to be found.

Alfred called Vicki's mother, who was somewhat sympathetic to his telephone lamentations. Initially, Constance Laney had disliked the man, but despite her initial threats and protests, she apparently succumbed to Alfred's charm and generosity. As time wore on, Bloomingdale was kind to her, polite and attentive. He referred to her as his "mother-in-law", something that both pleased and embarrassed her. Besides, there was no sense in fighting it out to the bitter end. Mrs. Laney knew her daughter and knew she could never prevent her from doing what she pleased.

Vicki was never certain whether or not it was Constance who gave her up. But Alfred discovered that she was staying with Emmy and Alan in their house in Beverly Glen Canyon. He called, begging to see her. Vicki told him to forget it; the relationship was over. "What's done is done," she said.

Alfred wouldn't hear of such rejection. The following morning he was on the doorstep of Emmy's house, frantically ringing the doorbell. Vicki and Emmy spied through the peephole, as Bloomingdale muttered and fidgeted.

"Vic, I have to talk to you," he shouted for the world to hear. "Please...let me come in."

On the other side of the door, in whispers, Emmy and Vicki debated what to do. Finally Vicki recognized that he would never go away, at least not until she confronted him. She opened the door and looked into his face, taking note of the pathos and anguish. She was sympathetic, but she promised herself she would be resolute and unyielding.

To avoid disturbing Alan and Emmy, and perhaps the entire neighborhood, with what to date promised to be his greatest dramatic performance, Vicki insisted they sit and talk inside Alfred's car. She warned him that he'd better speak like a civilized man and not start ranting and raving. Otherwise she'd go back inside the house.

"I can't live without you, Vic," Alfred repeated with tears in his eyes. He was rubbing his mouth with the back of his hand.

"I'm sorry, but I don't want to hear it. You left me stranded. You say how much you love me, but you couldn't love me that much if you don't want to leave your wife."

"For Chrissakes, Vic, what do you want me to do? Beg you? In my entire life I've never begged for anything."

Vicki told him he could do what he wanted but it simply wouldn't do any good. She had been betrayed and exploited. They were finished and that was that.

This, of course, was the last thing Alfred wanted to hear.

He lost his composure, and Vicki trembled at the sight. He was red-faced, convulsing, and sobbing. Snot was pouring from his nostrils. Vicki was alarmed and speechless, nearly unable to accept what was happening. This was not the way it was supposed to be. Alfred, this embattled veteran of so many conflicts, was much too tough to reveal himself like this. He—the corporate warrior who had been born rich and to a grand tradition, who had helped make Ronald Reagan governor of California, and who with God's help and the assistance of others would see him as President—seemed the least likely man to be crying pathetically before a brazen, twenty-year-old girl.

Vicki slid closer to Alfred and gently placed her hand at the back of his neck. Her touch was soothing as she stroked his wrinkled skin. He stopped crying and lifted his head, pressed his face against her shoulder. Vicki stroked his cheek with the tip of her fingers and kissed him on his brow.

"No one can love you the way I do," Alfred whispered.

"I'd like a chance to find out, but I know that won't happen. Not when you make me so crazy."

"That's right," smiled Alfred, his eyes still red from crying. "I'll never leave you alone."

Alfred won her over again, and a few weeks later he leased Vicki another house, this one on Sierra Alta Drive in West Hollywood. This house was smaller than the last, a modest structure with quaint appointments, one she could maintain without the expense of a legion of servants. But she still needed a few things to get started. Furniture, dishes, linen, and various accessories, items she had previously sold or given away, were needed to fill this little house of hers. She needed some clothes, some artistic supplies for her dabbling on canvas. New photographs, eight-by-ten glossies, were also needed for acting and modeling auditions. She needed some money from Alfred.

Bloomingdale was only too happy to spend it in order to win back his girl. To him, money was only money, but a tug-of-war with a woman like Vicki was nearly impossible to find. For she had taken him further than any other, forced him to transcend at least part of himself, to acquire new tastes in gamesmanship. He loved how she would approach him, tease him and then withdraw. She was thrilling and unpredictable, fading, shifting, dodging and hiding among the illusory decoys. She would bluff him, or carry out threats by imposing her tremendous strength of will. If he tried to call her hand, she would merely up the ante. If he pressed her too hard, she would leave. Around and around they'd duel, a frolic among the brain cells. Vicki was more than a lover and more than a friend. She was the crutch supporting his crippled and withered soul. She was the drug without which he could not live.

Vicki took a roommate, a kid named Peter, who established his residence in a room on the side of the house opposite from Vicki's. It was a platonic affair, the first in a series of roommates Vicki would keep around for company. She would explain to Alfred that she was doing her best to economize. In this case it wasn't all that far from the truth, since Alfred was undergoing a particularly bad financial period. To compound it all, his eating, carousing and popping amphetamines had finally caught up with him, and he was scheduled to enter the hospital for a triple bypass operation. Afterward, he would require time to recuperate from his open heart surgery, which meant Vicki wouldn't be seeing him very often unless she visited him at his house when Betsy was out of town.

While Alfred convalesced, Vicki grew bored and restless. She tried her best to ignore what was ailing her, but hidden in the shadows of her daily routine, among the disguises, the dreams, the fleeting romantic imagery, she was plagued by the encroaching need for sexual release. Too many weeks had gone by in her life when her only sexual interludes consisted of her scenarios with Alfred and his chosen prostitutes, or a late-night, quality session of solitary, masturbation therapy. The Alfred scenarios had become intolerable and, while masturbation had its moments, it had its limitations as well. It was time, Vicki realized, to start looking around for a younger lover.

Her friends were eager to assist in her search for romance. Variety in Vicki's life served as the catalyst for adventure and intrigue. Her friends could indulge in their vicarious thrills as, privy to a front row seat, they watched Vicki take the risks and suffer the consequences. She was a great victim, an entrancing and prodigal martyr. She was the tragic actress, with the world as her stage in a collapsible theater. She was provocative and entertaining. She was their pal.

Emmy, who by now had left her husband and was living with Joe Cocker, the British rock star, offered to introduce Vicki to people she had met working in the Record Plant. Vicki at first resisted the idea, but Emmy's persuasion and the repeated nights of boredom were compelling enough for Vicki to give it a whirl. Among others on the music circuit, she met Lee, a rock and roll drummer, and soon they were dating steadily. Vicki, who had no time for getting acquainted, suggested they move in together after a month had passed, and it was clear that Lee was not adjusting well to her leaving his bed in the middle of the night. He grumbled unmercifully, demanding to know the reason she couldn't stay until morning.

When she told him about her ongoing relationship with Alfred, Lee was angry, hurt, and surprised. He demanded that she end it and stop seeing Alfred. This, she assured him, was not about to happen. He better learn to live with the reality or forget about seeing her. Ever again!

Lee backed down, just as Vicki knew he would. Men always argued and threatened, but in the end they always gave in. She had no respect for their acquiescence to her demands that they share her with someone else. Where was the strength and virility that men were thought to possess? Where were their principles and convictions? Where was their love? Certainly not present in Lee, the rock and roll drummer who was persuaded to allow Alfred Bloomingdale to mitigate this passionate love affair. Vicki already knew their relationship was over before it had even begun. Months would pass, almost a year, before she would finally admit it. Meanwhile, to keep Alfred happy, she told him Lee was gay.

# 11

VICKI BEGAN TAKING drama instruction at the Lee Strasberg Theater Institute. At about the same time, Earle Lamm was arrested on suspicion of smuggling a planeload of marijuana from Mexico into the United States. Unfortunately for Earle, he and his partners had hired an undercover narcotics agent as their pilot. Fortunately, Earle wasn't present at the landing site when dozens of agents surrounded the plane and arrested his partners in crime. Earle was later taken into custody while dining in an all-night restaurant on La Cienega Boulevard. Hours later, an anonymous caller telephoned Vicki and asked if she would please retrieve Earle's car, which the parking attendant insisted must be removed from his lot before morning or else he would have it towed. The caller insinuated that the arresting officers had been rather casual while searching Earle's car and hadn't discovered the additional drugs that were stashed inside. Cocaine was one of the substances, which, if discovered, would naturally escalate the charges against the captured man.

"Also," the caller implored her, "is there some possible way you can help Earle make his bail?"

"How much is it?" she asked apprehensively.

"Twenty-five thousand," he answered before hanging up.

Vicki cursed Earle for being so stupid. He was almost fifty years old and here he was, the star of an illicit venture. Earle knew nothing about smuggling and had never before tried anything like this. Guilt crept over Vicki as she realized what it was that made him take the risk. He was that desperate to win her back. Well, he should've known better. Whether he had money or not, it still was over between them. Better to delude himself with fantasies, rather than attempt something as stupid as this. Vicki shook her head, put her face in her hands and felt the tears running down her cheeks. Poor Earle. Poor, crazy Earle! She loved him for all the good she had found in his soul. Deep down, perhaps, camouflaged by his vices and his lunacy, but it was there nevertheless. She couldn't possibly ignore his call for help and allow him to rot in jail. Besides, Vicki lived for the times she could come to the rescue. Midnight heroics fulfilled her deeper sense of devotion, made her feel cleansed and whole. But this time she was stymied. Where in the hell would she come up with twenty-five grand?

Alfred Bloomingdale was out of the question. He hated Earle, especially after Earle had assaulted him for the second time, the last time in the parking lot at the Century City Hospital. Alfred had just come from visiting his friend Sammy Colt, when Earle, who had been lying in wait, suddenly jumped from his car and pounced on Alfred. They were wrestling on the ground when a security guard interceded. Bloomingdale was so incensed afterward that he called Vicki and threatened to have Mayor Sam Yorty run Earle Lamm out of town. Alfred would have Earle put away for life, before he would ever go his bail.

So Vicki took the hour's drive to Montclair and proceeded to beg her mother to put up her house as collateral so Earle could get out of jail. Constance finally relented, and by the following morning Earle was back on the street. He appeared bewildered and shaken as Vicki rushed to greet him at the station. He embraced her, swore his love, and expressed eternal gratitude. Otherwise, the couple had little to say to each other, things being what they were.

With Earle a free man, Vicki returned to her hillside house, and to Lee, the rock and roll drummer. Lee, who was experiencing angry desperation, was certain Vicki had been out diddling around with Norman, her acting instructor from the Strasberg Institute. Recently, Lee had seen them walking together on Sunset Strip. Nervous and jealous, he had accused Vicki of deceiving him. She denied it at first, but when Lee refused to buy it, she finally admitted the truth, adding that truth was stranger than fiction; it was time for them to go their separate ways. In another week or so, she was to be admitted to the hospital where she was scheduled for breast surgery. When she was discharged, she would not be returning to Lee. Her possessions would be cleared from his house and placed in storage.

"No hard feelings," she said. "I'll try my best to keep in touch."

Vicki thought her career as an actress would be boosted if her breasts were made larger, and she entered Cedars Sinai Hospital for implant surgery, and emerged days later—with no home, no identity, and no direction. She was weak from the operation and needed a quiet place in which to recuperate. Jim Brown, an old friend from Vicki's days at The Candy Store, put her up in a spare bedroom in his house. Brown, the football legend and a popular movie star, offered her comfort and solitude. When post-operational complications forced a long convalescence, he let her stay the extra time. He liked Vicki. He had to have liked her, or otherwise he could have never put up with an ebullient Alfred Bloomingdale, who, while dropping by for his afternoon visits, liked to corner the former running back and engage him in chats about football. Jim was uncomfortable with Alfred's boyish adulation, his exhaustive recollections of the glory days during Brown's career. To him it was history, and he was much too busy to listen to Alfred, a former varsity lineman for Brown University, expounding on his love for the game. But Jim took it in stride, remaining patient and courteous for Vicki's sake, if not for his own. She was troubled enough as it was.

More than three years had passed since Vicki Morgan had first met Alfred Bloomingdale. She was twenty-one now, going on forty. Each day she was growing older. Each day she was spinning her wheels. She was at the crossroads, and if she was to change her life, she must break free from Alfred's domination or otherwise be swallowed up in his world. Of course, she would need his help to get started. She wouldn't need much, an apartment instead of a house, something cute, but spacious enough for Vicki and Penny, her devoted housekeeper. With her life streamlined and simplified, Vicki would have time to pursue her acting career. She was determined to refrain from playing the dilettante; to bear down instead, and work hard at developing a proper future for her and her son, who was still living with her mother. She would acquire an agent, someone strong and influential, who would send her on interviews and keep her motivated. Lord knows, Vicki had the looks for it.

It would take me months, if not years, before I came to understand the severity of what was happening, the predicament she was faced with at this particular point in her life. And even now, after phone calls and meetings conducted with the utmost discretion, the only thing I can safely determine is that I'll never know it all. Vicki apparently was afraid to tell me certain things about her relationship with Alfred. What she did divulge, in her typical Vicki fashion, was related in bits and pieces, in the content of her offbeat intimations and her repertoire of personal aphorisms. These were the things that perhaps were less sympathetic, but much more in keeping with the spirit of their relationship. For she was a woman in love with danger, aroused by power and intrigue, and he was a man who, among other things, was in the information business. They lived in a world where careless mutterings and spontaneous indiscretions could be particularly revealing and ultimately exploitable in exchange for favors and capital gains.

Vicki, I believe, was cultivated as Alfred's personal listening device, an instrument of subterfuge as well as one of pleasure. Alfred, being who he was, certainly knew how to use her as this, taking advantage of her intrinsic insecurities to employ her to his best advantage. He would encourage her to serve as an escort for his powerful business associates. She would sleep with them if they attracted her, or when she thought it necessary. But most important, she would get them to talk to her, and she would listen. Vicki had an excellent memory. She would often say to me, "Men will reveal things to women...things they wouldn't tell their best friends."

In addition, according to several handwriting analysts, on documents available in the public record, involving business transactions related to some of Alfred's corporations, there are as many as five different signatures—male and female—that were possibly written in Vicki's hand. On several occasions Vicki mentioned to me that Alfred would stop by with papers for her to sign.

"Sometimes, Gordon, he'd come over with like two briefcases stuffed with documents. I'd be all dressed, thinking we were going out to dinner or somewhere, and he'd sit me down with a pen and a stack of papers and say, 'Go to it kid.'"

"Did you ever read the documents, or ask why he wanted your signature?"

"Read them? No. Back then, I never had the patience for that. Now I wish I had."

"What did Alfred say when you asked him about it?"

Vicki paused and smiled enigmatically. "He said it was part of the job."

Whenever I pressed her, Vicki would switch subjects and start an argument about things unrelated. However, I believe this, and his genuine love for her, are the reasons Alfred paid her what he did. He paid her when they were together as lovers, and he paid her when they were hardly together at all. When she lived with other men, or went off on her adventures both here and in foreign lands, the checks kept right on coming. Dutifully he paid her, as if he had to, until Betsy finally cut off the checks, two months before Alfred's death. Maybe she wasn't supposed to do that. After years of looking into it, I still find it difficult to say, but when he died, there was no money left to Vicki Morgan. She was no longer necessary, at least not to him. Only two contracts, which Alfred had entered into with Vicki, remained. They would be posthumously judged in her favor, and the money awarded would be given to her son. Finally, a year and a half after her death, a jury made Vicki the sentimental favorite. However, that decision is still under appeal.

But at twenty-one, Vicki had no sense of consequence. She leased an apartment in a high-rise building on Doheny Road in West Hollywood. She had found what she wanted with the help of a friend of hers, a man named Alan Smiley. Smiley, a reputed underworld figure had the dubious distinction of being present the night his close friend, the Las Vegas futurist Benjamin "Bugsy" Siegel, was shot to death in the Beverly Hills home of his girlfriend, Virginia Hill. Vicki had met Alan on an airplane, while flying to Palm Springs for a vacation. She was attracted by his looks and she found him charming. He was an elderly man, brimming with a particular kind of insight and colorful talk of the "old days." They dated each other for a couple of months before Vicki, under Alfred's influence, decided it was time to move on.

It may have been Alan Smiley who found the apartment, but it was Alfred who paid the bills. Initially, sensing Vicki's restlessness, he was all for her serious pursuit of an acting career. He wanted to see her happy, or at least not so distressed that she refused to see him. He feared she might decide to run away for a spell. He may have tolerated Vicki's impetuous excursions, but he certainly didn't like them, especially when she stayed away for any length of time. It made him disconsolate and nervous to think she wasn't neatly stashed and easily accessible. And now that she was in one of her restless periods, he knew he had to accommodate her in every possible way in order to keep her happy.

Alfred made arrangements for Vicki to sign with Joyce Selznick, a tough and effective talent manager, who liked her style and admired her looks, and who would send Vicki out on a number of auditions for leading roles in motion pictures. But Vicki, unlike when she was a child posing for catalogues, now became much too self-conscious when standing in front of a camera. By her own admission, she couldn't act her way out of a paperbag. None of this seemed to have any disheartening effect on Joyce however, and she kept sending her out, but to no avail.

"Your problem is," said Joyce, "that you're much too insecure. You're a beautiful girl with a terrific personality. You can captivate anyone you meet. But when they put a light on you and stick you in front of some know-nothing sonofabitch, you come apart at the seams. What you need is a psychiatrist."

"Joyce, I'm already seeing one."

"He's a man, Vicki. What you need is a woman."

Vicki relinquished her former psychiatrist and started visiting the one who had been recommended by Joyce. The woman worked out of her apartment in the Hollywood Hills, which afforded a view of the Sunset Strip and the contour of Los Angeles as it slipped from the hillsides toward the basin at the center of town. Vicki took in the view and talked for over an hour while the doctor listened intently.

"You're too used to having men fuck you over," the doctor informed her when the first session had finally concluded.

The psychiatrist then went on to suggest Vicki undergo therapy five times a week, for a while at least.

Vicki complied and began attending therapy sessions five times a week, while Selznick did her very best to promote the starlet's shaky career. One thing Joyce did was to arrange for Vicki to meet with Michael Gruskoff at his office on the lot of Twentieth Century Fox. Having planned to do some shopping later that afternoon, Vicki had brought along her housekeeper Penny to assist with carrying the packages. In addition, Vicki was dressed to the nines. She covered herself in a print silk dress and layers of gold jewelry. After shaking hands, she took a seat opposite the producer's, while Penny sat quietly in a chair by the door.

The producer sat in silence and stared at Vicki. "Daddy says you can be an actress, so you'll be an actress? Is that it?" he wondered. "You have a lot of nerve to come to an interview dressed like that."

"You know, you're awfully goddamned rude," Vicki told him. She glowered at the producer, her eyes widening. Scornfully, she curled her lips, aware she now had his attention.

Gruskoff, a former agent and movie packager, had seen some talent in his time. This one he didn't know what to make of, as he lowered his eyes and wondered what he should say. He rubbed his eyes and sat back in his chair as the morning sunlight gave a saintly aura to his prematurely ashen hair. "You have no business being here," he said. "You're not serious about being an actress."

"And that still doesn't keep you from being an asshole," Vicki retorted. With that, she was on her feet, signalling to Penny it was time for them to leave.

Gruskoff, alternately angry and sheepish, walked Vicki to the door. "Do you want to go out sometime?" he asked to no reply, as Vicki and Penny stalked off down the hallway.

When Vicki returned to her apartment she found Joyce Selznick had already left several messages with her answering service, all claiming it was vitally important that she call Joyce right away. Selznick had already spoken to Gruskoff and now wanted to know Vicki's side of the story.

"He was rude to one of my girls?" Joyce, upon hearing her client's version of the meeting, shouted so loudly that she may not have needed the telephone. "I'll take care of that," she said, and then went on to threaten in graphic detail what she would do to Michael. She ordered Vicki not to move, that she would get right back to her as soon as she finished with Gruskoff.

In less than ten minutes Joyce was back on the phone. "You were five minutes late," she scolded. "I told you a thousand times, you can never be late for a meeting. But that's no excuse for the way he talked to you. No one talks to you like that. Not ever!"

After hanging up with Joyce, Vicki poured herself a glass of wine and climbed into bed for a little contemplation regarding the trials and tribulations of the road to movie stardom. She reflected on her meeting and considered what Gruskoff had said to her. What bothered her most were the things that were true. She never dreamed that in the future, she and Michael would be living together. As for Joyce Selznick and Michael Gruskoff, they never spoke to each other again.

Soon after the episode with Gruskoff, Alfred arranged for Vicki to begin private dramatic instruction with the director Mervyn LeRoy. A distinguished gentleman from Hollywood's golden years, LeRoy was taken with Vicki from their first meeting. He had been willing to do Alfred a favor, but this seemed more like a privilege instead of a sacrifice. Mervyn claimed Vicki was as talented as anyone he'd seen. Vicki thought right away that Mervyn was full of shit. Nevertheless, she enjoyed his company, and believed he was sincere with his efforts to teach her how to act. From leatherbound scripts of the films he had directed, Mervyn and she would play the parts of different characters. He was patient with Vicki, devoting hours of time to her dramatic instruction for the better part of a year.

Mervyn was an inquisitive man who would ask more questions than Vicki felt comfortable answering. But sometimes she would share with him the mysterious side of her life, exaggerating innocuous secrets and intrigues which she had colored specifically for his benefit. His eyes would brighten when she told him her fabulous tales of adventure. She became his excitement, a medium from which he could dream about the days gone by. While in the company of Vicki, he could portray himself as the aging confidante— sharing secrets he promised to never reveal.

One day Mervyn made a pass at her, which Vicki figured would happen sooner or later. It was on a day when she was hung over, having drunk too much because she felt guilty about a borrowed leatherbound script her dog had chewed to pieces. She smiled when he kissed her, and she let him take her by the hand and lead her to the sofa. For Mervyn, the scene that afternoon was undoubtedly Vicki's most rewarding performance. He praised her for being so kind to him. She knew he would tell her something like that, having known a few by now who were at least as old as Mervyn. Some of them she had been attracted to, and there were some for whom she'd felt sorry. But, like Vicki once told me, aging men are always so appreciative when they can make love to a young and pretty girl. They are always so eager, so happy for the chance that they seem to fall all over themselves. It made it easy for her to gain the advantage.

Mervyn had done his best to teach Vicki the finer skills of acting. For this she was always grateful. But what she appreciated most of all was the director's introduction to Cary Grant. Vicki, like most women, had considered Grant the epitome of gentlemanly sophistication, an emotional icon one dreams about but never meets in reality. Thanks to Mervyn LeRoy, for Vicki this would be no dream, no restless midnight fantasy. Cary Grant was very much for real and Vicki was thankful for it.

# 12

VICKI AND CARY GRANT had perhaps a dozen conversations over the telephone, all within the period of a month prior to their actually meeting each other. While good old Mervyn sat beaming in the background, Vicki, telephone in hand, listened intently to just about anything Cary had to say. Mainly, he spoke of the inconveniences he was suffering while he remodeled his house in the hills above Benedict Canyon. It was taking much longer than he expected, more than a year, and the place was still in shambles. He invited Vicki to come up and see him sometime, to witness the mess in which he was living.

At the time of their encounter, Cary Grant was seventy-one years old and in excellent physical shape. His epidermal trademark, a rich, golden tan, evenly covered his body. His manner of dress reflected both simplicity and elegance, complementing his wit and grace. He was wearing gray slacks, a white, silk shirt, and a single, gold chain around his neck when he greeted her at the door. With a light-hearted attitude, Cary apologized for the condition of his house, a long, white Mediterranean structure. He explained that the kitchen and two of the bedrooms were the only rooms in liveable condition. The rest of it, he said, was in complete transition.

Vicki could see he wasn't exaggerating. Floors and walls were torn out, and building materials were everywhere. There were rusty nails and chunks of plaster underfoot.

Wires were exposed and lighting fixtures were suspended precariously from the ceiling. It was nothing like the movies. Naturally, despite his warning that she wear something comfortable, Vicki had dressed to make what she considered her best impression. She wore a silk dress, a fur coat and nearly all of her favorite jewelry. She should have worn a hardhat and overalls instead. But what the hell? She wasn't complaining. It's not every day you get to meet Cary Grant.

"Would you like to see the work they're doing on the roof?" he asked.

Vicki nodded. "I'm a fun kinda girl, Cary. Sure, I'll climb up on the roof if you want. I'm not stuffy."

Cary chuckled appreciatively as he led the way to the rooftop. Vicki followed, her heels catching on chunks of ragged flooring. Once on the roof, she listened earnestly while Cary went on about the tasks and challenges facing the carpenters, electricians, and plumbers with this particular housing design. She agreed with his every explanation as she stood at the edge of the rooftop and feasted her eyes on L.A. at sunset, its horizon filled with the pearlescent majesty of blue, rose, and pewter. The sunset was awesome, as was the man who stood beside her. Vicki couldn't get over it. She was beginning a romance with Cary Grant.

Vicki thought of him as the last of the classic gentlemen. He was patient with her and enjoyed her company. He saw that Vicki was bright and inquisitive and permitted her to use charm and provocation to get him to talk on a variety of subjects relating philosophically to the greater significance underlying the common events in one's life. Among the things she respected in Cary was his ability to speak sensitively about delicate matters. He described his childhood, his humble beginnings in Bristol, England, as Archibald Leach, the son of a working-class family, who, with just a high school education, affected the manner of an Oxford graduate in order to advance his career. He told Vicki about

Jennifer, his daughter born to him and Dyan Cannon, with whom he was fighting for custody. Cary loved his daughter to such an extent he had rented a house in Malibu Colony, just two doors down from his ex-wife and daughter, so he could sit on his porch at seven A.M. and watch her go by in the school bus.

Vicki, out of respect for Cary's wishes, spent many nights sleeping in a separate bedroom. It puzzled her and troubled her that he'd remained sexually aloof, but she had never dared broach the subject. For the time being, she reconciled herself to waiting patiently. She wore his pajamas to bed and huddled beneath the quilts, shivering from the cold. Cary, to Vicki's chagrin, would always keep the heat off at night.

During much of the time they saw each other, they would remain at his house, dining mainly on TV dinners. Cary claimed he enjoyed their convenience, and thought the food wasn't half bad. But what he absolutely detested was Vicki's habit of stubbing her cigarette butts in the greasy aluminum tray after she'd finished picking at her meal. Smoking itself disgusted him. He hated cigarettes and considered them an evil menace. But what Vicki did with her cigarette butts really took the cake. Finally, it so outraged him, he insisted she could no longer attempt to kill him by filling his house with smoke. He removed all the ashtrays and placed them in hiding, just to make his point. Vicki, however, was not to be denied. She brought her own ashtray to his house and smoked near an open window, freezing to death in the cold night air while Cary laughed at her foolhardy gesture.

Cary was also very critical of the way she overdressed. "I don't understand it," he began one day in the midst of a discussion about fashion and clothing. "Why does someone like you, who's so naturally beautiful, wear that...stuff on your face? And all that jewelry. You'd look so much nicer in a pair of jeans or slacks and a white cotton blouse."

He paused to consider, then gestured toward the bathroom. "Go wash your face," he demanded. "You'd be so much prettier without that stuff all over your face."

Vicki tried to pass it off as an order she shouldn't take seriously. "Next time," she said, hoping it would placate his wishes, "I promise I won't wear any makeup."

"No. I want you to do it now."

Emitting a long, deliberate sigh of resignation, Vicki got up from her chair and shuffled reluctantly in the direction of the bathroom. In the doorway she was struck by a whimsical notion and turned to call over her shoulder. "Would you like me to shower and put my hair up in a towel, like Doris did in *A Touch of Mink*? I'll put on a pair of nifty striped pajamas and really look the part. How would that make your evening?"

Cary drew his fingers across his lips and gave it a moment's thought. He was smiling in appreciation of Vicki's wit, if not the actual concept. "Actually, my dear, that wouldn't be a bad idea."

What had started as an argument became an evening of sharing and tenderness. It was the first night she slept with him, no longer alone and curled up in the blankets, wondering why he didn't turn on the heat.

For the premiere opening of the MGM Grand Hotel in Las Vegas Cary Grant took Vicki Morgan. They flew there together on a private jet owned by Fabergé, the cosmetic and health-care products manufacturer, of which Cary was a member of the board. En route, he teased Vicki about her excess baggage, claiming its weight was so overbearing he was afraid the plane was incapable of remaining in flight. He simply couldn't imagine what she was doing with the three fur coats and the towering stack of luggage she had brought for the few nights they'd be staying in Las Vegas. Vicki responded by telling him that was the way she always travelled. She hated to suddenly be wanting something and not have it with her. This way she was prepared and secure.

Before leaving for Las Vegas, Vicki called Alfred and announced she was going away with Cary Grant. Cary knew nothing at all about her relationship with Alfred, and Vicki was doing her best to keep it that way. Alfred was angered and voiced his displeasure when she told him she'd be gone for at least several days. When he had first learned about her dating Cary he had patiently held his tongue, regardless of the jealousy that was welling up inside. Now it was becoming too much for him. He complained bitterly, claiming it was no good for Cary and her to be seen in public. Vicki, silent and gloating, listened to Alfred bluster over the telephone.

"Too bad," she retorted when there was a lull in his monologue. She reminded him that, until he divorced his wife and married her, she'd do whatever she damn well pleased.

Alfred started to argue, but Vicki cut him off. She was growing tired of his demands, his hookers, his broken promises and especially his attempts to monitor her every move. It was she who deserved to be angry.

"You'll keep supporting me, just like you're supporting me now." she shouted in reply. "You know it and I know it, so please don't argue."

Vicki's liaison with Cary Grant lasted for nearly eight months before they drifted apart. Years later she would regret not having spent more time with him. She blamed herself for not having kept in touch. Cary had been good for her, had bolstered her self-confidence and offered a vision of what was ultimately important in life. She could identify with his lack of formal education and was inspired by his successes. Cary had explained things to her, claiming there was no rule compelling her to make the same mistakes over and over again. She could make changes and redirect herself. She could establish a different perspective toward life.

But to do so meant escaping Alfred's domination, which was a tricky thing to do. Alfred, who had sensed her aloofness toward him, became more persistent than ever. He phoned her incessantly, leaving dozens of messages with her service. He asked her to go to lunch with him, but she usually declined, making excuses he didn't believe. He would argue, declaring his eternal love for her while pleading for her understanding of his sexual needs and desires. He claimed he couldn't reach an orgasm unless she was there, if not to participate, then to remain clothed and merely sit there observing him and his prostitutes.

Vicki explained she was tired of his weird scenarios, and that for her sake and his, he should give up the apartment on La Cienega Boulevard. She couldn't go through with it any longer. She advised him to seek psychiatric help, a suggestion that he loathed. Alfred recounted his hurt and annoyance, but sent her checks every month nevertheless. The more he pushed for Vicki to join him in his sexual escapades, the more determined she was to keep him from getting his way. It was a contest of wills and, eventually, a war of nerves. Neither would back down, and the game was locked in a deadly stalemate. Alfred teased and threatened and played with her emotions, while Vicki was at her vitriolic best whenever she disparaged him.

The conflict finally came to a head one day, when Alfred, under the pretext of taking her to lunch, tried to talk her into accompanying him to their apartment on La Cienega Boulevard, where two hookers were scheduled to join them. It was one step over the line. Vicki was outraged by his duplicity. She cursed him, dubbing his effort a classic cheap shot, an act of betrayal. The more she hollered, the more livid she became. She was bursting from the months of pent-up frustration. "Get out of my life!" she screamed. "I don't need this anymore!"

Alfred had never seen Vicki this angry. He mistakenly believed she was play-acting, exhibiting a mere imitation of outrage, and thought it cute, which made Vicki despise him for not taking her seriously. He was grinning and taunting her with threats of deprivation. "I won't be sending you anymore checks," he teased, "not when you treat me like this."

Vicki swore he'd be sorry. "I'll make it rough for you," she said. "I know things."

"I dare you to walk out on me," he grinned, seemingly unaffected by her threats to expose him.

"Alfred, don't ever dare me!"

He was all smiles now. "I dare you," he repeated before he turned and walked out the door.

Vicki curled her lips in silent fury and planned her course of action. The audacity of the man. Well, he'd be sorry. Real sorry! She was gonna sue his ass!

Abruptly, the checks from Alfred stopped coming, but this time Vicki was more relieved than worried. She was tired of being manipulated, of living under his scrutiny. She couldn't take his sex trip anymore. It was time to stand by her principles while preparing for the inevitable combat.

With Earle's assistance, Vicki had retained Paul Caruso as her attorney. Caruso was sympathetic, having distaste for older men who liked to abuse young girls. The attorney filed suit against Bloomingdale, and when the papers were served, Alfred's attorney Jacques Leslie, whom Alfred referred to as "The Judge," collapsed and died of a heart attack.

"He took it well," Vicki noted when she heard the news about old Jacques Leslie. Apparently, "The Judge" knew more about Alfred's tainted history than even Vicki was aware. He must have feared what would happen if the suit came to trial. For there were times when, according to several sources, Alfred had gotten a bit overzealous with his beatings of women and had been forced to pay them off in order to keep them quiet. These women, Leslie knew, were lurking around somewhere. God only knew what would be exposed, or who would come forth and serve as a witness against him. This case was a potential disaster, for lawyer and client alike. How could an attorney successfully defend what, essentially, in the eyes of most people would be indefensible?

Long before her breakup with Alfred, Vicki had learned there were certain friends and members of her family who resented her whenever she was short of cash. And now, while they ostensibly supported her action, Vicki perceived in some their concealed disenchantment, as if her loss of income was their loss instead. Perhaps it was the way Vicki squandered her money on trinkets for family and friends. Only now there was no money to piss away, which meant no more fancy lunches or shopping sprees in limousines. The good life, courtesy of Vicki Morgan, was rapidly slipping away.

Vicki, least of all, seemed to mind her new way of living. She busied herself with an active social life, dating three men during the same period of time, something she hadn't done until then. She and Cary Grant were still involved, although they did not see each other as regularly as before. In addition, she was dating Hal, the plastic surgeon whom she had met during her stay in the hospital, and Michael Gruskoff, the producer with whom she had an altercation just several months before.

A blind date had brought Vicki and Mike together again, a match-up arranged by a committee of four, including Michael's accountant, Fred Altman, his wife Barbara, and Vicki's attorney, Michael Dave, and his wife Lorraine, whom Vicki had first met when she was still working as a manicurist at Ménage à Trois. There were promises, expectations, and assurances that Vicki was in for a marvelous evening. What Vicki was in for was a rude awakening when she opened the door and discovered Michael Gruskoff standing in the shadows of love, eager to take her to dinner. At their last meeting he had labeled her a daddy's girl, a shallow-minded dilettante who would never make it on her own. She considered him rude and presumptuous, short both in stature and patience, especially in dealing with women. But she went out with him anyway, for an evening mixed with hostility and romance. She had been attracted to Gruskoff, if not for his sensibility, then at least for the challenge. Something clicked, and they began seeing each other on a regular basis.

Meanwhile, Bernie Cornfeld had just been released after spending eleven months in St. Antoine's, the prison in Switzerland, and was ensconced once again in his mansion in Beverly Hills. Vicki had gotten the news from Leslie, who had married a Swiss jeweler while Bernie was in jail. Vicki was genuinely glad to hear of Cornfeld's return, and sent him flowers as a gesture to welcome him home. Soon after, Bernie called to express his gratitude and to invite her over for lunch that following day. Vicki, who had assumed it would be a private reunion, arrived at Bernie's house to discover that the press as well as his friends and associates had come to pay their respects. The photographer from *Newsweek* took a picture of the diminutive Bernie leaning against the willowy Vicki Morgan. The following week it was in the magazine. Alfred Bloomingdale undoubtedly was thrilled.

Vicki, during a moment alone with Bernie, had described her ongoing troubles with Alfred, including the lawsuit. Fear and embarrassment prevented her from confiding in him the real reason for bringing legal action against her patriarchal lover. Instead, she'd allude to something about his breach of promise, coupled with his refusal to honor his commitment, and his failure to send her the promised money. Bernie was sympathetic and invited her to stay at his mansion. Obviously, there was plenty of room and the price was right, an attractive offer since Vicki's money was rapidly dwindling.

At first, she refused Cornfeld's offer. She thanked him, but reminded him of their earlier encounter and said that wasn't her mood at the moment. What she really wanted was some peace and quiet.

Bernie assured her that he could provide it. "I just want to do you a favor, that's all."

Vicki smiled, regarding him with a knowing smirk. She puffed on her cigarette and considered his offer. "Bernie, you'd be all over me," she told him. "You do understand I'd never allow you to treat me like another one of your girls."

"Vicki, I'm offering it to you as a friend. You can put your own locks on your door."

"What about the telephone? Can I have my own private line?"

Bernie agreed that she could, and Vicki, after establishing the ground rules, moved into Bernie's mansion. She selected a large bedroom, separated from Bernie's by a hidden sitting room, accessible from their chambers only. As promised, Bernie permitted her to install her own locks on the door as well as her personal telephone.

Vicki was relieved, satisfied she had thwarted Alfred, at least for the moment, by getting out from underneath the bulk of her monthly expenses. If nothing else, she would have food to eat and a roof over her head, thanks to Bernie. What's more, he had assured her he wouldn't interfere with her life, that she could come and go as she pleased. A nice arrangement, a comfortable situation that, if she was lucky, would give her the chance to catch her breath. Besides, when he heard she was living at the Cornfeld estate, Vicki thought Alfred would simply die.

# 13

AS THE MONTHS passed I noticed changes in Vicki's personality. She claimed that being with me had restored some of her confidence and had given her a different outlook. She was starting to believe that even without money she could overcome the obstacles and achieve success. She said she relished the hours we spent together, all the talking we did, and missed me when I was away. But she feared she had become too dependent upon me. This, she assured me, would only lead to conflict.

"I'm used to getting my way, and you don't give an inch," she laughed. "If I depend on you for everything and start making demands...well, you know how you'll deal with that."

"Not well," I acknowledged. "Besides, that's not what you want from me, to get your way. Your way you can get any place in town."

"It's your attention. That's all I want from you...your attention. And your respect. You're right, the rest of it I can always find elsewhere. Once I get my head straightened out."

"And that's where I come into this delicately contrived landscape? The reorientation process? Getting your head straightened out?"

She smiled before she leaned over slowly and kissed me. "That's part of it. You may drive me crazy at times, but you're really very good for me."

BEAUTIFUL BAD GIRL

"Until you get your head straightened out, or get some money. Whichever comes first."

A different expression came over her face; she assumed the countenance of universal wisdom. She was smiling, only differently than before; it was the delicate smile of a gentle buddha, as she affectionately clasped my hand. "You still don't think you can trust me, do you?"

"Yeah, right now I do. But conditions change with time. You may get desperate."

Vicki tapped my leg. "One day you'll realize you could've trusted me more than you thought."

"Meanwhile," I asked, "what are you going to do for money?"

"Oh, I don't know. At a time like this I won't let my pride get in the way. I won't do anything seamy or ugly, but if I can get a loan from somebody, then terrific. If we sell the book...better still. Until then, a few dollars, a bag of groceries, thank you very much...I'll take what's being offered.

"Except from you. I don't want to depend on you for money. Like I told you, I need your respect and I want your attention. Money I'll find somewhere else. Not much, just enough to cover my rent, Todd's schooling, food, whatever. Maybe two thousand a month would do it. God, what I used to get from Alfred in one month's time would last me close to a year right now. I was so stupid with money," she sighed. "The way I pissed it away."

"It happens like that if you don't pay attention."

"Oh, I paid attention, but to the wrong people, for the wrong reasons."

"I meant you should've paid attention to your own instincts."

"I know what you meant. And I know what I did. Let's just say that I don't want to do it wrong anymore. I need to trust myself. Trust my own judgement."

"You'll catch on. You've got enough to make it on your

own. You've got brains, despite what they say, and you've got style. There'll be no stopping you once you get on the right track."

"I know," Vicki replied. "Sometimes it's just so hard to accept that things have changed so much."

Within herself, Vicki had finally admitted that Alfred was dead and that period of her life was over. There was no going back and there was no second guessing. There was the future or nothing at all. Vicki was starting to loosen up in view of her recognitions. Even her walk was relaxed, more the shuffling gait of a her pugnacious adolescence than the formal rectitude that she had employed for so many years. As a residual effect of my influence, at times she cursed like a sailor, giving vent to her anger; a better choice, I guess, than keeping it locked up inside. When her friends complained that she was being much too casual, not taking life seriously and getting down to business, she ignored or rebuked them, depending on her mood.

"None of them can begin to understand what's happening to me," she remarked one afternoon as we walked from her condo to the parking lot. "They never understood it. They think, after all the weirdness I've been through, that I can just settle down into some normal, boring existence. God forbid that I should spend some time trying to find myself and pick up the pieces. No, that would be asking too much. All I keep hearing from my friends, my mother, and everyone else is how responsible I have to be. Responsible? Hell! Some of them I supported for years. I gave them money, cars, vacations, drugs. You name it...what they didn't get from me.

"But now that stuff isn't happening so easily. Makes them nervous. What is Vicki gonna do with herself if she doesn't get married? Where's she gonna get her money? It's a big panic, believe me.

"They want to teach me recipes," she laughed, " so I can learn to cook and find a man. Can you imagine? Or they'll help me find a job. A job? I didn't finish high school. What kind of job am I gonna find? I'll be a waitress in a doughnut shop or something, and then they'll all complain that I'm not living up to my potential."

"That's why we have to finish the book," I laughed. "Otherwise...it's the doughnut shop for you and God knows what for me."

"You know I want to do it," she assured me, turning serious as she went on to explain. "But talking about my past is so damned difficult. Especially now that you and I are...."

"Sleeping together," I interjected. "Makes it tough to come out with the intimate details, right? Well, that's what you get for getting involved with me," I chided as we laughed together. "Not that I blame you for feeling uncomfortable," I added. You've got some pretty hairy stuff to discuss. But, so what? You've gotta do it. If you believe in it, then you've gotta tell your story."

Warily, she glanced at me. "That's easy for you to say."

It was. I could come and go as I pleased, while Vicki was forced to remain and endure the pressures applied by friends and family, who were growing impatient and expecting the book to be written within a few months. Over the years, they had heard most of Vicki's stories. Reconstructing her life appeared simple enough to them; just make it fatuous, neat, and easily marketable. Write something that wouldn't be too...revealing. What did they care that she didn't see it that way, that she needed time to gain perspective, or that there was potential here for a volume of depth and magnitude? Forget substance, they thought. Just scribble a supermarket masterpiece, a mundane but salacious chronicle that left their own lives undisturbed.

It irritated me that they were being coercive in a backhanded sort of way. Never would they confront me directly, these brave souls, but instead, during my absence, they pounded Vicki, voicing apprehensions about my ability as a writer, while fretting about my influence on her and what she might divulge about their supposedly exemplary lives. Needless to say, they didn't make things any easier on Vicki by making her doubtful and self-conscious while trying to cover themselves.

But I could see for myself what was going on here. There was good old Mom and Michael Dave, Vicki's attorney, who by his own admission had lost his way in drugs and rock and roll before he discovered the spiritual teaching of Sy Baba and the enlightened Hindu path. There was Mary Sangre, Vicki's lesbian lover, who disappeared, either because I stepped in or the money ran out. And there was so much more in this action-packed adventure, behavior and attitudes that I almost didn't believe. I watched, I listened, and I even engaged them in conversation. With Vicki winking at me and scribbling notes for my benefit, I listened to her speaking to them on the telephone. These were her friends? I silently mused. No wonder for the most part she was ignoring them and spending her time with me.

And we were having a helluva time, I must confess. We made love often, joking, claiming we'd better get as much in as possible before the novelty wore off. Our romance, we knew, was a quarterhorse, running hot and fast and finishing quickly. There is no holding back, no pacing in a quarterhorse race. Like the one-hundred-yard dash, it's all out from the starting line. And we were running day and night, compacting as much as possible into what time had been allotted. On many occasions, I've reflected on the offhanded references, the important things that are sometimes conveyed by ostensibly insignificant statements. It's the tangential phrases that have gained importance for me with the passage of time. I am haunted by Vicki's and my subconscious motivations, the nonverbal recognition that the party would soon be over.

Frequently, I stayed overnight, or long into the wee hours of the morning. I'd watch her stretch out on the sheets, her toes pointed, her arms above her head. "The Bad Seed" was how she would refer to herself, elongating the words for their greater impact. She'd be laughing, or acting mystified, staring at me and shaking her head, acting as if this was all too much for her.

When it came time to leave, the trouble would start. "I hate it when you leave," she'd inform me. "It's the time that I hurt the worst. When I resent your being married."

"So what do you want to do?" I'd ask, aware of her feelings, but knowing neither Vicki nor I was about to see it end just yet. "Every time we get into this it ends up going nowhere. You know how I feel about you. You know what the story is. And you know it's not about to end so easily. We're really wrapped up in this," I laughed. "Blame it on love."

"You don't know what love is," she contested, as if I had profaned a sacred concept. "No man does."

"You're supposed to be the authority. Not me."

She disliked me when I was being contrary, when I was in no mood for being cast in "The Edge of Night" or one of Chekov's dramas. If she wasn't sulking, she was glowering in my direction, hoping that somehow she'd involve me in this melancholy intrigue which would keep me there at least for another hour or two. Sometimes tempers would flare and the sparks would fly. She could rival James Joyce's *Ulysses* with her soliloquies on the heartbreak of romance, going on for days about my impatience and lack of tolerance. She was right. I didn't buy all the schtick, or really understand to what extent the years of being manipulated and cultivated like a thoroughbred had made her reluctant and skittish. She was used to having it easy, getting other people to keep her life in order. Over the years, Alfred had built it into the system. No wonder she was in such a mess. The components of daily struggle, the

141

common experience of urban survival, had been lost on Vicki Morgan. Her tools of survival were her powers of attraction: get the attention of men and then get them to do your bidding.

Instead of working a job like most other people, Vicki had spent her days practicing, honing her vampish skills. I think, as part of it, and to pass the time during all those years of quasi-isolation, Vicki got used to amusing herself with character transformations. At times it was scary to observe the changes. Over the years it escalated to the point where she didn't always have control. In an hour's time, she could interface with a gang of personalities and make me deal with everyone of them. I thought she was playing a game at first. And then I learned she wasn't. These schizophrenic bonzai charges were serious business. For these were more than your average mood swings. She could change in both appearance and demeanor, literally altering her facial features to match her characterizations. Her eyes would seemingly vary in size and intensity, her cheekbones would sharpen or soften and her mouth would widen or purse, its corners turning up or down. In one instant she could be the sweet coquette, the petulant beauty, while in the next she was the convivial matron or the cynical whore. She could also appear as the fun-loving tomboy or the stylish and gracious lady. "Sybiling-out" was how she put it, referring to the best-selling book and popular television movie depicting a woman with as many as seventeen personalities. It was a regular blitz on the nervous system. Fascinating, but also distracting as hell.

Fuck it! She could make her demands, but I still recognized my other responsibilities. I knew I had things to do. There was a script to write, and time I wanted to spend with my family. I never denied my affections for them. That always seemed ridiculous to me. Obviously, I didn't go home for nothing. But I didn't remain there either. I kept going back and forth, walking the groove and praying I wouldn't fall into a rut. Hell, there was no denying I was having my difficulties. Just keeping up with it was bad enough, but trying to explain it, even to myself, was impossible. It is what it is, I determined, and that, in itself, is unavoidable. When confusion mixes with passion they start a riot in the psychic cellblocks. There were days when the voices in me debated like scholars over the Talmud. What was I thinking? Where was I going? What the hell was I doing, anyway? Damn if I knew. And damn if I was gonna stop.

"I guess you'd just better go now," Vicki would say every so often, when the tension got high, or when she was trying to impress me with her existential sense of despair. Maybe Vicki couldn't act when the cameras were on, but in person she could render a spellbinding performance. She'd be wan and pouting and none too talkative, lying with her back turned, her face buried in the pillow. I would stand and watch awhile before I made for the door, wondering as I departed what part of it was real and what was another performance.

Marcia and I were still sleeping together, and Vicki knew it. As for what Marcia knew, she later claimed she had suspected it, though not because of the odd hours I was keeping with Vicki. Marcia was used to my schedule, since for many years I had worked on offbeat assignments. Her suspicions had more to do with that certain sense women have when their lover's attentions are divided. But considering our twelve-year marriage, she decided not to challenge it; she would go for the advantage of the long run and let it all take its course. It was a respectable decision, an act of self-confidence. Whatever happened, she believed, would ultimately be in her favor. Still, she wasn't exactly stoic about it, and there were moments when conflict seemed imminent. Along with periods of concern and affection, there were periods of tension and times of momentous silences. I knew, as Marcia and Vicki did, that sooner or later, something had to give. Naturally, I was hoping for later.

But mostly it was Vicki and I monopolizing each other's time. We were going out more often, seeing movies, eating dinner in casual restaurants. We would take long drives, gazing at life through the windshield, looking up at the stars. We'd cruise Mulholland Drive, the winding road cresting the Hollywood Hills. I always kept binoculars in the trunk of my car. One night I took them out and passed them to Vicki, who held them up to the waxing moon and then peeked into the sparkling lights of the city. It was the first time she could remember ever having used binoculars, and she marvelled at the wonders in science and optics.

"What about a telescope?"

"No," she shook her head. "For some reason...it just never happened," she explained, as if American kids had to go out of their way to look at the stars through a telescope.

"All the money and the places you've been and you've never looked through a telescope? That's hard to believe."

"Gordon, who was I with who ever wanted to gaze at the stars?"

Going for drives was the best way to get Vicki out of the house for awhile. She felt secure in the isolation and the mobility of an automobile. She'd become restless and paranoid in crowds and public places. Sometimes, within minutes, be it at a restaurant or a supermarket, she would hang her head and round her shoulders like a scared little kid, asking that we exit and head for the safety of home. I would try my best to reassure her, but seldom did it make a difference.

"C'mon," she'd whisper, "let's get out of here."

Out of reflex I'd glance around, looking for the source of her fear. "What's the matter?" I'd ask. With her glasses on, her hair straight, and dressed in jeans and a sweater, it wasn't as if people were approaching and asking for her autograph.

"I don't know. Just the feeling I get.…"

In a crowd she would be nervous, but Vicki thought nothing of walking her dog alone at night in an isolated spot by the river. If anyone came up from behind her and blocked her exit through the single gate in the cyclone fence, she'd be trapped with her back to a twenty-foot drop into the concrete walls that line the path of the waterway. Forget what the dog might do to protect her, Doberman or not. If she was grabbed, it was over. With the heavy rains that season and persistent downpours that flooded the streets, the river water was high and running swiftly enough to carry a body as far as the ocean.

So I walked with her when she took her dog for a mid-night stroll along Colfax Avenue. It was a well-lighted, four-lane thoroughfare frequently travelled by people work-ing at the nearby CBS studios. So what if on the opposite side of Colfax the hills were alive with the sounds of nocturnal Los Angeles, replete with the distinctive growl of meandering Porsches belonging to gangs of Columbian smugglers trying in vain to live discreetly? They were never any trouble really, preferring to keep to themselves rather than be singled out by the stake-out teams of police. There were all kinds of police, from local and federal agencies, who from time to time parked on Colfax Avenue.

It was partly out of my years of habit and partly for security reasons that we were living at night and sleeping during the day. The late evening, I believed, was the time when we were most vulnerable, and with the odds as bad as they were to begin with, we wouldn't stand a chance if surprised in our sleep. But awake in the silence of the night, I would hear every movement, know the sound of every vehicle that, with any regularity, would be passing through the driveway. In case of trouble I kept a shotgun stashed in Vicki's closet. I was no stranger to weapons, and although I never expected to use it, I felt better that it was there. If attacked, I'd shoot to kill. Morality would never inhibit my aim. Since I can first remember, I've been possessed by the Alamo mentality, the concept of taking a few of them with you before you go. No shutouts here, not if I could help it. At the very least, I'd make a lot of noise. Let them explain all the bodies and the commotion the following day on the news.

Only one time did I ever feel the threat of imminent danger, and that was toward the end of her life. Late one night, a gray Lincoln Continental stopped outside the rear of the house and left its engine running for close to fifteen minutes. Neither the driver nor his passenger ever got out of the car, but they were staring up through the windshield at Vicki's bedroom window. Whether they saw me watching them or not, I wasn't certain. My nerves tingled with that inimitable sensation, that ass-grabbing rush of adrenalin, as I stood motionless in the darkened room, peering out the window with the shotgun cocked and ready.

"Oh shit!" I thought. "Here we go. Now it's gonna start."

"What is it?" Vicki asked me.

"Don't know yet," I whispered, just as the Lincoln took off in a hurry and headed down the driveway.

"Maybe they were just delivering pizzas," Vicki quipped, fully aware of the tension. It was a fine time to try and lighten the mood.

But then, Vicki was always less concerned with security than I was. Either she tried to suppress it or she genuinely didn't worry about a serious attempt on her life. She alluded to her guardian angel, who she claimed had protected her for all these years. Her fate, she said, was mainly in his hands. It was a grand occasion when she left the house and remembered to lock the door.

"Don't take it so lightly, Vicki. They may be coming back."

"The government's not interested in killing me," she protested, "if that's what you're thinking."

"The hell with the government," I said. "I'm not concerned about them. You know enough about Alfred's business to get your ass shot off and mine along with it. Let's face it, he was a high-powered money collector, a bag man. You told me so yourself...he'd come by your house with money practically hanging out of his briefcase. And you think no one's concerned about what he might've told you? You gotta be out of your fucking mind."

"Gordon, with my life as messed up as it is, I can't deal with it now."

"You'd better deal with it, because if anything happens, it'll happen fast. They're not the kind to advertise. They've got too much to lose."

"The hell with it," she laughed with a show of false bravado. "You just like to stay up all night. And now, you've gotten me used to your schedule. Oh, boy, if Alfred could see me now. He'd have to put off his nine o'clock call until noon."

Sometimes in the morning, on the way home from Vicki's, I'd drop Todd off at Notre Dame High School. Though posing as one of the punk minority on campus, and despite his acts of rebellion, he was a good kid. He had been living continually with his mother since he was eight, and now at fourteen he was beginning to establish independence. He was standing up for himself, learning the ropes on the street, seeking answers to questions he had previously not dared ask. Cautiously, he would pick at my thoughts and ask me about his mother. The public exposure had severely distressed him. Vicki had lied to him and told him that what the papers revealed wasn't true. Later, she had to recant her denial and explain what had been happening for all those years with "Uncle Alfred." Todd was confused, searching for a grip on reality and a balanced evaluation of

Vicki, or at least something that reduced the animosity he felt for her betrayal.

"She screwed up," I told him. "She should've been honest with you and not have lied about Alfred. She was afraid of hurting you. There were things she couldn't bear to tell. She was afraid of the way you'd react."

"Keeping it from me didn't make it any better. I hate the way she dealt with it."

"You can't go on blaming her forever. You know her at least as well as I do. After awhile, she'll quit feeling guilty and only resent you for being intolerant, for bearing a lifetime grudge. Remember, Todd, neither you nor anyone else in your family had any problem with her lifestyle as long as she was giving you money."

"I thought Alfred and her were friends," he relented. "I didn't think she was. . .doing all that with him."

"She did. Now he's dead, and she doesn't anymore. People have been known to do worse in this world. Just bear in mind that your mother tried her best to provide for you. Pass your judgements from there."

Throughout her life, to protect her son's innocence, Vicki had refrained from having men stay overnight. She would always go to their houses and return before dawn so Todd would awaken to find her in bed. Vicki at first intended to preserve the image of chastity in the household. She wanted me to be out of her bed in the morning, either gone for the day or resting on the living room sofa. She refused to believe her son knew we were sleeping together and that he mainly took it in stride. However, the pre-dawn charade only served to confuse him and make him suspicious of her behavior. At fourteen, he was experiencing his own sexual awakening, a fact Vicki found extremely difficult to face. He knew what we were doing. He told me as much one day when we were alone in the car. It wasn't until she saw him with his girlfriends that Vicki understood that her son had entered a precocious adolescence.

"I'm thirty, and I have a son who's fourteen," she'd tell me. "It's a problem. His friends' mothers are five and ten years older than I am. It's weird for him sometimes. I'm afraid if he knows you're in bed with me, it'll make it even tougher."

"The kid knows already. Don't pretend he doesn't."

"He knows you're married and that you have a son."

"He also knows that people fuck around. You should talk to him more and ask him what he really knows; ask what he's thinking now that he's a rebellious punker living in the Valley, and not another spoiled kid from Beverly Hills."

"There're things I don't like to discuss with him. I'm afraid of what he'll think of me."

I grew impatient with her. "Don't be such a coward. Let him get a sense of your experience so he'll appreciate it when you try to give him direction. He won't respond at all to bullshit. He'll feel cheated and trouble will start. You've got to make him respect you for the things you've come to know in life."

Vicki was lost, guilty and diffident when thrust in the face of authority. She was always polite, be it to her creditors or the dean of the high school, maybe too polite and therefore unable to put them off or assauge their fears. It was making her crazy that Todd would soon be expelled from school, and that the landlady was nervous about her rent.

"I wish Todd wouldn't grow up so quickly," Vicki lamented. "If I could have just a little more time to grow up myself, then maybe I wouldn't feel so pressured. I feel like a kid myself when I'm talking to his teachers. I keep thinking it's me who they want to throw out of school."

# 14

VICKI DIDN'T DARE have a bank account for fear the collections people would hound her for payments on the overdue charge cards. Her debts was overwhelming, to say nothing of the millions the Internal Revenue Service could sue her for in unpaid taxes, which made the thought of clinging to her few remaining possessions that much more absurd. She wished the moment would come when she could say, "Enough of this already," divesting herself of those remaining possessions to assume once again her gypsy way of life. Screw all the responsibility. She'd rather depend on the kindness of strangers than remain like a sitting duck. She claimed she'd be content if she could stay with friends, sleeping on their sofas or camping in their driveways, in the back of her Jeep Wagoneer. She said if she got some money she would travel awhile, spend some time in Europe. I could come with her if I so desired.

I told her I didn't much see the point. There was work to do before vacations were taken. When the book was finished, then we'd see where things were.

Vicki stared incredulously at me, as if I should know better. "You wouldn't want to go to Europe?"

"When this is all over, that's probably what I'll do."

"With me?"

"I don't know. I could even be going alone by then."

Suddenly, she was horrified as a certain recognition slowly dawned on her. "Oh!" she cried with genuine fear in her voice. "I can see where I'll be too old for you."

"Too old for me? What started that?"

"I will be," she insisted, pensive and gazing with a faraway look in her eyes. "I know it. You'll be involved with other things. We'll be friends, but that's all we could be."

"You think so, huh?"

Vicki didn't answer me. A powerful recognition had come over her that enhanced her fears and ruined her expectations. So I said nothing and observed her in silence, wondering what she was contemplating.

"What is it?" I asked, when I grew tired of the silence.

She shook her head. "Just thinking about Europe and Bernie Cornfeld. When I think of Europe, I always think of Bernie. He and I spent some time over there. Good times, when we were getting along with each other. When we didn't, we fought like hell. But Bernie was good to me. A better friend than he was a lover. He took me in when I needed a place. Just like I need one now."

"So call Bernie," I laughed.

"I can't. We had some trouble between us."

Bernie had fallen in love with her during her stay at Grayhall. He was overcome with feelings that perhaps he'd rather not have had. He wanted her badly, and Vicki knew it. She demanded his attention and, in exchange, offered no guarantees. She allowed him to dangle, to yearn for her when she went out on dates with other men. Weeks passed before she as much as hinted that she might be willing to sleep with him. Anticipation, she knew, served to whet the appetite, and Bernie, with all his girls, would have to learn that Vicki came first. Nearly a month went by before his nervous patience was finally rewarded. For him, she was worth waiting for and they soon became companions on a regular basis. According to his coterie, he felt more for Vicki than for any other woman. He was charmed by her reticence, her conservative posture. She was insouciant and mischief burned in her eyes. She was taller than he. She

151

was a beauty. She was a lot more than just another conquest. She was a prize, a worthy tribute to his status and power. For the man on the move, for the man who had it made, she was the final testament to his taste and prowess.

Before moving in, Vicki had stipulated he must allow her to come and go as she pleased. If she wanted to skip dinner and remain aloof, tucked away in the privacy of her room, then he was not supposed to disturb her. Bernie had agreed to her wishes and he obeyed them for almost a full week before he began requesting her presence whenever he had company. Vicki grumbled, but mainly she went along with the program. She knew he wanted his friends to believe it was his charm that kept her at his side and not his money. Unlike the other women whom Bernie saw, Vicki wasn't struggling. She already had the furs, clothes, and jewelry. She even had a Mercedes Benz; that is, until a spiteful Alfred Bloomingdale had it repossessed after she walked out on him. Bernie, as consolation, presented her with his yellow Maserati. A skeptical Vicki asked if it was really a gift or merely a loaner. Bernie was appropriately noncommittal. Vicki accepted the car.

When the ice finally broke and they became paramours, Bernie suggested that Vicki accompany him to Europe. He would first take care of business there and then they would go on vacation. He talked of leasing a houseboat in the South of France and cruising the Riviera. He made it sound inviting, but Vicki was initially reluctant to go. She feared that their friends would misinterpret the trip. She worried about Alfred's reaction. She knew such a junket would be seen as a romantic commitment, and although she liked sleeping with Bernie and keeping him company, she wasn't quite ready to be his steady girl. The thought of it made Vicki nervous. Not because of Bernie so much, but because she feared what any relationship might do to thwart her own desires. She was hoping to take things easy, have fun and explore the possibilities of independence. She wished to experience a variety of men and she enjoyed the freedom it gave her. And last but not least, she was hoping to discover something meaningful to do with herself.

But Bernie was tenacious and very persuasive. When she insisted that none of the other women go along, Bernie obligingly complied. The last thing he wished to do was upset her and lose his chance to consolidate their relationship. Vicki was making it difficult enough as it was. Repeatedly she had bent his ear with her reservations and her warnings against a steady romance. He knew his timing was bad. For one thing, there was Alfred's lingering spectre and, for another, there were jealous women, skilled opportunists who had already tried to come between him and Vicki. One, according to Bernie—Charlene La Seine— had even gone so far as to serve as Vicki's procurer by setting her up with rich and elderly men. When Bernie objected, an argument ensued, creating animosities that would later help to destroy their relationship.

During the first leg of their journey abroad, Vicki discovered she was an asset to Bernie in ways she hadn't expected. She should have known better when they arrived in Geneva and Bernie magnanimously offered to exchange suitcases and carry hers through customs.

"Here, you carry this, and I'll carry yours," he offered, sticking his bags in her hand. "Mine are lighter," he went on to explain.

Vicki, followed by Bernie and his two business associates, caught the guardian eye of the Swiss inspector and put him to rest with the charms of a pretty young girl. She tried not to think about what might be concealed in Cornfeld's luggage. If it was undeclared money, then she certainly did not want to know.

"Just get it over with," she told herself, and with pounding heart, shaky legs, and sweaty palms, Vicki hoisted the bags and entered Switzerland uncontested.

From Geneva they flew to Paris and remained a few

days in Bernie's flat, a few blocks away from the Champs Elysees. Vicki was alone much of the time, while Bernie conducted his business. It gave her time to think, to wonder what she was doing. She was growing increasingly uncomfortable with the situation. Tension had been building between her and Bernie. She was missing her son Todd and was missing Alfred Bloomingdale. She tried to deny it, but the more she discounted the notion, the more she felt like a fool. She knew better. Alfred was under her skin. On one hand it tormented her, on the other she was grateful for someone to love. It was the same terrible dilemma, choosing between passion and practicality. She could strive for independence or live her life as Alfred's mistress. It was getting tougher all the time to try and do both.

Despite its relative size and its modern conveniences, Vicki found she wasn't thrilled with the houseboat Bernie had leased in St. Tropez. After three days of tooling about the coastal waters, she demanded to be put ashore. She would take a hotel room and properly wash herself, do her makeup and fix her hair. She would get a good night's sleep for a change.

Bernie did his best to persuade her not to go. "You'll get the hang of it. It just takes time."

"Too bad, Cornfeld," countered Vicki. "I'm getting the hell off this boat."

Bernie continued to protest and Vicki continued to argue. At one point Bernie threatened to leave her stranded, but Vicki, undaunted, told him he didn't have to stay on her account. She was certain she'd get by. She disembarked and carried with her only one small bag, having left the remainder of her luggage with Captain Bernie. This was the last she'd ever see of her things, for that night Bernie piped aboard a couple of ladies, who later escaped with Vicki's luggage and whatever else they could steal. Vicki was livid when she returned that following day. She demanded

Bernie compensate by doubling the quantity of things that had been stolen. Otherwise, it was over then and there.

Bernie diplomatically countered with an appropriate offer. "If I buy you new things, will you stay on the houseboat with me?"

Vicki interpreted this as a sign of surrender. She was moved by Cornfeld's boyish self-pity and had no need to embarrass him further. Reluctantly she agreed to sail with him and Jim Webber to Monte Carlo, which was further north on the Côte d'Azur. It would have been an easy trip if someone only knew how to sail. Bernie, in his five days of cruising the harbor had yet to get the hang of it, and he drifted out to sea until evening fell and they finally lost sight of the coastline. There was no radio or running lights aboard the craft. As time passed and tension mounted, the members of the trio gradually became more worried that a ocean freighter would suddenly emerge from the midnight fog and smash the hell out of their pitiful houseboat.

With lantern in hand and armed with a compass, Bernie climbed into the dinghy, which had been attached by rope to the mother ship, and tried by rowing to pull the boat toward land. Jim Webber manned the rudder while Vicki kept a flashlight trained on Bernie. She was laughing hysterically, taken with the absurdity of it all. There he was alright, Bernie, the felonious cherub, rowing for all he was worth, straining in the distance, amidst the sinewy, rippling waters of the open sea. Unfortunately, he was pulling the boat in circles. It was the story of her life, a perfect allegory, direction without intention and motion without results. It occured to her that she may die out there, miles away from her dreams.

"I'm coming back," shouted Cornfeld. "I think I've spotted land."

This time they all climbed into the dinghy, and with Bernie on one oar and Webber on the other, the lusty swabs pulled for shore, goaded by Vicki's laughter. Soon they were able to see the lights dotting the coastline. They pulled harder, struggling to keep the boat pointed straight ahead. They were getting closer to land, where the waves were swelling and breaking on the jagged rock formations that extended outward from the darkened beach. As the dinghy reached the shoreline, it swayed and trembled, scraping against the rocks. The dinghy was breaking apart, so they abandoned it and waded ashore.

At last they were on the beach, soaked and ragged, with minor cuts and bruises, the result of unstable footing in the swelling tide. Nevertheless, they were safely on land, standing on a narrow beach beneath a sloping cliff formation. They climbed the winding trail until they reached the top and found refuge in a lesbian nightclub, the only place open for miles around. It was the perfect ending to an imperfect journey. The ordeal at sea was finally over, and with it, the end that would soon come to Vicki's affair with Bernie. It was enough, she thought. He, like the others, with his desires and his jealousies, had worn her down, chewed up her insides. The persistent demands of all these rich and powerful men were like so many songs for which she had been forced to learn the different dances. To do so, she had assumed a variety of personalities, causing her to fragment and break apart.

Be it Alfred, Bernie, this one or that, they had all wanted so much from her, to partake of her rare and special qualities. For she was more than just another pretty girl, more than a mere embodiment of vapid pleasure to be enjoyed and discarded or retained like a personal charm. Sure, she was appealing enough and sexy, but she was also strong enough to mother them in times of their personal crises. She was different, alright, something goddamned hard to find. And a girl like this invited tough competition. This was no game for brow-beaten nerds. To find a girl like this, you had to play hardball. To keep a girl like this, well...you had to be kidding yourself. But even so, despite the improbable odds, men would ante up, risking self-destruction to play a game without rules, hoping to win what they could never possess.

Vicki returned alone to Los Angeles, having left Bernie in London to finish up with his business. At first he would not let her go, fearing she'd split from him and disappear as she had done earlier in London. It had taken him days to track her down before he had found she was hiding out in Margaret's flat, a lady friend Vicki had met through Bernie. Quite a scene had ensued that evening, with Bernie pounding on the door and his associate, Jim Webber, calling from the corner pay phone, telling a frightened Margaret that, "Bernie wants to talk to Vicki."

Vicki refused to let him in, and Bernie remained in the hallway, demanding he have his say. For nearly an hour, the exchanges took place on opposite sides of the door until Vicki finally relented and permitted Margaret to open up and let Bernie come in.

"What's wrong?" asked Bernie, after he had stepped inside. He was red-faced, petulant, and very confused. "What did I do?"

"I'm tired of it," Vicki told him. "I'm tired of your ego, the girls and all the hangers on. It's a circus with you, and it's time for me to get out."

Bernie attempted to win her back. He furrowed his brow, narrowed his eyes, and glared at a quivering Margaret, voicing his anger that she had assisted with Vicki's escape. Before he could work up another full head of steam, Vicki interceded on Margaret's behalf, demanding Bernie cease with his accusations.

"C'mon, Bernie," she relented. "I've had enough of it tonight. If you want me to come with you, then let's go now."

So it was with great trepidation that Bernie consented to Vicki's return to California. He made her promise him that she would be waiting at his mansion upon his own return to L.A. Vicki, he knew, would always keep her word. This time was without exception, and she was there to greet him when Bernie walked through the door.

Having met her commitment, Vicki left Bernie a few days later, absconding with the Maserati, her jewelry, Penny, her housekeeper, and several bags of clothes. She was on the run again, in need of a place to hide since Bernie would certainly try to find her. She also needed money and, for that, there was only one person to call. She would be the portrait of suffering humility, explaining her plight, detailing the personal indignities, the enumerable inconveniences with which she had to live. She would lay it all out before Alfred Bloomingdale, hoping he'd pick up the pieces as he had done in the past.

Vicki took a room at the Holiday Inn, where she stayed up all night waiting to call Alfred. She was hoping to reach him at five A.M., when he first arrived at his office. He wouldn't remain there for long, unless he was having hookers drop by for a torrid sunrise scenario. And then with the hookers gone, Alfred, having worked up an appetite, would make his important, long-distance phone calls before taking off to Duke's in West Hollywood for his usual breakfast. Vicki had known his schedule for years. She was even aware of the hookers visiting his office in Century City. Although they had never discussed it, she was wise to Alfred's moves, having found him winded and nervous on the occasions when she had gone to bed late or awakened early and surprised him by calling first.

Vicki gobbled down Valiums and snorted cocaine as she waited for morning to come. She was nervous. Her eyes burned with exhaustion, her hands were clammy and the drone of the television was starting to get on her nerves. She paced the room and stared out the window, observing the eerie silence of a vacant Westwood and the sprawling UCLA campus. No one was walking the streets. Nothing moved out there but a few cars and trucks on Wilshire

Boulevard, whisking past the Holiday Inn. The hollow sounds of an empty midnight stimulated her fears of isolation. She kept evaluating her game plan, just to pass the time. It would be their first conversation in months, since she had taken legal action, except for their few "chance" meetings at the car wash on La Cienega Boulevard. She believed that once she explained everything, he would never leave her stranded, if for no other reason than to keep her away from Bernie. It didn't necessarily mean he'd be gracious about it. He might want to teach her a lesson. She knew he could make it tough.

Vicki's anxieties were soon put to rest. It was like old home week when Alfred picked up the phone. He was elated that she had called him. He had missed her and he didn't mind telling her so. He went on and on, in his deep, raspy voice, about the void in his life since she'd been gone. He thought of her constantly. He had been enraged when he discovered that she was living with Bernie. "Vic," he said, "you really hurt me by moving in there."

"Alfred," she reminded him, "I warned you never to dare me. Look...I had to get out of there. I couldn't take it anymore. I need your help."

"I would never leave you in a bad situation," he assured her. His voice was filled with sentiment. He was so excited he could barely catch his breath. "Only because I love you...and believe me, I know how stupid I am for loving you...that's the only reason I'm giving you money to get away from Bernie. I'll give you some money, but only so much. Until you drop the law suit. If you do that, then everything's fine. If not, then I won't let you do this to me. I'm not going to keep giving you money."

Vicki agreed to meet him at Duke's to talk things over. Duke's, a modest café in the Tropicana Motel on Santa Monica Boulevard, draws an assortment of actors, rock and rollers, and businessmen, who come in droves each morning for their ritual serving of good, basic food at inexpensive

159

prices. It's a place where patrons sit at the counter or share crowded tables with friends and strangers. Duke's was one of Alfred's favorites, and he had been going there for years. He was eating alone at a corner table when Vicki finally arrived. She was jumpy and ragged from being up the night before. She was conscious of the other patrons, mostly men, staring at her with veiled curiosity. She saw them drop their eyes and go back to what they were eating the moment Alfred stood and beckoned her to his table. She was reminded that life was so easy when Alfred took care of things.

Alfred couldn't have been happier than when Vicki embraced him and kissed him warmly on the mouth. She was back in his arms, squeezing him tightly, pressing her face against his chest. Alfred stroked her hair and glanced around him, taking pleasure in the envy he saw in the eyes of the silent observers.

"I can't tell you how glad I am to see you," he chortled. He returned to his chair and bade her to sit in the one next to his. He took her hand in both of his and squeezed it tightly. "I get crazy when you're not in my life," he whispered in that deep, raspy voice. He raised his head and stared at her, allowing the silence to wash between them. "I hope you're dropping the lawsuit," he said.

"I will, when you stop forcing me to go along with that perverted trip of yours. You know I don't like it."

Alfred was quick to change the subject. He started laughing, as if something had suddenly just popped into his mind. "You know you killed my goddamn lawyer," he roared.

Both were hysterical over old Jacques Leslie's sudden demise. But when the laughter faded, Vicki was frowning, her eyes were wide with fear and dismay. She grew numb as she listened to Alfred's instructions, his assurances that all would be well and that he would call his friend, who

*Alfred Bloomingdale* (AP/WIDE WORLD)

(GRAHAM/OUTLINE)

NAME—NOM

**VICKI LYNN LAMM K-A VICKI LYNN MORGAN**

SEX—SEXE  BIRTHPLACE—LIEU DE NAISSANCE

**F     COLORADO, U.S.A.**

BIRTH DATE—DATE DE NAISSANCE

**AUG. 9, 1952**

ISSUE DATE—DATE DE DELIVRANCE

**NOV. 7, 1977**

WIFE/HUSBAND—EPOUSE/EPOUX

**X X X**

EXPIRES ON—EXPIRE LE

**NOV. 6, 1982**

MINORS—ENFANTS MINEURS

**X X X**

SIGNATURE OF BEARER—SIGNATURE DU TITULAIRE

*Passport Vicki used to visit Earl Lamm while he was imprisoned in Mexico.*

*Executive producer Michael Gruskoff on location during filming of* Quest for Fire. *Shortly afterward, Gruskoff sent author Gordon Basichis to collaborate with Vicki on her story.* (ACADEMY OF MOTION PICTURE ARTS AND SCIENCES)

*Cary Grant with Margaux Hemingway at the Royal Lancaster Hotel, London, in 1976. (A similar photo of Cary and Vicki Morgan taken a few years before at the opening of the MGM Grand in Las Vegas was destroyed in that hotel's disastrous fire.)* (AP/WIDE WORLD)

*Vicki with Bernie Cornfeld and his retinue outside Cornfeld's Los Angeles mansion, built for Douglas Fairbanks, Sr. Cornfeld had just been released after serving eight months in a Geneva prison.* (AP/WIDE WORLD)

*Vicki in two of the many houses she would live in but never own.*

*Betsy Newling of Beverly Hills becomes Mrs. Alfred Bloomingdale in 1946.
(Inset) Betsy in 1974 with Claude Roland at opening of Las Hadas Resort
in Manzanillo, Mexico.* (AP/WIDE WORLD)

*King Hassan of Morocco shortly after meeting with President Reagan in 1982.* (AP/WIDE WORLD)

*Celebrity lawyer Marvin Mitchelson holding photos of Vicki after filing palimony suit against Alfred Bloomingdale in 1982.* (AP/WIDE WORLD)

ALFRED BLOOMINGDALE

1888 CENTURY PARK EAST, SUITE 1018
LOS ANGELES, CALIFORNIA 90067

February 12, 1982


Mr. William McComas
Marina Bay Hotel
2175 State Road 84
Ft. Lauderdale, Florida 33312
Dear Bill:
As per our conversation, if we finalize Showbiz
Pizza, then Vicki Morgan, now residing at 1611
Tower Grove, Beverly Hills, California, is entitled
to ½ (one-half) of my interest in the above.  Her
name should be included in all contracts so that
this cannot be taken away from her, in the event
of my incapacitation or absence.
Regards,

Alfred Bloomingdale
cc:  Vicki Morgan
     David Rousso
     Barry Rubin

WITNESS                          WITNESS

_Alice Valenzuela_               _Charles F. Chandler_

_1918 PLANT AVE_                 _2615 Hampton Ave._

_Redondo Beach, CA_             _LA. CA. GCC7L_
                _90278_

*Letters (see facing page) from Alfred Bloomingdale authorizing payments
to Vicki. After Alfred's death, Betsy Bloomingdale's refusal to honor these
led to Mitchelson's suit, public scandal, and the events that followed.*

ALFRED BLOOMINGDALE

*1888 CENTURY PARK EAST, SUITE 1018*
*LOS ANGELES, CALIFORNIA 90067*

February 12, 1982

Miss Vicki Morgan
1611 Tower Grove
Beverly Hills, Ca. 90210
Dear Vicki:
I agree to pay you $10,000 a month for two years
beginning March 1, 1982.  This money will be paid
to you by the 28th of each month from the proceeds
of my profit from Marina Bay, etc.
Bill McComas has been authorized to do this.

Regards,

Alfred Bloomingdale
cc: William McComas
    David Rousso
    Barry Rubin

WITNESS
*Alice Valenzuela*
*1918 PLANT Ave*
*Redondo Beach, CA*
*90278*

WITNESS
*Charles F. Charles*
*7615 Hampton Ave.*
*L.A. Ca. 90046*

*Vicki poolside at one of the homes Bloomingdale furnished for her.*
(GRAHAM/OUTLINE)

*Marvin Pancoast hearing police testimony that his fingerprints were not found on the baseball bat that was used to kill Vicki Morgan. He is presently serving 26 years to life for her murder.* (UPI/BETTMAN)

owned the Holiday Inn, and explain what was happening. Vicki would have a suite where she could stay until she sorted things out, get everything settled and started all over again.

# 15

FOR OVER A month, Vicki hid out at the Holiday Inn. She ordered up meals from room service, watched television, and spent hours talking on the phone. Every now and then she'd brave the world and go for a ride in the Maserati. She knew it was a matter of time before Bernie would discover her whereabouts and demand she return his car. Alfred, meanwhile, was taking a hard line when it came to giving her money. Until she agreed to drop the lawsuit, she could forget about getting another Mercedes from him or, for that matter, receiving anything but a subsistence income. Instead, she would be living her life on a designer shoestring—the cloistered damsel of the Holiday Inn. He would keep her there until she understood what she could and couldn't do in the life she had chosen. He would teach her that it wasn't wise to get too uppity in this world, and that there were better ways to resolve their differences than hashing them out in court. He made all of this quite clear to her each day when he called to keep tabs on her, to see how she was making out.

Vicki had apologized, had claimed she was sorry for letting it all get out of hand. But...he never should have dared her and, what's more, she would no longer be part of his sado-masochistic encounters. She would no longer mingle with his legion of hookers or in any way sanction his sexual proclivities. If they were to have sex, it would take place in an intimate setting, with just the two of them present.

Otherwise, they could be only friends. Although Alfred, till the end of his days, would continue with his bizarre sex practices, Vicki was never again a part of it.

But before the issue was settled, an irate Bernie Cornfeld showed up at the Holiday Inn to confront Vicki Morgan and take back his Maserati. Vicki bought time by asking Bernie to wait in the lobby until she was dressed. When he agreed, she immediately called Alfred and asked what she should do.

"Don't worry about Bernie," Alfred assured her. "He won't give you any trouble, not if you tell him you've come back to me."

She was trapped again, caught in a squeeze play with only one move to make if she was to save herself at all. God help her if she went against Alfred and went along with Bernie, especially at a time like this when the two massive egos were at the flashpoint. For this was a struggle far more severe than two men competing for a woman. This was a classical rivalry between Alfred, the old monied socialite, and Bernie, a product of the *nouveau riche*. Jealousy, animosity, and the taste of dried blood from previous disagreements were all at work here. Winning Vicki's hand was more than the taking of flesh. In a struggle of this magnitude, hers was the hand of gold.

Vicki would soon drop the lawsuit and return to the dominion of Alfred Bloomingdale. She returned the Maserati to Bernie Cornfeld and thanked him for his companionship and hospitality. She predicted that they would always be friends. But Bernie wanted more than that, and he wondered why he lost in the end.

"Because Alfred needs me and you don't," came Vicki's reply. "I have to go back to him."

With the lawsuit gone and Bernie thwarted, Alfred staked Vicki to a furnished apartment on Doheny Drive. Alfred was pleased that she had come back to him, but Vicki was lost in her frustration, guilt and despair. She sensed she was on the brink of a nervous breakdown, and she went into seclusion, seeing few friends and spending most of her time in bed. She now understood that she couldn't get out. She had chosen a life of adventure and intrigue; she had experienced wealth, the machinations of power, and through it all, she had gotten to know too much. She had been buffeted about and she now dreaded mingling. She seldom left her apartment, and she got the shakes when the telephone rang. Her suitors were put on hold, and she told Alfred Bloomingdale that, since nothing had actually been resolved, she couldn't see him for fear she'd go over the edge. She agreed to talk with him on the phone, however, while maintaining a nice, safe distance. Sometimes her nerves were so bad she would get dizzy and vomit as soon as she hung up the phone. Vicki was twenty-four years old.

After living on the brink for several months, Vicki had an emotional breakdown. She recovered with the aid of her friend Sally Talbert, who, along with her husband Art, took her in and provided shelter until Vicki felt secure enough to go back into the world. By this time, she was bored and restless, remaining aloof from Alfred and the different men she had dated. She had lost touch with Cary Grant and Hal, the plastic surgeon, had faded into her memories. Mike Gruskoff still called every now and then and Vicki surprised him one day by accepting when he asked her out.

She dated Gruskoff frequently and eventually moved in with him at his house in the Hollywood Hills. She perceived in him a rare opportunity to break away from Alfred, for Mike was a man of maturity and promise. He, like Bernie Cornfeld, was a native of Brooklyn, New York, and obsessed with the images and trappings that come with success. He was an up-and-coming producer, a former hotshot agent who, like Vicki, had suffered a rugged childhood and lacked much of a formal education, but by using his wits and ambitions he had made his way in the world. Michael was younger than Alfred, Bernie, and Cary Grant. He didn't have a fraction of their money, and he certainly wasn't a worldwide power. But he did have potential beneath the crusty layers of fear and distrust. He might have been gruff, intransigent, and often insensitive, but underneath it all, like gold in the hills, she believed he possessed qualities worth bringing to the surface. With a little help from her, Vicki believed Mike could realize a spiritual awakening. She would help him find himself, get him in touch with his deepest thoughts and emotions. If nothing else, she could help him make a lot of money.

To placate a nervous and curious Alfred Bloomingdale, who all this time was still sending Vicki her monthly checks, she used her standard explanation and told him that Michael was gay and therefore no competition for Alfred. She argued that Michael could help with her acting career by using her as an escort whenever he made the rounds to the important Hollywood parties. It was all bullshit, but Vicki made it work just the same. And, since Michael never objected to her relationship with Alfred Bloomingdale, harmony was maintained.

Michael, like Bernie Cornfeld, often had trouble with Vicki. He had been attracted to her for her status and beauty, but he was intimidated by it as well. He knew little of the world from which Vicki had fled, and virtually nothing of how to live up to her expectations. But Michael offered Vicki the visceral side of life, unlike the others who had gone before him. He made her doubt and he made her wonder. He could be as unpredictable as she was, and he kept her on the defensive. Vicki loved him for it and saw it as a challenge. Michael was critical of her, and she strived for his approval. Believing that she failed him would affect her for the rest of her life.

"I hope you're not here for the money," Gruskoff had warned her soon after she moved in with him.

Vicki, laughing, spoke softly as she patted Gruskoff's

hand. "Mike, I love you. Don't you understand? You don't have the kind of money I'd expect, if that's what I was interested in. I have more than you."

Mike had recently been divorced and he swore to Vicki that he'd never remarry. Especially, he would never marry her. He claimed it was because of her high-minded attitude and her ostentatious habits, but she believed there were other reasons, things that Michael would never admit. She knew he was nervous when Todd was around, due mainly to the strain of his previous marriage. Vicki, like Michael's ex-wife, had brought a child into their relationship, and he made her feel that she burdened him, leaving her anxious about losing her man. Sensing Mike's discomfort, Vicki neglected her son and avoided having him stay over with them on the weekends. Instead, she would sneak off to Montclair and visit Todd at her mother's, or drive him back to the city for an orgy of shopping and juvenile treats. In the aftermath, she would cry at night in frustration. Her mother was grumbling, claiming neglect and applying pressure, once again threatening to sue for custody of the child.

In order to distract herself from the gnarly traumas of despair and uncertainty, Vicki steeped herself in Gruskoff's domestic life. It was wholesome behavior, but exhausting nevertheless. Michael, having the responsibilities of his career, his three children, a son, and two daughters, was only too happy to accommodate Vicki's wishes and teach her what the real world was all about. The children, Vicki learned, were having emotional problems; Gruskoff's ex-wife was erratic and difficult and his dog kept getting lost. The maid, who was Vicki's responsibility, couldn't speak any English, and Vicki's Spanish was yet to be heard. However, Vicki stuck with it, believing these trials were necessary to demonstrate her love for Michael, while revealing to him her true emotional character. Despite his critiques, his complaints, the countless orders and myriad commands, as errand girl for Mike Gruskoff, Vicki ran around the city and did whatever he asked.

In addition to Valium, Vicki started taking Quaaludes. It was as good a way as any to pass the time, especially on location in Guaymas, Mexico, where Mike was filming *Lucky Lady*, his latest production. Gruskoff didn't encourage her appearing on the set, except for special occasions, so Vicki remained at the hotel sunning herself on the beach. In the beginning, she'd take half a Quaalude and sleep while one side tanned, and then awaken, swallow the other half pill and roll over for the second part of the day. She was soon building a tolerance for methaqualone, needing more each day to relax and feel dreamy, but she did look terrific. She was the darkest she had been in her life.

The end to Vicki's relationship with Michael Gruskoff came abruptly. He had gone to New York on business and, during his stay there, had made a point of calling Vicki and telling her he was going out on a date. When he returned to Los Angeles he found Vicki dressed and standing in the doorway, waiting to take him to dinner.

"Are you in love with me?" she demanded, once they had ordered drinks. Her brow was raised, and there was a narrow, expectant smile on her face as she awaited his reply.

Mike took some time in thinking it over. His face flushed as he stared at her, the candlelight flickering on his reddening face. "Of course I love you, but . . ."

Vicki cut him off and pointed her finger as she issued final judgement. "Anything you say before the 'but,' Michael, becomes totally irrelevant. Thank you very much, at least for being honest."

Puzzled, Michael wrinkled his brow and waited for her to continue. He watched her sigh and rise from the table. Vicki glanced around the restaurant and then looked back at him. Standing over him she announced, "I'm leaving you tonight."

"Where will you go?"

"I have reservations," gloated Vicki. "My bags are already packed and in the limousine. You see, Michael, I knew the answer you'd give me, even before you came home."

On a particularly spiteful evening, about a month after walking out on Michael Gruskoff, Vicki proposed to John David Carson, a struggling young actor she was dating. She knew by marrying him she could kill two birds with one stone; she could drive Alfred crazy and really piss off Mike. She didn't have to accept the hurt and disappointment she had realized during her affairs with these two men. She would show them what they were missing and all the fun she was having in life.

John David at first was taken aback by Vicki's proposal. He had not imagined earlier in the evening that this might be his wedding night. Dinner and a movie would have been enough for him, but Vicki was very persuasive and he listened intently as she made her pitch.

"Marry me now, because it won't happen tomorrow, or next week. Tonight's the night, if it's for real. If not, then we should forget about it, here and now."

Carson wasn't used to ultimatums. With Vicki, he wasn't prepared for much at all. Although they were the same chronological age, he was a kid in Vicki's eyes. Being young and inexperienced, he was susceptible to Vicki's influence, the manipulation and elements of mind control she wielded so effectively. This gave her the opportunity to let out her frustrations on John David Carson, avenge the things that men had done to her.

When he finally agreed to marry her, Vicki suggested they fly to Las Vegas right away. But John David called his mother to tell her the good news, and she offered to drive them there instead. A well-dressed woman, chic and attractive, she arrived an hour later and inspected her future daughter-in-law. Instantly, both women knew there was more going on than John David was aware of. His mother, during the six-hour drive to Las Vegas, asked many questions and reacted with alarm to some of Vicki's answers. John David, she hoped, would reconsider and change his mind about getting married. But John David, meanwhile, said almost nothing as he drove his mother's car toward Vegas and the fleeting chance of marital bliss.

In the beginning Vicki enjoyed her marriage. Her husband, she believed, was tender and loving, but also indecisive and insecure. John David, however, tried his best to make her happy. In addition, unlike the other men in Vicki's life, he demonstrated genuine affection for Todd. They would go for long drives, play at sports, and horse around together. Vicki was pleased for her son, grateful her husband cared enough to try and behave like a father.

To reciprocate, Vicki threw herself into the marriage. She bought cookbooks, and with the utensils received at the post-dated wedding shower she attempted to cook for the first time in her life. For groceries she went to Gelson's, the expensive gourmet supermarket, which for Vicki seemed like a belt-tightening operation. It wasn't too long before she gave up her culinary artistry and allowed her husband to do the cooking. She did the dishes instead.

She was three months into the marriage before it started to get on her nerves. Money was tight and she was craving the thrills and intrigue of the life she had previously known. Vicki likened her desires to a drug she was kicking, believing the addiction might very well pass with time. She vowed to stick it out. However, to tempt fate, she did call Alfred Bloomingdale every now and then, something she had promised herself she wouldn't do. He had offered her cash to provide for the household, but she refused it. She was hoping to turn the tide by helping boost her husband's fledgling career. She pushed and prodded, even dressed him in drag one night and took him to dinner to see if he could act out the gender he was to portray in a "Police

Woman" episode: that of a man disguised as a woman who murders people until justice once again prevails.

With Vicki there to coach and inspire him so that he would achieve, become a star, and be able to support her in the style to which she was accustomed, John David worked hard and boosted his career. He was getting more work on episodes of various television series and some in feature films. One, an independent production to be filmed in Lawton, Oklahoma, would be on location for weeks. John David invited Vicki to come along and she agreed.

The filming was barely underway when a local sheriff arrived on the set one day with a subpoena in his hand. Vicki had been summoned back to Los Angeles by the District Federal Court as a witness for the prosecution against Bernard Cornfeld, who was on trial for the illegal use of a blue box, an electronic device he had allegedly used to bypass charges for his long-distance calls. These cases were often treated lightly, with fines and such, or the offended telephone companies were willing to settle out of court. But not in their case against Bernie Cornfeld. No leniency was ever implied, and Bernie, if convicted, was facing additional time in prison. The prosecution, he found, had been relentless in pursuing its case, as if some vindictive and influential soul was pushing it, had set it up, and now refused to let it drop. Bernie's troubles could have come from Alfred Bloomingdale, but Vicki was never sure. She only knew she had received her first subpoena to appear as a witness before the grand jury a little more than a year ago, shortly after her midnight departure from Cornfeld's palatial mansion. It was Alfred, she remembered, who had hinted at vengeance.

At her appearance before the grand jury, Vicki had lied on Bernie's behalf. She claimed she knew nothing about a blue box, or what one even looked like. Bernie, as far as she knew, paid for all of his calls. What Bernie ultimately refused to pay was the $1,500 that Vicki had demanded to hire her own attorney, rather than use the one Bernie had retained to protect his entire clan.

Bernie, claiming she was holding him up for money, refused to pay for Vicki's attorney and left for Europe, a fatal mistake that would cost him more than three months in jail.

Vicki, enraged by his refusal to comply with her wishes, really went to work on Bernie. Prior to her second appearance before the grand jury, Vicki let agents of the FBI know she had recovered from her bout with amnesia and now was ready to talk. She added, with vituperative candor, that she was ratting out of spite, believing Cornfeld had lied and abandoned her, leaving her stranded to fend for herself. The FBI agents didn't care about her grudges, had little concern for her underlying motivations, but they were delighted to accommodate her wishes, grant her immunity, and, therefore, milk her for what she was worth. They were indulgently patient with her, friendly and quite impressed with her memory. They found it convenient, too, that Vicki, having met him through Alfred, knew the presiding judge on a first-name basis. It was also helpful that Alfred was in constant contact with Vicki throughout the entire trial.

But in the end, Vicki regretted what she had done. She had obtained her vengeance and lost a friend in Bernie Cornfeld. Bernie's conviction and sentencing came as a hollow victory, an unsavory and unnecessary condition that should have been avoided. She should have known better, should have realized that she and Bernie were both alike— obstinate creatures who can be stubborn to the point of stupidity. Bernie had been negligent rather than arrogant, Vicki believed, and she had overreacted. She had been impetuous and moved too quickly. The government, she realized, had played her for a fool.

As the days passed and self-revelations began to puncture her dreams, the youthful zeal of John David Carson was losing much of its appeal. In Vicki's world, that of

171

power and crisis, John David didn't belong. And now Vicki longed to return to that world. She was bored and restless, trapped and uninspired. She had hoped for the best, but she had gotten what she'd feared. John David was not to blame; the blame fell on Vicki Morgan. She had tried to hide out in the simple life, but that, like everything else, had failed. She hated to be without money and she was bothered by the obscurity. She felt herself getting older, running out of time. She was no longer the sharp, flexible little girl she had been when Alfred found her. There was a brittle permanence to her character. There was really no escape.

John David went away on location to work on a horror movie that was shooting in Florida. Vicki had stayed home and allowed herself to be talked into a supposed modeling assignment in the Middle East. Vicki was told by Charlene La Seine, the woman she had met through Bernie Cornfeld, that the work would be easy and the pay would be good. Needing money desperately and wanting to get out of town, Vicki boarded a commercial jetliner and, along with several other women, began the first leg of her journey to Marrakesh. She knew nothing about Morocco, having travelled mainly in Europe, but, after speaking to the other models and picking up their vibes, she determined something strange was taking place. She was suspicious and worried as she neared her destination. But never did she imagine that she had been singled out for special reasons long before she had boarded the plane. Nor did she consider that, as she crossed different borders, her travels were being monitored, and that word eventually would be getting back to Alfred Bloomingdale.

# 16

ABDELSLAM JAIDI, a spiffy Arabian diplomat in a natty suit, was waiting to greet her when Vicki stepped off the plane in Marrekesh. Jaidi was courteous to the other women, but Vicki Morgan was the focus of his attention. He introduced himself as the Moroccan Consul General to the United States. Jaidi ordered the chauffeur to carry her bags while he escorted her to his limousine. Little English was spoken between Jaidi and his chauffeur as they drove Vicki to her quarters. The two men conversed in French and Arabic, which aroused Vicki's suspicions.

"What's going on here?" she wondered. Why was she going alone with Jaidi while the other women stayed in a bunch? The Consul General was keeping silent. He shrugged and smiled noncommitally, pretending he, too, had no idea what to make of it.

They drove out of the city, into the surrounding mountains and arrived at an isolated, modern building complex that had been developed for the needs of the heads of the Moroccan government and their guests. For many years, royalty and dignitaries from the various Arab states convened in Morocco to discuss their different political strategies and to settle national differences. It was also a place known for its recreation, where good times could be had by all.

Vicki's living quarters were a large, modern house made of concrete and glass, set harmoniously into the landscape and highlighted by a lush, exotic garden, something unique in the middle of the desert. The house's interior was accented by rich woods and colorful Moroccan tiling. Persian carpets were strewn on much of the floor space, interspersed with potted palms and other foliage. Pillows made from colorful, Mediterranean fabrics were scattered about or covered the upholstered furniture. The mixtures of pattern, color, and texture gave Vicki a sensual uplift after all the wearisome hours of plane travel. Exhausted, but oddly satisfied, she stood gaping at her surroundings. She barely noticed Jaidi when he approached her.

"I'll return after nightfall," Jaidi was explaining. "You should be dressed. We're going to dinner."

With Jaidi gone, Vicki ventured a walk around the premises. Outside, she discovered armed guards were posted at every strategic location. Inside, a bevy of servants was eager to wait on her hand and foot. They were everywhere, nervously fumbling about like spasmodic chickens, seeking her approval by unpacking her bags, trying to undress her, drawing her bath, even applying the paste to her toothbrush. For Vicki, who normally enjoyed being catered to, this was overkill. She found it all pretty embarrassing.

It would be hours before Jaidi was scheduled to pick her up for dinner, so Vicki, resigned to the whims of fate, succumbed to the inviting comforts of the oversized, marble bath. She closed her eyes and luxuriated among the bubbles, allowing the two women servants to wash her hair and sponge her body. She felt like the maiden being prepared for the ritual sacrifice, a notion that at the moment she didn't consider as all that unlikely. She wasn't there for modeling, that's for damn sure. She wondered if she had courted danger once too often, and now, trapped in isolation, with nobody apprised of her whereabouts, she was about to disappear? She knew the stories about American and European women who had gone away on such assignments and supposedly had never come back. She knew the Arabs still sold women into slavery. But that seemed unreasonable, since she doubted they would treat her to so much luxury before putting her up on the auction block. Then what was she doing there? She pictured Alfred at his office, sitting in ignorance, frowning because she didn't answer her phone. He'd be angry, Vicki imagined, and possibly alarmed, but not frightened enough to begin searching the globe for Vicki Morgan. At least, not yet.

Dinner was served in the banquet hall, a large, vaulted chamber, mixing traditional with modern architecture. In keeping with the Arab custom, the long, rectangular tables were set near the walls as an exterior perimeter, so the center of the room was left as a vast, empty space. Rich linens covered the tables adorned with flowers, silverware, and china settings. Guests sat and chatted and drank at the tables, as dignitaries arriving from nearly every Arab country greeted each other with broad smiles and stylish embraces.

Vicki sat beside Jaidi and gazed at the awesome spectacle. There were Arabs dressed in traditional robes and *burnooses*, and Arabs attired in tailored business suits. Palace guards stood with swords and rifles. These were hardened soldiers who seemed immune to fun and games. There was music and belly dancers, gyrating squadrons of veiled Arab women snapping their fingers and popping their navels. Aromas mingled in the air, the steaming food blending with that of incense and the pungent smell of hashish. Huge quantities were being inhaled as it was passed around the crowded tables. Vicki had taken a couple of tokes. She smiled and tried to look dignified as Jaidi introduced her to a series of inquisitive men. They were charming, these men, and very polite, but not the kind who would be needing fashion models for anything other than personal reasons.

175

"You'd better tell me what this is about," Vicki demanded when she had a moment alone with Jaidi. "I hope this is not what I think it is, otherwise, there's gonna be a problem."

"Excuse yourself from the table," whispered the Consul General, "and meet me inside the ladies' room. We must talk."

"We sure must."

After giving Jaidi enough time to graciously disappear, Vicki stood and excused herself. She wandered down the long, glowing corridors, her heels clicking on the polished marble tiles. At last she came upon the ladies' room where she found Jaidi, nervously waiting inside.

"When you're finished with dinner, say you're tired and be prepared to leave."

"I am tired. I could leave right away, and it wouldn't bother me."

Jaidi, sensing her anger, attempted to assuage her fears. "Be patient. Everything will be alright."

"Why aren't I with the other girls?"

"Please. Be patient."

Jaidi was the first to return to the banquet hall, leaving Vicki behind to smoke a few cigarettes and ponder her fate. She was angry, tired of riddles and smiling men. The thought of being sold into slavery wasn't appealing at all, and by now she believed in the possibility. She pictured herself, the tall, lanky blonde, as an evening's entertainment for a dozen Arab gentlemen, held captive or murdered, depending on their whim. Vicki winced at the notion and finally returned to the banquet hall. She figured for the time being, at least, she was the safest with Mr. Jaidi.

Vicki had returned to her seat just a few moments, when she sensed a sudden change in the ambiance. People had stopped talking and were directing their attention to the main entrance where a segment of the palace guard stood in alignment on opposite sides of the doorway and presented their arms, a high, flashing archway of rifles and bayonets.

The hush in the room was overpowering, as with great ceremony the doors swung open and the palace guards snapped to attention, as a man, followed by his aides and bodyguards strode into the room. Everyone in the banquet hall stood as he entered. Everyone except for Vicki Morgan. She had been accommodating enough, thank you, and was drained of pomp and patience. She wasn't about to stand for anyone.

The Moroccan gentleman, diminutive and balding, wore a dark suit—more a uniform, really, than a suit—with epaulets and sashes made from gold brocade. His eyes focused straight ahead, and he walked directly toward a bemused and seated Vicki Morgan. Curiously she watched him, aware of the tension exuding from the other guests. Their eyes, filled with expectation, bore down on her as the gentleman stepped forward, bowed, and kissed her hand.

"You're a lovely lady," he offered. He had a soothing voice, a comforting presence. "How was your flight to Marrakesh?"

"Not bad."

Vicki knew this was no time for lodging complaints or asking foolish questions. Grandstanding before an audience was not her strongest suit. Better to wait and see what happened. If he could be charming, then so could she. Besides, she could smell power from a mile away, and this one wore it like cologne. It appealed to her. She wondered who he was.

The man nodded and glanced around the room, pausing to acknowledge certain dignitaries who were seated at the tables. Before long, he returned his attention to Vicki. His eyes bore into her as he gently bid her goodnight.

"You look tired," he suggested. "Why don't you try to get some rest?" With that, he turned and left the banquet hall, with his aides and bodyguards following him.

"Who was that?" Vicki inquired of Mr. Jaidi.

"A friend," he answered, not wanting to say anymore.

The following day Vicki awakened to a huge breakfast, composed of mounds of lamb, rice, dates, cakes, cheeses, coffee, and wine. To her dismay, it was hell to convince someone that all she wanted was some tea and some toast. While attempting to explain things, she entered the kitchen, which caused the servants to grow wide-eyed with fear. To them, it was not the custom for house guests to casually chat with the help. Something was wrong, they worried. Perhaps they had insulted her in some way, an act for which they could be severely punished.

"Toast," Vicki kept repeating. "Tea...toast."

Jaidi's chauffeur, who had arrived unannounced, popped into the kitchen and mediated on Vicki's behalf. In Arabic he explained her needs to the servants before turning and speaking to Vicki in broken English. At the sound of his rendition of her native tongue, the bells rang and the lights flashed inside Vicki's brain as she realized the chauffeur could be her only chance to communicate with the outside world. She was all smiles in seconds, lightly taking his hand as she led him toward the telephone.

"Mr. Jaidi forgot to show me how it works," she gestured, lying about her intentions. "I have to call my son, in America. I promised, and he'll worry if he doesn't hear from me soon."

The driver nodded and obligingly lifted the receiver, instructing the operator in Arabic to get the number Vicki had provided. "It's ready," he said and handed her the phone before departing for reasons of her privacy.

"Alfred, it's me," Vicki whispered as soon as he answered the phone. She was vastly relieved that he was still in his office this late in the day. "I'm in Morocco, supposedly on a modeling assignment, but I think it's something else. If something happens to me, then you'll know where to look."

Alfred as yet had heard nothing from his sources in the Customs Department that his girlfriend was trotting the globe once again. He became so alarmed by Vicki's disclosure he nearly leaped through the telephone line. "What?" he boomed in his old, familiar style. "Do you know what white slavery is? I'll call the embassy. I'm scared to death for you. They'll take you away and that's that. You're never heard of again. It goes on all the time. Believe me, I know."

Vicki was both amused and frightened by Alfred's concern for her safety. She knew he wasn't behaving this way for nothing, and yet despite the potential danger, she felt it was worth it, just to get under his skin. This time she had really gotten to him, had dug right into his nerves. She was feeling better already.

"Alfred I have to go now. Someone's coming."

Hurriedly, she slammed down the phone, leaving poor Alfred blustering in the middle of his diatribe. Well, he'd certainly have something to think about, she gloated, now that she had gotten through to the outside world. She could relax now, take it a little easier, and actually enjoy the Moroccan hospitality. She wondered what would happen next.

A half hour later Mr. Jaidi came storming into the guest house demanding to know the name of the man Vicki had called in Los Angeles.

"How do you know it was a man?" Vicki wondered, hoping to play for time.

"Who was he?" pressed Jaidi.

Vicki was delighted to see him unnerved. He was solemn and very formal, his mind working so hard she could almost hear the wheels turning.

"Who was he?" Vicki asked, recalling the incident the night before when she had asked Jaidi that very same question. Well, hell, two could play that game. "A friend," Vicki answered, echoing the Consul's response from the previous evening. "Just a friend."

The Consul General wasn't amused. "You told him where you were?"

"Yes, I did. Why? Do you have a problem with that?"

He did. Jaidi insisted she should not have called until she had asked his permission. Vicki responded by arguing he would have never allowed her to make the call. She reminded him that she didn't like to be treated this way, that she was an American citizen and not some anonymous entity who could be easily had and then disposed of. Wisely, the Consul General decided not to argue.

That night Vicki again was escorted to dinner by Mr. Jaidi. Only he wasn't as festive as he'd been the night before. He guarded her much more closely, and whenever possible he avoided introducing her to anyone. Something ailed Jaidi, filled him with a sullen disturbance. Vicki saw it in his movements, his listless speech, and the way he picked at his food. This wasn't the same crisp man, erect and authoritative, who had greeted her at the airport. This man had troubles. She may have ruffled his feathers, but apparently someone had trimmed his tail. Good! His discomfort was providing her with needed satisfaction. Alfred would teach them not to mess with her. Boy, was she glad she had made that call.

Early the following morning Vicki went for a brief shopping tour in downtown Marrakesh. The driver and an additional bodyguard were constantly at her side. She was grateful for their protection, for the eyes of the men she had passed in the streets revealed her fate if she was ever left alone. In their dark eyes and leathery faces she understood the value of tall blondes in that part of the world. Before their scrutiny she felt naked in a white linen dress cropped at the knee. Veiled women were staring at her hair. Children followed after her. "Fuck me," she muttered to herself. "What am I doing here?"

When she returned to the guesthouse she went back to sleep. She had been dozing for less than an hour when she was abruptly awakened by Mr. Jaidi.

"Come, please, Miss Morgan?"

Vicki sat up and rubbed her eyes. She hated to be

awakened, especially when it was always so hard for her to fall asleep in the first place. Once she was out, they could march armies around her and she might not even stir. But Jaidi was impatient, and more persistent than any army. He couldn't believe it was taking her so long to become coherent.

"What do you want?" she finally grunted.

He wanted her out of the country—right away—sooner if possible. Before she had a chance to respond, Jaidi had snapped his fingers and summoned the briefcase his driver carried. In a flash he had it open and began removing stacks of one-hundred-dollar bills, slamming them down on the bed without counting.

"Is that enough?" he asked.

"Yeah. Sure," she mumbled, staring at the money.

"Where do you want to go?" he asked. "Paris? London? Rome?"

"Los Angeles!"

"Los Angeles?" frowned the Consul General. "You should not go back there right away."

"Why not?"

Before he could answer, Vicki offered him a compromise. She gestured toward the briefcase and flashed her triumphant smile. "Throw a couple more stacks on the bed and I'll take a hotel suite at the Westwood Marquis. I'll tell only my son that I'm home."

Jaidi relented, and by early evening Vicki was ready to leave for the airport. Jaidi came by to see her off and take care of any possible foul up. He was gracious and smiling once more, now that things were resolved. He did his best to flatter her and assure her it was nothing personal that she must leave the country, just something that couldn't be helped. As dusk was turning into nightfall, he led Vicki from the house into the dry, night sky where the chauffeur waited by the limousine. His arms folded, his chin on his chest, he was leaning against the fender and staring at the ground while Vicki and the Consul General said their goodbyes.

"The driver will take you to Rabat, where you'll stay the night. I've already seen to the hotel accommodations. You'll leave on the first plane tomorrow morning."

Vicki shrugged and shook his hand, avoiding the temptation to ask why the need for her hasty departure. A look into the eyes of her diplomatic escort ruled out any probing. Yet she was slightly surprised when he suggested they would meet again, that he would call her once she was back in Los Angeles. With other men, under different conditions, she would've chalked it off as bullshit, a cheap way out of an awkward situation, but in this case there was no need for Jaidi to make such promises unless he meant to keep them. Well, thought Vicki, we'll just have to wait and see.

The miles clicked by as they passed through the desert on their way to Rabat, the chauffeur performing his task in silence while Vicki relaxed in the air-conditioned comfort, swigging straight from the bottle of Dom Perignon champagne she had taken with her for sustenance during the three-hour ride. Having polished off the entire magnum, Vicki stretched out on the back seat and soon was asleep. She awakened hours later, stared out the windows into the darkness and started to panic. Why hadn't they arrived in Rabat? They had left at eight P.M. for what was supposed to be a three-hour drive, and now it was four in the morning. Vicki lowered the glass partition and tapped her driver on the shoulder. "Where the hell are we?" she desperately wanted to know.

The chauffeur shrugged and mumbled something in Arabic and then something else in broken English. Vicki grew suspicious and very afraid. "My God," she muttered. "It's all over. Murdered and buried in the middle of nowhere."

BEAUTIFUL BAD GIRL

She was mistaken. The chauffeur had missed the turn-off and gotten lost. An honest mistake. Within a couple of hours she was in Rabat and safely ensconced in her hotel room. It was almost dawn and Vicki was hardly in the mood for sleeping. She thought about going for a stroll in the lobby, but when she opened the door and found a guard with a submachine gun posted outside, she reconsidered. Still dressed, she fell on the mattress and closed her eyes, her thoughts on the guard in the hallway. By this time she was so exhausted she didn't know whether to feel paranoid or simply well protected. Somehow, she drifted off to sleep.

Early that morning Jaidi arrived and escorted her to the airport. Naturally, being Vicki, she was late in getting started, and the Consul General telephoned from the limousine and delayed the plane's departure. Once on board, with the five grand she had received from Jaidi tucked in her carry-on luggage, Vicki sat back, ordered wine, and indulged in the hospitality offered for her comfort during the long flight home.

When she landed at New York's Kennedy Airport she was handed a telegram, a note of thanks from Mr. Jaidi. In the brief message he reiterated that he'd be in touch, that he would soon like to have her return to Morocco for a much more pleasant stay. In addition to the telegram, Vicki was presented with four cases of vintage French wine, compliments of a "friend."

Once she was settled in the Westwood Marquis Hotel, a familiar stomping ground for her and Alfred, she picked up the phone and called him. Alfred was thrilled to hear her voice once again, delighted she was back in Los Angeles. But before he could start making plans with her, Vicki dropped the bomb.

"They want me back in Morocco."

This was almost more than Alfred could handle. He was nearly apoplectic as he stammered wildly on the other end of the telephone line. He told her someone very high up was interested in her and once she returned they would do whatever they liked.

"They'll marry you," warned Alfred. "And then that's the end of it. There's no way out from there."

Vicki knew there was more to Alfred's anxieties than his concern for her safety. She knew him well enough to understand his fear of competition, that someone with equal or greater wealth than he would steal away his lover. And from what she had seen in the banquet hall, these Arabs were in possession of some very serious cash.

"Vic, tell me where you are," Alfred implored her. "I'll be right over."

"Alfred, I can't. I promised I wouldn't tell anyone."

And with that, Vicki hung up the phone. She knew he would be dying, cursing and pounding his desk in exasperation. She knew it, and she loved it. It was just too bad. If he didn't want to leave his wife and marry her, then fine, let him pay the price for the trouble she got herself into. She paid a price for their relationship. So could he. There was more to the game than money.

An hour later the telephone rang. It was Mr. Jaidi, who had just arrived in Los Angeles. He wanted to see Vicki right away. She didn't know what to make of it. It was as if he had been there all the time and had followed her back to the States. If, en route, she had changed her mind and gone somewhere else instead, she was certain he would have been there as well. Jaidi was moving swiftly and making no bones about it. Vicki was impressed with his relentless pursuit. She realized it wasn't for his own sake that he was going to so much trouble. Someone else was pushing him, probably the man who had approached her in the banquet hall. Screw Alfred's warnings. She had to find out who wanted her. Things were getting much too interesting to just let it go, to refuse to go back there...to just walk away. After busting Jaidi's balls for a couple of minutes, Vicki agreed she would see him. As a matter of fact, she would pick him up at the airport.

On the way back from Los Angeles International, Vicki began the bargaining process. She explained to Jaidi that a friend of hers would like to see him, a man who had been intimate with her father and had known her family for years. The Consul General at first refused her request. In hushed tones, he warned her that she shouldn't be discussing this with anyone.

"I'm sorry then. I can't go back to Morocco."

"Miss Morgan, please. You must...."

"If you want me back there, then you'll talk with my friend."

Thirty seconds into his phone conversation with Alfred Bloomingdale, the Consul General was getting nervous. He was wide-eyed, his face ashen and pale, as he listened to Alfred make it graphically clear what would have happened if any misfortune had befallen his mistress. Yards away from where Jaidi was standing with the telephone next to his ear, Vicki could hear the menace of Alfred's deep, guttural epithets. She sensed that he loved going to work on the Consul General, taking out the frustration he'd been stuck with for the last couple of days. What a sight for Vicki to behold—Alfred's true wrath and formidability. When the storm was over, a solemn Jaidi surrendered the telephone, explaining Alfred wanted to talk to Vicki. He bowed his head attentively as he listened to her conversing with Bloomingdale. She was certainly making out better than he. His shoulders drooped as he stared at the floor, his face contorted like a punished little boy.

Vicki found Alfred frantic and raving. "The king wants you," he was shouting. "The goddamned king!"

"You've got to come back with me," Jaidi was pleading in counterpoint to Alfred's warnings.

It was enough to make her crazy. Vicki started to laugh.

185

For Alfred's benefit, she was loud and deliberate as she started bargaining with Jaidi, demanding cash and proper accommodations, insisting that a few of her friends come along for the ride. The Consul General acceded to all of Vicki's demands. He made it easy for her, never tried to argue. Alfred, meanwhile, was cursing at the other end of the line.

"Look Alfred," Vicki hollered back at him. "Since you never left your wife, and you can't marry me, then I'll do what I damn well please. But, if something should happen to me," she added in a lower voice, her eyes trained on Jaidi, "then you know how to take care of it. I trust that you will."

The following day, Vicki and three friends left for Paris, where an entire floor of the lavish Ritz-Carlton Hotel was reserved for their stay. The other women were assigned to rooms, while Vicki had a suite to herself, with bodyguards at the doors. This, among other things, would later provoke hidden jealousies among her friends, women who believed that Vicki had it far too easy in life. Just leave it to her to get the best of everything. She made them feel like second stringers. She made them feel like fools.

When Jaidi arrived that afternoon, he appeared much more relaxed now that he was in Paris and not L.A. Here he was known and easily accommodated. He also didn't have Alfred breathing down his neck.

"Look your best, tonight," he encouraged Vicki. "We're going to a friend's house for dinner."

The friend's "house" was actually a country château more than an hour's drive from Paris. It was a huge, sprawling estate, dwarfing anything Vicki had ever seen before. A palace, most definitely, a remnant of the halcyon days of the French monarchy. Stone chimneys protruded from the heavy slate roof and large metal gates blocked the entrance to the driveway. Armed guards in military dress approached and peered suspiciously into the limousine, but relaxed as soon as they spotted Jaidi. The driver moved on across a bridge, passing more guards as the limo arrived at the palace doors.

The stunning interior was a paean to wealth and power, an ambience elusive to the bonds of time. European and Middle Eastern traditions and histories were intertwined, accented by the cultural mix of the priceless decor, adding luster to the dynamics of modern living. People were gathered, mostly men, from all over the world. On marble floors and classical artisan tiling, dignitaries stood with drinks in their hands, discussing business and politics. On the ceilings above them, religion and history were depicted in Renaissance frescoes. Gilded woodwork outlined the arches and vaultings, and paintings from the great western masters hung on the walls. There were tapestries, golden *objets d'art*, and various displays of precious stones. On one table sat an immense crystal frog, inlaid with rubies, diamonds, and sapphires. Beyond it the staircase ascended to the mezzanine, boasting a serpentine lucite bannister encrusted with virtually hundreds of precious gems. It was rich and spellbinding, an experience to take the breath away. Vicki stared in awe, afraid to risk a glance at her girlfriends, for fear they would blow her act.

Suddenly there was someone calling her name. It was the charming man from Marrakesh, immaculately dressed, looking optimistic as he took her hand and kissed it.

"Miss Morgan, it's so lovely to see you again," he offered, before listening to Mr. Jaidi introduce Vicki's friends. He listened patiently, but it was clear his attention was focused on Vicki. She allowed his eyes to lock in with hers, so without speaking they could express what was on their minds. Vicki could sense his desires, feel his anticipation. She smiled, allowing him to take her arm and lead her into the ballroom as her friends watched and tried to hide their growing discomfort.

"I'd be honored if you'd dance with me," he had said, and

now they danced slowly, waltz-like, apart from each other, their hands clasped high in the air. The entire dance floor had been vacated. They had it all to themselves. And as they spun and dipped and glided about, Vicki took note of the golden crown the man wore in the buttonhole of his suit.

"Alfred wasn't lying," she mused. "This is really the fucking king."

"I am Hassan, King of Morocco," he smiled, as if he were reading her thoughts, "and I find you to be a beautiful and charming woman."

Vicki wasn't sure how to answer him. The best she could do was smile.

When it was announced that dinner was ready, the King escorted Vicki into the dining hall, where he insisted on serving her meal. From golden platters piled high with assorted, exotic foods, the King selected portions and to her amazement laid them on Vicki's plate. He was standing while serving, and when the King stood, except for Vicki, so did everyone else. Hundreds of people were on their feet observing in silence, their eyes bearing down in wonder, studying the young lady from a small California town.

The night wore on and the crowd thinned, but the King remained at Vicki's side. They were a regular item for all to see, but not to speak of. No one dared betray his thoughts or reveal his curiosities. Party guests, formal and reverent, smiled in his presence, complimented his hospitality and thanked the King for a wonderful time as they bid their farewells and departed, without so much as sneaking a peek at Vicki. Surely, the lesson didn't go to waste on her. Authority was always attractive to Vicki, if not to obey its ruling order, then to get away with breaking its laws. But this was truly intoxicating. He was the epitome of supreme confidence, the rarity of absolute rule in such an abstract and chaotic period of time. And she was part of it, a set piece in a moment of history, having stood within the ring of power as the world went marching by.

In the quiet moments, the King spoke to Vicki about his family, the wife he loved, his children. He talked of life, of love, his view on American politics. He spoke of his cultural, political and emotional ties to France, which, for nearly forty years, had included Morocco as part of its colonial empire. Now it wasn't the French who were settling in North Africa, but the colonials who were settling in France.

The King was impressed with the taste of Vicki's brand of cigarettes, and in Vicki's presence he instructed Jaidi to order him a dozen cases. Vicki was pleased she could contribute her share in furthering international relationships. The King, in reciprocation, let her in on one of his most guarded secrets. To keep from drinking too much, he would always put ice in his glass of champagne.

"I was wondering," laughed Vicki. "I didn't think it was to keep it from getting warm."

They made love that night in a canopied bed, in a chamber that was nearly half the size of a Broadway stage. Rich Siberian incense and the artful, Moorish décor were a lush and seductive mixture. Vicki had been stirred by the mood of the evening and was aroused and inspired, pleased by the skills of the King. As they made love, she felt herself drifting through abstract sensations, as if she were embodied in different incarnations, changing suddenly, erupting through space and time. The alluring sense of the mystic, the timelessness of erotica, enshrouded her naked skin. She had been in different beds with different people, but never before had it been like this. Opulence, elegance, and sensuality were the pillars of an exotic culture, a legendary mystery that the aesthetics of history had refused to destroy.

During that year they saw each other several more times before fate and circumstance took Vicki once more in another direction. Until then, she was always delighted to receive his phone calls, his assurances that he would always be of service. In contrast to Alfred's foreboding, Hassan II, King of Morocco, was always the perfect gentleman. He, like the others, would give her money and buy her jewelry. At one point he gave her Fatima, a live-in maid.

Nearly two years later, Fatima would split with money, jewelry, and everything else she could carry. She claimed to have stolen these things because Vicki owed her back pay. Vicki claimed it was a lie and that the woman was a pain in the ass and a bad influence, having wedged herself between Vicki and Todd.

I once asked Vicki if Fatima was a spy. She merely shrugged and slid away from the question, brushing it past with a wave of her hand.

"How the hell do I know?" she said a bit too brusquely, hoping to convince me that she was annoyed.

"I thought maybe you did," I retorted. "I mean, why does he decide to give you a maid in the first place?"

Vicki didn't offer any answers, and I had run out of questions, so the matter dropped between us, making a thud like a lead balloon. But for years after her death, I would think about Fatima, along with the other things, the bits and pieces I had gathered like so many crumbs along the way. I would think and I would wonder. Just what was Vicki up to? Just what the hell was going on?

"The King had once offered his assistance in time of need," I reminded her one evening. "How come you never asked him for help?"

She told me she had considered calling him in Morocco, but it wasn't too long before she had ruled it out. Shrugging, her arms outstretched, her palms turned up toward the sky, she explained to me in that bittersweet voice of hers, "I figured it's best to leave it alone already. It had its place and time."

# 17

FATIMA, THE MAID, wasn't all that concerned me. As time wore on, the novelty of our romance faded and the reality of the long haul began to take its toll on Vicki. There were increasing periods when she was reluctant to talk about the past. Book or no book, it hurt her too much; she was too embarrassed to delve into subject matter that either had long been forgotten or never viewed in a critical light. Subjects, moments in time that used to appear like isolated incidents, now added up, combining and interweaving to form a disconsolate tapestry that alarmed and discouraged her. She'd be distracted for days by past misfortunes. During my absence, when she was alone, she'd lie in bed for hours dwelling on problems, real or imagined, that left her cynical, distant, and occasionally paranoic. She believed her friends were deserting her. They had little respect for her intelligence, her instincts, or any cerebral pursuits. She believed she was a threat to them, now that she was thinking seriously rather than flitting through life spontaneously. She believed, also, that I would eventually abandon her.

"When I was stupid, people thought I was terrific," she initiated one evening. "The minute I start thinking and, more importantly, start relating what I feel...then nobody wants to talk to me. When I spend time with my girlfriends, they go on about clothes and condominiums, like that's what I'm concerned about right now. I'm not, but no one wants to accept it. I can't find anyone who'll deal with me out in the open, except for you, and you could get tired of this and leave at any time."

"What makes you say that?"

"Because you know I'll make you miserable just to prove my point."

"What point? That you can screw up any relationship? I know that already. You don't have to go out of your way to prove it."

"Suppose I start going out?" challenged Vicki. "What would you say about that? Would you be jealous if I started seeing other men?"

"Yeah, I'd be jealous. I'd feel bad. I wouldn't like it. I'd feel a definite sense of loss. I happen to be into this up to here. Anything else you want to know?"

Vicki was smiling now, preparing to launch her frontal assault, backed by a now familiar diatribe regarding her need for independence and her demands for emotional equity. "But you have Marcia."

"That's right. I have Marcia. And Marcia has me. But only part of the time, since the rest of the time I've been staying with you."

"That's not fair. How could you be jealous if I dated other men?"

"If you want a logical answer, then forget it. Things like this are never logical. I'm possessive and jealous. Like most men, when it comes to this, I'm a regular goddamn fool. But at least I admit what I am rather than pretend I'm this great libertarian. If I love someone, I feel this way. If I don't, then fuck it, they can do whatever they want."

"Alfred used to tell me he loved me. He claimed I was his reason for living."

"I think he got carried away."

"He left me stranded is what he did. That sonofabitch! What makes you any different? Why should I listen to you?"

"You shouldn't. Alright? Feel better? You know how I

love it when you try to press my buttons. You want to go out, then go out. Have yourself a ball. Just remember what I've told you."

"About what?"

"About getting involved with the wrong kind of people and leaving me exposed to trouble. I don't need to get blind-sided because you thought it was smart to try pulling off a move like blackmailing someone. Because if you ever do something like that, without giving me the option to split or stick around, then there's gonna be hell to pay. Believe me."

Vicki demurred and tried to lighten up the mood. She was disturbed by my attitude, aware that I meant every word. There were things I wouldn't tolerate; there were schemes I feared that Vicki, in desperation, might be persuaded or driven to consider. I had enough to be concerned with. I didn't need any more trouble.

"I have no intention of going out," she promised. "I was only testing you, to see how much you cared. Because if it didn't matter to you whether I see other men or not, then we'd really have trouble."

Vicki was drinking heavily at this point. The years of desperate living were catching up with her. A magnum of dry white wine or a fifth of vodka was being consumed on a daily basis. Her monthly prescription for Valium, assuring her twenty milligrams a day, no longer satisfied her cravings and she doubled her intake, leaving her short toward the end of the month. The effects of her dependency were startling to me. Days before she was due to run out of pills, Vicki would become despondent, irritable, and inaccessible. At this point, obtaining more Valium became her top priority, and she would call friends, asking them for extras, conniving, promising to return what she had borrowed. She was so desperate that she contacted Marvin Pancoast, a friend of hers who, months earlier, I had inadvertently scared away. She began seeing him again on an increasingly frequent basis. Marvin, who would later be convicted of murdering Vicki Morgan, was under the care of various doctors, and capable of obtaining a Valium prescription to supplement Vicki's.

One night, following a particularly depressing afternoon, Vicki challenged the demons by swallowing as many as fourteen Valium. She took two at a time, pausing to gauge the sensation, the effect it had on her mood. She washed it all down with a handy bottle of Smirnoff vodka. She had done something like this once before, and had called her girl friends who, *en masse*, had come to the rescue, discovering a half-written suicide note and a missing quantity of pills. This time she decided to call only me. She phoned at four in the morning, very soulful, very calm, to see what effect her slurring speech would have on me.

I sped down the freeway and reached her house in a couple of minutes. I found her upstairs, lying in bed in a white satin robe, neither awake nor asleep, appearing serene and comfortable. "Shit," I thought to myself, "she's liable to die on me."

It took some doing to rouse her so she could stand and I could walk her over to the medicine chest where the Ipecac, a vile-tasting liquid used to induce vomiting, was waiting to be pressed into action. Vicki, sultry and congenial, was feeling much too romantic to be concerned with such banalities as saving her life. She put her arms around my neck and started to kiss me. "Please don't make me drink that stuff," she pleaded in a coy and silvery slur. "I can't handle throwing up right now."

I glanced down the hall to the door leading to Todd's bedroom and hoped he was sleeping soundly. There was no need for him to witness this. Lightly I closed Vicki's door while, with pressure from my hips, I kept her standing, braced against the wall between bedroom and bathroom. I removed the Ipecac from the medicine cabinet, opened the bottle and made her drink a couple of swigs. I never thought to read the label for directions. No sir, instead of diluting it with water she got it full strength; it was a message, if there ever was one, not to pull this again. In seconds she was on her knees with the dry heaves. Try as she might, nothing came up. "I can't," she groaned, her agony echoing in the toilet bowl.

"You'd better," I exhorted from my seat on the lucite bench. "You can't be dying on me."

"Fuck it," she laughed, despite fourteen ten-milligram Valiums, stomach convulsions, and nearly a fifth of vodka. Now she had me laughing. Suddenly it all was funny. I knew she was gonna be all right.

"It's a dumb thing I did," she apologized, several days later. "I promise not to do that again."

Instead, whenever Vicki got depressed and was fed up with lying in bed and pouting, she'd run across the street to commiserate with Mary Sangre. Sometimes Mary was a comfort and sometimes she and Vicki argued. Of course, I'd hear more about the bad times than the good. And after the few occasions when Vicki had stayed at Mary's for a couple of days, I'd hear nothing at all. I knew better than to try to find out what was happening. Ultimately, it was none of my business what Vicki did with Mary Sangre.

But what Vicki did with her other friends often became a matter of discussion. She was hurt when they treated her differently and paid less attention to her stories and her suffering. In some ways I couldn't blame them. Her theatrics at times could overwhelm them, her litanies about her and Alfred could bore them unmercifully. I saw it in their faces, their sighs and the nodding of their heads. Vicki's going on about Alfred Bloomingdale was not so much the disturbing issue, since for years they had listened to that. The disturbing thing was that the Vicki Morgan Show lacked the glitz and the drama of the salad days. It was one thing to put up with her when there was something for them to grab onto, and quite another when it was she who was taking from them.

Janis, a friend Vicki had met at Bernie Cornfeld's, claimed that Hartley, her fiancé, a jeweler from Seattle, considered Vicki a bad influence, and didn't like it when Janis spent too much time in her company. This I thought was rare. Despite the many years Janis had hung out at Vicki's house, had lived with her and, at times, lived on her generosity, Janis was reluctant to stay overnight for fear of losing her boyfriend. When Vicki's son Todd temporarily ran away from home, Janis, rather than deal with it, disappeared, leaving Vicki frightened and worried. I had been upstairs with Vicki attempting to determine where Todd had gone. It was the first time the kid had done this and, rather than accept it as rebellious adolescence, she blamed herself for his surreptitious departure.

"He hates me," she lamented, "for having lied to him about Alfred. Christ, I'm barely sixteen years older than him. It's not that I don't know what it's like to be a kid." With that, she started laughing as the tears welled up in her eyes. "Hell, I've been one all my life."

"I'll get us some coffee," I offered, "and we'll stay up until we figure this out."

I went downstairs to put on coffee and discovered Janis had departed in the middle of the night without so much as a word. I stared at the empty sofa, the rumpled sheets and the pillow that had fallen on the floor, wondering how she could pick a time like this—with the kid missing and Vicki in tears—to make her point. Ascending the staircase, I was morose and disgusted, fearing the worst of reactions when I told Vicki the news. She surprised me by taking it in stride, claiming it was just another time, another place where something like this had happened.

"I guess that's what happens," she sighed, "when you try to buy your friends."

Another friend, under the pretext of intimacy, invited Vicki to dinner in Malibu. Before dessert was served, she introduced Vicki to an intermediary who offered to fix her up with some wealthy and curious foreigner who was eager to meet the notorious Vicki Morgan. In the midst of his sales pitch, the intermediary let it slip that he and her friend, who were receiving a broker's fee, were also expecting a percentage of the take from Vicki. She fled the house and returned to her bedroom, refusing to answer the phone. Worried, having not been able to reach her, I went to her house and was relieved when she answered the door. I followed her inside and watched quietly as she puttered about the kitchen. Her face was taut, her movements quick and self-conscious. There was a faraway look in her eyes.

"What's the matter?" I asked finally when it was clear nothing would be volunteered.

"I don't want to talk about it," she replied, pausing from her duties at the sink to glower in my direction.

"It's the dinner party, isn't it? Something happened?"

Tears moistened her cheeks as she fought in vain to keep from crying. She sat down beside me, her head bowed, her clasped hands supporting her chin and her elbows digging into her thighs. I could see how disturbed she was, how badly she was hurting. I waited patiently for Vicki to gather her thoughts. Before long, she told me the entire story.

"I never knew how much she hated me until tonight. I felt so low, so dirty. The two of them—she set me up and he made the pitch—were like real estate agents handling property. They were pimping, selling me off, and he has the gall yet to mention a percentage. All those years I was friends with her and this is the way I'm treated. I should've known, I guess. But I didn't. God, where was I all that time? What was I thinking of? What was I doing?"

I was seeing signs of a breakdown and I didn't know what to do. It disturbed me to see her drinking so heavily and lamenting her financial decline. Conversation and uplifting pep talks would only go so far before she gave in to her morbid temptations. She needed to see results—something divine—to lift her from the throes of poverty and land her, once again, on Rodeo Drive, or more important, transport her to the redwood mountains of Big Sur along the California coastline, where she entertained dreams of residing in seclusion and luxury. Unfortunately, there was nothing immediately forthcoming that held that promise. Selling the book appeared to be a long way off, thanks to various pressures and silly distractions, while the story itself, as it unravelled, became more confusing with each passing day. Her tale was a mysterious puzzle, composed of refracted perspectives. Insights were varied and contradictory, with injections of new information being subjected to Vicki's changing attitudes. There were times when Vicki proposed we shelve the whole thing and take off for Europe, or write one very serious sample chapter and, if we sold the book, do the rest of it as a burlesque. This, she found hysterical.

To get her away from the monotony of her daily routine, I took her to Las Vegas. It's a place neither one of us had frequented over the years, although Vicki had three times been married there. But this was to be a business trip. It was a chance to make some money by playing a system for betting at craps that a friend of mine had inherited from a guy who had developed it out of sheer desperation in order to pay his creditors. He had parted from his wife and wandered off alone into the outlying Vegas desert. After living like a monk and testing his grueling system day after day at the different casinos, the inventor committed suicide. And, after playing his brilliant system for only a few days, I began to see why. The system was exhausting, but it did work.

By the end of the weekend, Vicki and I had made enough to pay for the trip. She had worked hard at it, standing there from the early evening until the break of dawn, leaving the tables for drinks and meals and an occasional walk down the Vegas Strip. We strolled among the crowds of geeks and hookers, loving couples and badly dressed tourists. And as we stared into the molten flow of the colorful neon scripture fronting every hotel, we felt removed yet oddly in touch with America's mainstream as depicted on the Vegas Strip. It was intense, but reassuring, as if alienation had provided us with the insight and sensitivity to better understand the hopes and motivations of those who live the types of lives we had escaped from while back in our teens. Perhaps, as outcasts, we had learned to scorn the insipid hypocrisies and love all the more the values of sentiment and tradition. Ostensibly, Vicki's philosophy may have differed from mine, but ultimately, the results of our quest were still the same. We had wanted to be different and we had gotten what we wanted. Long ago we had reached the point where, simply, there was no return.

"If we could only blend into all this," I offered, "just like two little bulbs in a big neon sign. Then we wouldn't feel it so much...."

"You mean we were fucked before the race got under-way," she laughed. "It's gonna be a long time before we sell that book," she said, turning very serious. "I know. I can feel it. I hope we're not wasting our time."

"If we are, at least we're having some fun while we're at it."

Vicki nodded. "For now. Maybe. But that won't last forever. I need money, and I have to get it soon. I'm destitute. I can't afford my rent. I'm not used to living like this. Sometimes, when you're not around, I just lie in bed and cry. I try to hold up against it, but I can't. Not all the time. It just gets to me."

"So what do you want to do?" I asked, believing I knew where she was leading.

"I think about getting married," she stated matter-of-factly, as if she was discussing the prospects of buying a car.

"Find a rich cornball and get him to marry me. Like I've told you, within five weeks from the time I meet him, I could get a man to propose to me."

"Is that five working weeks, or does that count the week-ends as well?"

"I'm serious."

"I know you are. That's what worries me."

"Why? You're not gonna marry me."

"Even if I did, that wouldn't solve your money problems."

"Then I wouldn't care. At least not so much." She put her arms around my neck and kissed me passionately, as the Saturday-night crowd of tourists did their best to walk around us and leave us undisturbed. "You're a good kid," she said as we parted. "And I love you. I may hate your guts for it, but I love you just the same. We're in trouble, you know. You do understand that?"

"What kind of trouble?" I asked, perhaps too casually. "What are you trying to say to me?"

Vicki shook off the questions and took my arm instead. Her body pressed tightly against mine as she led me in the direction of the MGM Grand Hotel. "It's time we stopped taking this trip so seriously," she said. "Let's play around for awhile."

# 18

I HAD LEARNED a lot about Vicki during that trip to Las Vegas. I had noted the ease with which she had acclimated herself to any given condition. She was not a gambler per se, yet she was able to stand calmly at the tables and place bets with the discipline required for winning with the system. Winning and losing were taken in stride. When given a chance, she'd work hard for her money. She had enjoyed the time we spent together. She had enjoyed it too much, for when we returned to Los Angeles she became distant and aloof for a couple of days. When I asked her why she was acting like that, she answered it was her way of dealing with the uncertainty of our love affair, that circumstances prevented us from getting away as often as she would like. She hated the fact that I was married and caustically lamented that, just like Alfred, she would always be the mistress waiting for my call.

I didn't know what to say to her. Or, if I did know what to say, I didn't want to say it. I wasn't sure if I lacked the nerve or just the desire. I only knew that I wanted her, but apparently not badly enough to call it a day with Marcia. And I knew that I had an infant son who stood in his play pen and made growling animal noises—comic sounds of aggression I had taught him when we roughhoused—as he struggled to get my attention whenever I passed him by. I knew that he needed me, more than anyone else ever would, and that I couldn't do what so many others had done with their children, abandon him to statistics, with half-hearted rationale.

Vicki, having sensed my resolution, was caught in her own dilemma. She wanted me, but not on a part-time basis. Increasingly, she was becoming hostile, starting arguments over nothing, causing tempers to flare which resulted in angry midnight departures, followed by a series of telephone calls and a round of elaborate discussions rivaling negotiations at the SALT talks.

"I've had it," she said one night in early May, about the same time the Comet IRAS-Araki-Alcock was passing closer to the earth than any other comet for more than two hundred years. I had spent hours on Mulholland Drive, at the crest of the Hollywood Hills, peering through my binoculars at this vast and cloudy block of ice and its long, fiery tail. I was awed, excited and also alone, since Vicki didn't feel like coming along to witness this particular spectacle. I returned from the hills, prepared to relate what I saw, only to find her angry and prepared for a confrontation.

"It's all caught up with us," she went on to say. "I'm more concerned with this than I am with the book or anything else. I lie in bed and think about you. I wonder if you're coming tonight, or if you'll be early or two hours late. I wonder if we'll sleep together, and if we do, whether you'll leave in the middle of the night or wait around until morning. And when you stay for a day or two at a time, it only makes it worse for me. I start to relax and get used to it, then it's snatched away. We can't see each other anymore."

"You're sure, this time?" I asked, knowing she wasn't but also believing that she meant what she said. Usually, she never responded to the question, but would sit there, gazing petulantly off into space; I would wait around until her mood shifted, and before the night was over, there was usually a change of heart.

But this time she was particularly adamant, insisting not only did she not want to see me, but that our working together also must end so that she could restore order to her life, achieve independence and come to grips, once again, with reality. She made me laugh, which pissed her off.

"You don't believe me, do you?" she challenged.

"Oh, I believe you're being sincere, only it strikes me funny when you go on about this great life you had before I came stumbling along. Makes me feel kinda bad to think you were so organized and at peace with the world until I ruined it all. Maybe I did. I made you think...about your past and about your future. Maybe I should've kept quiet and left you alone, instead of involving myself and stirring it up. Maybe the ignorance was bliss and it worked to your advantage. Well, that's typical for me, starting out with good intentions and being damned as I get carried away."

She lowered her eyes and with shaking hands reached for a cigarette. "I didn't mean it that way," she muttered.

"Yes you did. It makes it easier to talk yourself into a change. Believe me, I can understand it. There's no money here, only hard work and romantic uncertainty. Why struggle with this when there's some rich cornball out there just waiting to be had? I've thought it over a lot. It's probably the only way you can survive."

"Then why didn't you mention it?" she asked.

"Because...I'd rather keep hoping against it."

Vicki was surprised to hear me go on like this. She was used to my arguments, my arrogance, but certainly not my resignation. She looked up from the floor, her eyes on fire as they bored into mine. She maintained her stare, fascinated, I believe, by the fact that I wasn't kidding. She was growing worried now, as her anger abated.

"You mean you'll just walk right out of my life, leave the book and everything else behind?"

"Yeah. I sure will."

"Gordon, you don't understand....I need to do it on my own," she explained. "I can't have you helping me."

"Fine," I said. "You got it." In seconds I was on my feet

and moving around the house, gathering up the various things I had kept there, including the shotgun and a couple changes of clothes, and set them in a pile by the staircase.

Vicki watched as the pile grew. She was wide-eyed and silent. I barely glanced in her direction, fearing eye contact would give away my hurt and disappointment.

Fuck it. It was better like this. I was tired and had nothing left to say.

"Do you have to take all of it with you?" she whispered, frowning and looking away. She was rubbing her hands together, hoping to dry off the copious perspiration.

Jesus Christ, I thought. Here she was, telling me one thing and fearing another. The girl couldn't stand it when anyone walked out on her, even if she had asked them to leave. I was exasperated beyond words, a rare instance for me, and sat down to collect my thoughts.

"Vicki, what the hell do you want from me?" I managed after seconds ticked off the clock.

"I don't know," she answered.

I was back on my feet again. "When you do, then give me a call."

"Gordon...please don't leave."

I sighed and cursed and ultimately ended up sitting out on the patio watching the comet flash by with my pal, Vicki Morgan. She was relieved and excited as she peered through the binoculars. She couldn't get close enough to me. She was the model of tender, loving care. What did I do that brought all this on? I wondered. Something that the others hadn't done, I guessed. I've often thought about her other relationships and the reasons she had given me for wanting to see them end. With the exception of Alfred, the best of them lasted slightly more than a year. First Earle, then Bernie and Michael and, when the King started footing the bill, John David Carson had also gone by the wayside.

The end of her marriage to John David Carson had come abruptly, but certainly not on an impulse. According to Vicki, what love there was had faded long before, but she had kept it together for Todd's sake since John David had been more of a father to him than anyone else.

"Does this mean I have to go back and live with my grandmother?" Todd asked after learning about Vicki's plans to divorce John David.

"No," she answered. "You'll always be with me."

Todd was not so easily reassured. Much harm had been caused by their years of separation. In her quest to insure his material security, Vicki had neglected his more substantive needs. By blinding herself to the overall picture, she abused the one person for whom she cared the most. She had tried to be strong and protective, but she had failed, creating instead suspicion and insecurity. He didn't trust her and she didn't blame him. She had cared too much and tried too hard, and she ended up ruining her own best intentions. With horror, as she studied the look in his eyes, she realized it was a terrible price to pay.

Soon after she had returned to Los Angeles in 1978, Vicki phoned her lawyer, Michael Dave, to arrange for her divorce from John David Carson. Dave claimed he was unable to handle it personally and referred her to his brother, Jamiel, who was also an attorney. That was fine with Vicki. However, before hanging up, she casually inquired about Robert Schulman, a real estate developer to whom Dave and his wife had introduced her.

Barely a day had passed before Schulman was on the telephone to Vicki Morgan. He asked her out and they started dating. She liked Bob Schulman and thought of him as a decent guy, a family man, the kind of man with whom she thought she could be comfortable. Of course Bob was not exactly "Mr. Excitement," and perhaps he was a little rough around the edges, but he was good-hearted and smart, with strength of character and a successful business.

Dating Bob, however, didn't preclude her seeing Alfred Bloomingdale. After nine tumultuous years, he was still the man in her life. And although the King was providing for her, there was no need to stop Alfred from kicking in as well. Once again the checks started coming. Once again they started looking for a house for Vicki. This time she wanted something in a more family-oriented community, a wholesome environment for Todd and herself. She found what she was looking for in the Beverly Glen Estates, a new housing project located near Bel Air at the crest of the Hollywood Hills. There were houses and condominiums, all with the identical Spanish terra-cotta roofing, set neatly in rows on interweaving hillside streets. Vicki selected a house for its privacy and its yard space, in consideration for the dogs she owned and the Dobermans she intended to buy.

Alfred gladly sprung for the lease. It may have been expensive, but the Beverly Glen Estates was not without its advantages. The houses were modern and required very little maintenance. It was easy to reach from Alfred's office. He was always concerning himself with Vicki's safety and here the security was excellent. More important, he wanted her satisfied, believing if she wasn't she'd soon run off and get married again. And that, at the moment, with his business difficulties and the political pressures of helping to organize and obtain financial contributions for Ronald Reagan's presidential election campaign, would be extremely hard on his nerves.

Bob Schulman had also been up to inspect the house in the Beverly Glen Estates. He liked it right away. In fact it was perfect for the two of them. He urged Vicki to rent it, so they could move in together. It sure beat the hell out of commuting each day from Westlake Village, a distant suburb, or trying to live in the apartment he had rented in Westwood. Bob was excited, committed. At forty-one, divorced, and with two children from a previous marriage, he was in no mood for playing games.

He wasn't aware Vicki had gotten herself in a jam. Not wanting to be stranded, she had played both ends against the middle and now she was caught in a squeeze. Bob was already hinting at marriage, and Alfred, who was afraid of losing her, was working hard to change his image. Not only was he as sweet as could be, vowing his love and eternal support and promising Vicki whatever she asked for, he was spending more than twenty grand for appliances and accessories for her rented house in Beverly Glen. As soon as he could afford it, he'd be laying out more for her furniture.

Vicki didn't know what to do. Night after night she'd lie awake and weigh the pros and cons of each relationship. She loved Alfred, but hated the life of a mistress. Long ago she had stopped kidding herself. He would never leave Betsy. He would never marry her.

Bob, on the other hand, would relieve her from the fear and the stress of being a single parent. He loved her and he offered stability and a final chance to break away from Alfred and the world she had entered when she was just seventeen years old. He asked her to marry him the evening before she and Alfred were scheduled to leave for New York. It was Alfred's plan to take Vicki to Europe for a couple of weeks, mixing business with pleasure. Vicki did not want to go but had tacitly agreed, having succumbed to Alfred's persistence. She hadn't yet told Bob about the trip, nor, for that matter, about her long and strange relationship with Alfred Bloomingdale. And since he had just proposed marriage to her, the situation was even more delicate than it had been just a minute before.

"Before I give you my answer," Vicki started, "there's something I'd better tell you. It's not all my ex-husband's money that I'm living on. Do you know more than that?"

Bob was smiling, much to Vicki's surprise. "You mean, about Alfred Bloomingdale."

"Yes," nodded Vicki. "That's exactly who I mean."

"I knew it when I first met you three years ago, at

Lorraine and Michael Dave's. I knew exactly what and who you were."

"And you still want to marry me?"

"Of course I do!"

That night Vicki took Bob home to her house. Previously she had always gone to Bob's for the evening, but now it was different. She had agreed to marry him, which made it okay for him to spend the night at her place. She also wanted him there in the morning, to bolster her conviction when Alfred Bloomingdale called. But when he did call, Vicki didn't answer. She sat there instead and stared at the telephone. It rang incessantly and then stopped just minutes before Alfred's flight was scheduled to depart. Six hours later, it started ringing all over again.

"Answer it," Bob instructed and, standing with his arms folded, he waited to see what Vicki would do. This was the tale of the tape, the proof of the pudding. If she could stand up to Alfred under these conditions, then there was a reason for Bob to be optimistic.

Vicki was trembling when she picked up the phone. She did her best to act calm, as if she was in control, for any sign of hesitation, any nervous chink in her armor, would be sensed immediately and then Alfred would never get off the phone.

"Where were you?" he demanded. He was angry and blustering in a raspy staccato. "I waited so long I nearly missed my plane. Do you know it's snowing so hard they've closed the airport. I'm not sure I'm able to get into town. And all this morning I tried to call you, but you didn't answer the phone."

"Alfred..." she tried but he ran right over it.

"I've had it with you! You're always late. You're never on time. I wish you'd grow up already."

"Alfred...I wasn't there because I'm getting married."

She could have died waiting for his reply. She could hear the hustle of the airport, the bleating static of the public address system and Alfred coughing, grunting and wondering how to respond.

"Vic, don't do this to me again," he pleaded. He was self-conscious, faltering, hollow. "Vic, I mean it. I'll die without you."

"Alfred, do you know what's happening to me? I'm starting to fall apart. If something doesn't change, if I can't just lead a normal life.... Alfred, I'm marrying Bob."

Alfred, in tears, insisted this time he would divorce Betsy and marry her. Betsy would get all the money, of course, but they would have each other.

"Alfred, it's too late...."

He insisted it wasn't.

"Why didn't you leave her three years ago? I have my son living with me now, and I won't send him away like I did in the beginning. Not for you, or for anyone else. It's bad enough with all the mistakes I've made and the things I have to live with. I have to break away."


This time Vicki planned to have a real wedding and not another impromptu excursion to the chapels of Las Vegas. For her wedding invitations she went to Francis Orr, the oldest and most exclusive stationery shop in Beverly Hills. She ordered her wedding gown, beige and beaded, from Holly's Harp on Sunset Strip for $3,500. Her wedding would take place in the Hotel Bel Air, and the flowers were ordered from David Jones, the exclusive florist who serviced Nancy Reagan, Betsy, and nearly all their friends.

While Vicki busied herself preparing for this grand matrimonial spectacle, Alfred Bloomingdale sat it out in his Mercedes sedan, which each afternoon he parked down the street from her house. He would wait for Todd to come by on his way home for school, so he could inquire about Vicki. It rattled Vicki to learn of Alfred's proximity, and she was further agitated when Alfred called, in spite of her changing to another unlisted number. He was terse and business-like, requesting to speak with Bob.

"How much is it?" Vicki heard Bob inquire just moments after he'd come to the phone. "Twenty thousand? Fine. I'll put a check in the mail tomorrow."

"What was that all about?" Vicki asked, after Bob had hung up from Alfred.

"He wanted me to reimburse him for the appliances."

Vicki was proud of Bob for handling Alfred the way he had. She was smiling, feeling comfortable. "You know it blew his mind when you said you'd mail him a check. Alfred's not used to hearing that from people."

"I don't care what he's used to," Bob responded. "He'd just better not start calling here."

Vicki thought it useless to try and explain it to Bob. The trend had started years before and the habits were simply much too hard to break. Vicki knew Alfred well enough to understand his ploys. He didn't care about the $20,000. He cared about her; he wanted Vicki back and he'd persist until he had his way.

As the weeks passed and the wedding neared, Vicki was becoming increasingly apprehensive. The old anxieties were beginning to plague her. She feared her marriage would fail. What sexual attraction Bob held for her was already beginning to wane. She found him boisterous and good natured whenever they went out together, but lacking in the social graces. She picked on him endlessly, and although she hated herself for doing so, she was never one for self-restraint. Even in the company of friends she was compelled to ridicule his eating habits, his conversation, and the way he dressed—a matter of circumstance, since Bob, unfortunately, was color blind.

What Vicki did learn to enjoy were the boxing matches Bob attended Thursday evenings at the Olympic Auditorium in downtown Los Angeles. Bob was an avid boxing enthusiast who owned shares in a number of fighters. Vicki, who had never seen a boxing match, considered the sport grotesque and cruel. But Schulman persisted and she finally agreed to accompany him, dressing for the occasion as she would to go shopping in Beverly Hills. She was in for a rude awakening when she entered this grungy relic from the 1932 Olympics. As soon as she was spotted, she was welcomed with a resounding barrage of catcalls and whistles, the traditional greeting for women. Thousands of men, mostly urban Mexicans, were on their feet, hooting and shouting. It was enough to make her turn around and leave.

But she held her ground, found her seat and, from ringside, cheered and shouted with the rest of the fans. She loved the pounding, the sweating, and the roar of the savage crowd. There was spirit here, genuine visceral color, a miasmic frenzy of gambling, drinking, and fighting, in the seats as well as the ring. There was nothing she had to live up to, nothing chic, nothing trendy. This was basic and inexpensive—spontaneous blood and violence. Unlike so many things in her life, boxing was unpredictable; she couldn't be sure of the outcome or, for that matter, considering the mood of the crowd when the fights were over, if she would make it safely back to the car.

Boxing might have aroused her passions, but it wasn't enough to sustain her desire for Bob. Vicki was haunted by the feeling she was settling, accepting a tepid relationship in exchange for companionship and financial stability. It made her feel old to think of it that way, like a widowed geriatric, but she couldn't deny her habitual motives. She knew desperation had been at the source of her many different relationships, and it frightened her that she hadn't learned from past experience and lacked any viable options. Essentially, she had not made any real progress. There was no advancement, no expansion, and enlightenment was oblique if at all discernible. She had learned much and applied it in trivial pursuits. She had scant motivation, few goals; from past experience, a lively romance seemed impossible to sustain. She was twenty-seven years old. It was time to get serious. She would call Alfred Bloomingdale and arrange for a meeting. She'd offer to make him a deal.

# 19

ALFRED WAS ONLY too happy to meet with Vicki. He had missed her, and he hated it when she avoided him. Face to face, up close and personal, was the best way to regain control, to undermine her confidence and win her back. She never could stand up to him when he lapsed into begging and pleading. His was a coarse but polished act, very effective in terms of capitalizing off her guilt and ambivalence. Alfred enjoyed the contest, was stimulated by the challenge of thwarting her escape attempts and forcing her to acknowledge she'd never find in another lover the things she found with him.

The day she met with Alfred, Vicki brought a friend with her, an older woman who was to bear witness to the events that transpired, to the deal that was made. Polite and businesslike, Vicki entered The Old World restaurant, the place where they first met, and sat down across the table from Alfred. Vicki's witness was sitting between them. She listened patiently as Alfred rambled on with his usual platitudes—how much he missed her, how stunning she was, how she broke his heart. By the time lunch had been ordered, Alfred had temporarily appeared to run out of steam.

"If you give me a million dollars I'll walk out on Bob and come back to you," she offered, which was one way of filling the lull in conversation.

"That's a lot of money," Alfred muttered. He was

surprised by her demand but hardly astonished. Over the years they had bargained incessantly. Only this time the figure was higher than what she had ever demanded. It was also money that he didn't have. Despite all his years of playing the shell game, of finagling money by exploiting his good name, Alfred was hard up for cash. A million bucks would leave him on the short side, or, if he borrowed it, put him deeper in debt. Worse yet, all hell would break loose if Betsy ever got wind of it. Alfred knew he had to rise to the occasion. He had to stall for time.

"I know it's a lotta money," Vicki countered. "But that's my price for leaving Bob. I'm getting older, Alfred, and I have to be sure I can cover myself or my son if something happened to me."

"Vic, what are you worried about? Haven't I always taken care of you? I promised I'd always provide for you and I've always made good on my word."

Vicki didn't want to hear all that. She wanted cash, she wanted action, and no more verbal guarantees. "For ten years, Alfred, I've been at your beck and call. If I've been worth it to you, then now's the time to show it."

Alfred put up a fuss for several rounds of haggling before he finally agreed. Quite theatrically, with convincing humility and the air of one vanquished, he capitulated to Vicki's demands. Only he did get her to agree that he could split it up, a half-million now and the rest in, say, six months or so. And of course, since he was already tight for money, she did understand that it would take some time before he'd be able to raise it.

Of course she understood it. For Vicki, this was mainly an agreement in principle, another test to see if he loved her enough to fork over one million in cash, despite her knowing she'd never receive it. To a dreamer like her, it wasn't the reality but the thought that counted, the very idea that he would agree to paying the ransom. It was enough to get her to call off the wedding, leaving poor Bob with a broken heart and a stack of bills. He could have argued all he wanted; it didn't matter now that Alfred had agreed to pay her the money. The romance was over. Vicki felt horrible for hurting Bob. And when he was packed and leaving, she cried out in alarm. She hated to see him go.

But Bob departed and Vicki went back to Alfred. The million didn't come quickly, but the allowance was increased, and what's more, Alfred did his best to keep her busy by fixing her up with escorts so she could be in attendance at the social and political functions to which he escorted Betsy. So, while Alfred sat with his wife, Vicki made small talk, tables away and out of touch. The reality of what she had again gotten herself into was overwhelming, leaving her bitter and masochistic. She had affairs with several escorts. She relied more heavily on drugs. From all the self-abuse, she fell ill and had to be rushed to the UCLA hospital for what, among other things, was a burst appendix. While the doctors worked to drain the poisons from her system, her right lung collapsed. She remained for days in critical condition. It would be weeks before she could leave the hospital, weakened and drained from the experience. As a reminder of the operation, there was a five-inch scar running vertically from her pelvis to her navel.

To cheer her up and keep her busy, Alfred suggested they have a party. This, next to marrying him, was her sincerest desire. They would invite people so all could see they were not ashamed of being together, of functioning out in the open. Hollywood mavens, corporate and political movers and shakers all would come at Alfred's behest, mixing and mingling with Vicki's assortment of friends. Before it was over, she would spend $15,000 on the party, a homage to the grand illusion that everything in the end would be just fine. It sounded right, it felt good, until the one hundred and fifty invited guests began arriving. Then she panicked. After greeting them and welcoming them to her home, Vicki sequestered herself in the bedroom where she spent the night talking with Penny, her Oriental housekeeper, and Fatima, the Moroccan maid. So much for any more parties.

Bob Schulman, meanwhile, was angry and disconcerted. It was his turn to complain about the downside of laying out $20,000 for Vicki's appliances. He called Alfred Bloomingdale and demanded his money back. Alfred loved it. For some reason, it was different now that Bob was calling him. It was another opportunity to be magnanimous, to buy out a husband or lover, to make him feel small. It was one more suitor he was "getting out of the picture" with just the stroke of his pen. This, he claimed, was proof not only of his commitment to Vicki, but of his love for her as well.

Alfred might have gotten Bob out of the picture, but the picture itself was still the same. Vicki, having been relegated once again to solitude, or rather to the vicissitudes of escorting Alfred's friends and associates, could feel herself nearing the edge. She was crazy as hell, but no one cared or dared to perceive it. Vicki worked hard to keep up appearances. Only she was cognizant of her irretrievable split into multiple personalities. Each one she had created to fulfill a different task.

So it was in this state of mind that she proposed to Robert Schulman. Bob, who had once been jilted, was back on the scene, after being summoned one night by telephone. Vicki was panicked and very confused. She claimed she had made a mistake by going back to Alfred. Bob, she said, was a pillar of sanity, someone who could keep her together. She wanted to date him again, on a gradual basis. She talked him into leasing the sample condominium just down the street from her house. They became neighbors in the Beverly Glen Estates.

One night, on the way home from disco lessons, having taken Quaaludes to tough-out the session, Vicki popped the question to a startled and dubious Bob. He asked if she was doing it out of boredom or because she was lonely.

"No," was Vicki's earnest reply. "I made a mistake by not going through with our wedding. I just hope it's not too late for us."

It wasn't. Later that evening they were in Las Vegas, standing inside an all-night chapel listening to the justice pronounce them husband and wife. Vicki couldn't remember being there, or even what was said. All was not lost, however. A prudent Bob had bought a recording of the ceremony.

The day after the wedding, Bob returned to work and Vicki returned to her self-imposed isolation. She had time to contemplate what she had done and how she would break it to Alfred. Her son, when informed by a telephone call from Las Vegas, was vocal about his displeasure. He reminded his mother how he had predicted this would happen, and that she had denied it.

Fatima, the maid, didn't like it either. Bob, like Earle, Bernie, Michael, and Alfred before he converted, were all Jewish. To Fatima, this was a sickness, part of an aberrant syndrome. "You should devote yourself to your son," advised Fatima. "Forget about this marriage and stay with Alfred Bloomingdale. At least until your son becomes of age."

With all this invective undermining her resolution and starting the marriage off on just the wrong footing, Vicki still had Alfred to call. She did not look forward to dialing his number, especially after she had learned from Fatima that Alfred had been calling since early that morning and was demanding to know where she was.

"Alfred. . . it's me," she began, before he started cursing and threatening to cut her out of his life for being AWOL the previous evening. "I married Bob," she whispered when the furor died down. "Last night in Las Vegas."

Alfred should have been used to it by now. But he wasn't. News of her engagements and weddings always took the wind out of his sails. For the longest time he said nothing, waiting in the silence of his misery, hoping she'd laugh and say, "Sorry, just kidding." She wasn't kidding. He knew Vicki would never joke about something like that, not something as serious as marriage.

"I thought you agreed not to marry Bob," was the first thing Alfred could think to say.

"Where's my million dollars?"

"I told you it would take time," he protested.

"I'm out of time, " Vicki retorted.

"Alright," Alfred sighed in resignation. "Call me when you leave him."

Alfred wasn't about to sit around and wait for Vicki to call. Waiting, he believed, was for people who had nothing better to do with themselves. It was more in his nature to speed up things a little, pressure the opposition until a breakthrough was achieved. Alfred liked to rattle cages. Just a couple of days after Vicki had told him she was married, Alfred went to pay his respects to the groom. Armed with an itemized list of Vicki's yearly expenses, four pages worth, he called on Bob at his condominium, where Bob was busily packing, preparing to move the remainder of his things into Vicki's house.

"This is an itemized list of Vicki's expenses," Alfred explained on the doorstep. "It's everything I've spent during the last year...nearly half-a-million in cash. That's what it takes to keep her happy. Let's face it, Bob, you can't afford her."

Bob protested vigorously. "You have a lotta nerve, coming up here to talk like this!"

Alfred became impatient. He knew what kind of nerve he had. "Go ahead then, tell me if you've got the money."

"Alfred..." tried Bob, but there was no getting through to him.

"If you had any sense, you'd walk out now," Alfred ranted, "because if you don't, she's gonna kill you."

Exasperated, Bob demanded that Alfred get off of his doorstep. He shoved lightly and Alfred retreated, but not without a fuss.

"You can't afford her," he shouted, his heels dug into the ground. "What Vic needs, I take care of, until someone else comes along. And you're not that man. She'll only walk out on you, like she did with all the others."

"Get out of here."

"Write me a check," Alfred insisted. "Give me back my twenty thousand for the appliances in the house."

"No."

"I demand that you give me that money."

"Alfred, you can stick it up your ass."

At first Vicki believed she might have made the right choice after all. It was great, for a change, to have a man to wake up to, a man coming home from work who would talk to her and take her out at night. They even went on a honeymoon, to Vail, Colorado, for a skiing vacation. Bob loved to ski, but Vicki hated it. She seldom left the room, passing the time watching television and dreaming of warm, sunny beaches. By the time they returned to Los Angeles, Vicki was restless and Bob was disappointed. He promised they would soon get away to a warmer climate. Tahiti, maybe.

The only warm climate they experienced together was a brief excursion to Mexico. This was no vacation, but a rescue mission, an attempt to get Earle Lamm, Vicki's first husband, out of jail. For more than a year, Earle had been imprisoned in Mexicali, after being arrested for smuggling and allegedly bringing prostitutes into Mexico, which down there is an extremely serious crime. He had been arrested in Mexico City and sentenced to two years in jail. His friends and family had tried to get him out of it, but to no avail. They had lost thousands of dollars for their efforts, having been fleeced by the corruptive elements in the Mexican legal and political system.

Vicki had only recently been informed of Earle's troubles. She and her "ex" had drifted apart over the years, even fallen out of communication. Earle, Vicki thought, was heading for disaster, and ironically, Earle had predicted the same for her. They had argued and then they had stopped talking. It wasn't until Vicki received a telephone call from one of Earle's former cellmates that she learned of his fate. Being Vicki, she did everything she could to help him. She even called Alfred, to whom she hadn't spoken other than to tell him she was married, since her wedding to Bob.

"Alfred, you've got to help him," she implored, as the atavistic reminder of her dependencies impinged on her nerves. Not only was she calling him, she realized she was practically begging him to rescue Earle, the man out of all of Vicki's liaisons whom Alfred loathed the most.

Despite Vicki's pleading, Alfred remained consistent with his emotions. He reminded her how much he despised the man, recounted how Earle had assaulted him not once, but twice, no less. He said he loved Vicki, desperately. However, he'd do nothing for Earle.

"He should rot there," was Alfred's final word on the subject. That is, until Vicki begged and pleaded some more. Eventually he couldn't stand it and finally, reluctantly, agreed to see what he could do.

An hour later he was back on the phone. "I called my friend in Mexico," he related. "He said in this case there wasn't much to be done. Earle screwed up and someone wants him to pay for it."

It would be years later before it occurred to Vicki that that someone may have been Alfred, and that he might have been lying about his efforts to help. But back then she merely thanked him for his assistance and, with Bob as her escort, flew off to visit Earle. After Vicki filed for conjugal visiting privileges, enabling her to spend the night with Earle, Bob, who had been growing impatient, decided he

BEAUTIFUL BAD GIRL

had had enough of it. Despite her arguments, he returned to L.A. while Vicki stayed behind. He'd pick her up at the airport when she decided to come home.

As sundown neared, Vicki entered the prison and was led by uniformed guards through the dingy corridors to one of the larger conjugal cells in an isolated wing of the prison. The cell was dark, for there was no light bulb since that too was a luxury, something one had to pay for, along with the soap, the towels, the decent, clean sheets, and toilet paper Earle would bring for this festive occasion.

"How are you?" she asked, as she stood face to face with her former husband. It had all begun with Earle, she thought, reflecting on the hopes and dreams she had when she was still a kid. But the years had passed. Time had flown. The toll had been taken from both. Earle looked so much older, drawn and exhausted. But he was delighted to see Vicki. He could barely contain himself as he hugged and kissed her and started crying, more from joy than from self-pity.

They talked through the night, lying close to each other until the dawn, which for Earle came much too suddenly. Soon the jailer would be coming, announcing it was time for Vicki to leave.

"You know I've always loved you," Earle assured her as Vicki collected her belongings. "I might've done some stupid things, but I did them because I cared for you. I hated to see you ruin yourself. But I guess I had no way to stop it."

She kissed him and playfully prodded his ribs like she used to do in the good old days. "You did the best you could. The smuggling...the hookers...that was stupid."

"There were no hookers. I was set up. Believe me. We were having a party, that's all."

"And the smuggling?"

His head bowed, his eyes on the ground, Earle told her why he'd done it. "I thought if I made enough money, you'd leave Alfred and come back to me. You never loved him, Vicki. I know that and you know that. It was only for the money. Tell me! Wasn't it only for the money?"

"Yeah, sure," she lied. "You were right all along. It was only for the money."

After leaving Earle Lamm's cell in the Mexican prison and returning to Los Angeles, Vicki learned from Todd that Alfred was hanging around the house once again. Typically, he was parked down the block, sitting in his car. Vicki decided it was time to move.

With Bob she found the perfect house to lease. It was named Tara, no less, after Scarlett's estate in *Gone with the Wind*. In letters standing two feet high, its name was emblazoned on the wrought iron gates at the entrance. Max Baer, Jr., the movie producer and former star of the "Beverly Hillbillies," owned this grand stone house set on two acres of land, its boundaries rimmed by the most treacherous curve in Benedict Canyon, as the road wound up into the hills toward Mulholland Drive. There was the obligatory swimming pool, a tennis court, and a waterfall to grace the landscape. Simply lovely! A great place to start their marriage and set up for the social climbing, the parties, and sit-down dinners Vicki thought they would have.

She took it all very seriously. She bought new china and crystal glasses, and a Jeep for the help to use for their basic household chores. She hired a houseboy and a cook, and she retained Fatima, the Moroccan maid. Vicki enjoyed being the lady, the mistress of the house, the good wife behind the decent man. She bought things for the house and she did a lot of drugs. She was high all the time, with a great sun tan from lying around the pool on the days when she didn't go shopping.

Bob Schulman found it difficult to relate to all of this. He was uncomfortable with having servants. Fatima especially got on his nerves. And the way Vicki was spending his money was outrageous; it was putting him in a jam. As a feeble compromise, Vicki offered to get rid of Fatima. She would please her husband and accommodate herself. Rather than fire her, Vicki thought it best if she could find a job for the maid. She asked around and eventually she found a prospect, a Saudi princess who had been living in Beverly Hills. The woman's name was Jawajar Bint Saud. Her friends called her "J."

# 20

PRINCESS J WAS delighted to make Vicki's acquaintance. Like many Arabs, she was attracted to blondes. And Vicki, upon their first meeting, was the archetypical California blonde, with sun-bleached hair and skin of golden bronze, looking hot and sensuous in her white halter top and faded jeans. She was reserved and self-conscious after spending months in relative seclusion behind the gates of Tara. She certainly wasn't ready for the Spider, as Princess J would later be called. Emaciated and ghostly, the princess glided over the carpet as she crossed the room to greet Vicki Morgan. Her thick, dark hair was long and wild, swept to the winds in homage to Medusa. Her skeletal frame was covered by a tight, black jumpsuit, flared at the hips and under the arms. She wore rings on nearly all of her fingers, and a gold and diamond pavé watch encircled her bony wrist. Her dark eyes, intense and hollow from lack of sleep and dangerous living, carefully studied Vicki as the Spider sat down in the opposite chair.

The Princess spoke in a deep and throaty voice, the envy of anyone looking for work hosting the late-night horror movies. But the Princess didn't need to work. She was the daughter of former King Faisal ibn al Saud, a progressive killed by his nephew in 1975. J's sister was later beheaded for allegedly choosing illicit love over family concerns and would become the subject of the the controversial documentary, *Death of a Princess*. Princess J also had troubles at home, and was not likely to be voted Princess of the Year. Her mother, who resided in Switzerland, sent money to J and wisely urged her to stay clear of any family reunions. So the Spider lived in high style with a low profile. She, like Vicki, seldom left the house.

And what a house! Whether it was pre-punk or post-apocalyptic is difficult to say. The living room walls and the high arched ceilings were virtually covered with strips of black leather, interspersed with three-inch pieces of dia-mond-shaped glass. The chairs and the chaises were color-ful, in Moorish styling, and occupied by several women who sat around, talking softly among themselves. To Vicki, they appeared eccentric, slightly disheveled, and fashionably European. Now and then they glanced at Vicki and J, who were seated in the far corner of the room sipping tea.

"Darling, you are a very beautiful woman," J compli-mented after they had been talking for awhile. Her voice with its husky, educated timbre had a chilling effect on Vicki. She was intrigued, entranced, and scared of this woman and her whole, weird scene. On one hand, she wanted to pop out of her chair and break for the door, but on the other, she found the Princess a stimulating contrast to the dullness of her seclusion at Tara. After months of routine monotony, of hanging out with her girlfriends, of hiding out from Bob, Vicki's curiosity had been aroused.

"So what do you do with yourself?" J was asking. "Are you an actress?"

"I'm married," Vicki responded, feeling foolish as she did so. "Look," she said, hoping to change the subject. "I want to keep Fatima two days a week and sometimes for an extended weekend. Does that meet with your approval?"

"It's fine."

"So, do you want Fatima or not?"

"Of course I want Fatima," gloated the Spider, "because if I take Fatima, I'll see more of you. You will be picking her up and taking her, I assume?"

"She'll be here Monday," answered Vicki. Suddenly she was nervous, eager to leave. Fatima, who had been off somewhere while negotiations took place, was back in the living room standing over Vicki. She didn't seem happy at all. She curled her mouth into a scowl as she glanced furtively at her future employer.

"What was that all about?" Vicki asked, after she and Fatima had taken their leave. "She seemed so much like a man...the way she acted, how she looked me over."

"She's nothing," spat Fatima. "She's a disgrace to her people and their customs. You be careful with her," she added ominously, her finger wagging at Vicki. "She's very dangerous."

A month passed without further incident, when Vicki received an emergency call from a breathless Fatima. The Princess had thrown a wild, violent fit and had ejected Elizabeth, her girlfriend, and everyone else but the maid. J was shaking and vomiting, sick as a dog. Fatima didn't know what to do, and was afraid to call any doctors.

J, besides wanting something that would take the edge off, demanded only one other thing. "Call Vicki!" she hissed, until Fatima had picked up the phone.

Twenty minutes later, Vicki was ringing her bell. Fatima opened the door and let her in, while stammering about the disgrace of it all, the sacrilege. Vicki followed her into the living room where J was stretched out on the chaise. She was moaning, coughing, and in obvious agony, having snorted bad heroin, which her girlfriend had brought her, throwing her into convulsions. Their romance was over. She needed more heroin—good stuff—but unfortunately there was none in the house.

"Elizabeth always saw to these things," groaned the Princess. "You must find me something. Please."

Vicki started calling around, asking friends where she could score, until someone gave her the name of a doctor who was amenable to cash transactions. Within an hour the doctor arrived. He dispensed Methadone to the Princess, wrote a prescription for Dilaudid, a synthetic morphine, took his money and left. While the Princess sweated and grimaced, Vicki ground the Methadone pills into powder by pressing them with a spoon.

"Here, try this," Vicki offered, as she helped the Princess to a sitting position. J grimaced after snorting the ersatz smack, but gradually reemerged from the tortured throes of withdrawal. Although the Princess wasn't her old self again, Vicki felt she could leave her alone with Fatima and a friend, while she drove off to a shabby pharmacy in the San Fernando Valley to fill the Dilaudid prescription. She then returned to the house where she planned to stay until J recovered. She called Bob to tell him the story and found it was one he didn't want to hear. He wanted her home, a sentiment that angered Vicki.

"J's terribly ill. I'm not leaving her alone."

"Come back now, or don't come home at all," Schulman warned her.

"Fine," Vicki sighed, thankful her marriage was over. "Just let Todd stay with you until I straighten it out. Please, Bob, that's all I ask?"

Of the different men in her life, Bob had always been the most understanding. He agreed to care for Todd, for as long as necessary, and Vicki was grateful for the gesture. She was now free to remain with the Princess and consequently begin an all-out phase of self-destruction. She began snorting heroin along with the rest of the crowd. She smoked free-base cocaine and sometimes mixed it with heroin to make speedballs, an expensive killer if there ever was one. Now that J had recovered and was feeling chipper, the channels were opened, the connections were made, and enormous quantities of drugs were bought and consumed in an endless cycle. Day and night Vicki was high, losing all control. She was sleeping with J, whom she found to be extremely intense, more than most of the men whom Vicki had known. And the Spider was very demanding, obsessively possessive and sometimes cruel in her dealings with Vicki.

Earle Lamm was out of jail and back in town. Vicki had learned from mutual friends that he had been trying to get in touch. At the Spider's insistance, Vicki called him, since the Princess wanted to make a buy. Earle arrived in short order and was introduced to the Princess and the other women who lived in the house. He watched in horror as they snorted heroin, loaded glass pipes with free-base cocaine and heroin, and settled down for another nihilistic weekend. Surely they were potentially excellent customers, but it was all too much for Earle. He was sickened by what he observed and concerned for Vicki's welfare. He wanted her to leave with him.

"Vic, I'm begging you," he implored her as she walked him out to his car. "Leave this house and come with me. If you don't, you're gonna die here. You're gonna rot and go to hell, and that'll kill me. For years I've been afraid it would happen—that you'd die before me."

The smack and the free-base had already created dependencies. Vicki was too far gone to leave of her own volition. She tried to make light of it.

"You know me," she laughed. "I'll be okay."

Earle Lamm had aged in prison and was in terrible health. He didn't attempt to conceal the anguish torturing his soul. He clutched at his chest and tears filled his eyes as he stared at Vicki for what would be the final time in his life.

"Vic...for Christ's sake, I'm not a young man. I've seen too many of them end up dead or wasted. Don't do it, Vic. Don't end up like they did."

She smiled like the child he used to love and kissed him full on the mouth. Finally they separated, and Vicki watched as he climbed inside his car. As he was driving off,

Earle stuck his head out the window and looked back at his former wife. "I love you," he shouted. "Don't ever forget it."

Bob Schulman, meanwhile, was disgusted with Fatima and finally threw her out. She called Vicki to complain about the treatment and to declare that she hadn't been paid in a month. She threatened to tell Todd what his mother was doing unless Vicki made good on all her back salary.

"I'll kill you, if you tell him anything," Vicki responded. Fatima got the hint and took a powder, absconding with what valuables she could get her hands on. Vicki, fearful that Fatima had related it all to Todd, fled J's for consolation and solitude at L'Ermitage Hotel in Beverly Hills. But a few days later the Princess came to visit, suggesting they both leave town for awhile.

They chartered the *King's Point*, an enormous yacht, a luxurious vessel nearly two hundred feet in length, which they planned to sail to Hawaii. A friend of Vicki's, along with J's sister Desma and four other women, would also come along for the ride. To make do, the Princess withdrew over $250,000 from the bank to charter the boat and buy all the drugs for the voyage. She got it in cash and stashed it in her leather attaché case, which Vicki, needless to say, carried for her. Once again she was lost to the artifice of responsibility, the need to be relied upon, to be stimulated, and ultimately abused. It gave her a rush to be holding the bag.

The voyage itself was unadulterated weirdness, rivalling that of the *Ancient Mariner*, the *Mutiny on the Bounty*, or Ahab's ill-fated search for a whale named Moby Dick. There were dykes and drugs, a crazy captain, his girlfriend, whom he had managed to smuggle on board, and a motley crew of four. It would take them a month to reach Kauai, the first of the Hawaiian Islands; it was time enough for this leisurely cruise to be transformed into a macabre journey. The more drugs consumed, the crazier it got, as the

229

massive, two hundred foot yacht took on the proportions of an inflatable life raft, floating precariously in the stormy Pacific. To enhance their claustrophobia, torrential rainstorms swelled the ocean and waves crashed over the bow. Below deck, conflicts erupted among the passengers, and overtones of paranoia permeated everything but the food. There was bitterness and jealousy, and a Dutch captain who feared the women would seize the prized gun collection displayed in the stateroom, rape his girlfriend, and slaughter his hapless crew.

Meanwhile, Vicki got high and slept with the Princess, who kept offering to buy her houses and cars.

The days grew longer and the ship sailed on. "I feel bought," she confided in her sidekick.

Less than twenty miles from Kauai, the captain decided to radio the Coast Guard, informing them his ship was under siege. There were drugs, guns, and dangerous women aboard, he explained, hoping to put an end to the boat ride. "Hurry as fast as you can!"

His call for help must have been very convincing, for within hours, Coast Guard and Navy vessels showed up in force. Small countries have been taken with less than what was sent to board the chartered yacht. Eight to ten vessels were standing away from the yacht, ready if necessary to blast it to pieces.

When the ladies caught sight of this mini-armada, they began divesting themselves of contraband. Chaotically, like gunners on a frigate, they raced below deck and started flinging it out of the portholes. The Dutch captain, who was standing topside, shouted in vain to the Coast Guard, hoping to call attention to the floating debris.

"Be prepared for boarding!" came the Coast Guard's orders over their public address system. It made Vicki's skin crawl. Her stomach knotted in fear. She sat quietly with the others below deck, anxiously awaiting the boarding party. Before long she could hear the thunk of their boots, many boots, as they scrambled across the deck. With everyone in position, the commanding officer spoke again.

"Miss Morgan," crackled the portable speaker. "Drop your weapons and come out with your hands raised behind your head!"

It figured. She would have to be the first one called. She climbed the stairs on wavering legs and pushed open the hatch to find dozens of shotguns and machine guns aimed in her direction. One shotgun was prodding the back of her skull. "Lovely," she muttered under her breath. "Simply terrific."

A voice from behind was suddenly issuing commands. "Lie down on your stomach with your legs spread, and put your hands behind your neck," Vicki was ordered. She wasn't about to argue, and she remained with her face pressed to the deck for what seemed like an eternity. They handcuffed her wrists and told her she had better not move. She listened obliquely as the other women were called by name.

"My god," she thought. "First it was the ordeal on Bernie's houseboat, and now this." On the spot she promised herself she'd take no more ocean cruises.

As the petty officer snapped the cuffs on Princess J, she was filled with indignation. "How dare you put these on me?" she demanded. She then claimed diplomatic immunity and issued the appropriate threats.

Regardless, the ship was searched and the prisoners were interrogated before the commanding officer apologized and let them all go free. At the Dutch captain's insistence, he escorted the yacht to the Naval Base on Kauai. The pleasure cruise was over. The women agreed to fly to Honolulu before returning to Los Angeles.

However, Vicki learned on Kauai that she had an urgent message to call Sally Talbert. She did, to find out that Earle was dead. He had collapsed and died from a heart attack. Sally had been trying to reach her for days.

"There were storms at sea," Vicki explained.

"Vicki, the funeral is tomorrow."

Vicki was booked on the very next flight to Los Angeles. She checked into L'Ermitage and called Sally to let her know she was back in town.

"Did you call Bob? Or Todd?" Sally wondered.

"No, I can't," Vicki muttered.

"Why not?"

"'Cause I'm afraid to," was the only thing she could say.

At the funeral the following day, Vicki realized she was irretrievably breaking down. She could feel it happening. Whatever tenuous grip remained in her consciousness was rapidly slipping away. Vicki was frightened and paralyzed as she stood by Earle Lamm's gravesite, receiving off-handed condolences from people she hadn't seen in years. She was crying, overcome by guilt and despair. She hated herself and shouldered the blame for Earle's demise. She was ashamed for leaving Todd and Bob. She was at a new low and feeling suicidal. She wished it was she they were lowering into the ground and not Earle.

Burdened by guilt, embarrassed by her insanity, Vicki decided she must return to Hawaii and the Saudi Princess, if for no other reason than to finish the job of self-destruction she had started. Before her departure, she had a long talk with her son and then sat down to hash it out with Bob. Schulman asked her not to leave, to remain with him and seek help, and said he would pay for it.

"I'm sorry, Bob," she apologized, "but I can't stay with you. I'm booked on the morning flight."

But prior to her leaving, Vicki had second thoughts and called her husband, to no avail. The phone rang and no one answered. Bob had already gone to his office.

In Honolulu, the Princess rented a penthouse suite, with twenty-five hundred square feet of living space. It was the perfect hangout—registered in Vicki's name. Upon their arrival, the women stepped out on the balcony for a view of the beach and the surf. Very nice! They soon withdrew, shutting the drapes as they returned to their quarters for some serious drug abuse. The drugs were supplied by two women who had flown in from Los Angeles and stayed for the party as well. Vicki couldn't get over it. They had sailed across more than two thousand miles of hostile ocean to sit around and get high in the darkness. For this they didn't need Hawaii! The drapes were never opened again.

Vicki, in a moment of deluded sobriety, had invited her mother, Todd, and Barbara, her older sister, to join her in Hawaii. The trio arrived and Vicki booked them in a small motel, two blocks away from her den of iniquity. When her mother insisted they all go for dinner, Vicki promised to meet them later. She returned to her hotel suite and discovered her friend was leaving. Vicki pleaded for her not to leave, but the woman was adamant. She'd had enough of the girls, the drugs, and the Saudi Princess, who by now was dangerously insane.

"What's going on here?" Vicki angrily inquired.

"Money has been stolen from my briefcase," the Spider announced. She was ranting and cursing, breaking glasses against the walls. Suddenly she whirled and pointed her finger at Vicki. "And you took the money," she hissed to Vicki's amazement.

"I didn't steal your money."

"Yes, you did!"

Vicki started crying. She was sick and disgusted. "I'm leaving," she said and went to get her things. Quickly, the Spider was upon her, smacking her, wrestling her to the floor. At first Vicki struggled, trying to free her arms from the Spider's grasp and smack her in the mouth. But soon she changed her mind after thinking, "Oh shit, this broad is liable to kill me." She tried the rational approach instead, and eventually she was able to calm down the Spider. At least, for a while.

After she pleaded and promised, Vicki was allowed to have dinner with her family. She left the suite and started walking the two blocks to the motel where her family was staying. Somehow she lost her sense of direction. She couldn't remember where they were staying. She was so confused she walked in circles for nearly two full hours before she hailed a taxi in order to reach her destination.

She returned several hours later to discover all but the Princess were gone. Vicki's heart was in her mouth. The room was beginning to spin. What was she doing with this insane woman? Luckily for Vicki, J was packing, having decided it was time for them to leave.

It was close to midnight when the plane landed at Los Angeles International Airport, and Vicki, so she wouldn't arouse her suspicions, remained one last night with the Spider, before returning to Tara the following day. She never saw the Princess again. Once home, Vicki cried a lot, pouring it out to Bob who did his best to soothe her. After several days, she could see it was hopeless. She was too far gone for inspiring lectures and warm embraces. She called her psychiatrist, Dr. J. Victor Monke, and explained what had transpired for the past two months.

"Dr. Monke," cried Vicki. "I really need some help."

# 21

THE THALIANS Mental Clinic, like the rest of the Cedars Sinai Medical Complex, was the beneficiary of charitable patronage. Wealthy citizens, many from the show business community, had forked over bundles to have wings, rooms, and reception areas donated in their names. Thalians, the recipient of its fair share of tax-deductible contributions, was pleasant enough for a mental ward, having been designed to make its patients feel as comfortable as possible. It tried to be a home away from home, favoring a modernistic styling, offering kitchen and laundry facilities and other self-service conveniences reminiscent of the basic domestic environment. For Vicki Morgan, it would be her home away from home alright, for five months. It was her refuge, the one place she could find peace and quiet. It was her final chance to straighten it out.

At first the mental clinic scared her half to death. There were more than half a dozen people from the Hollywood community, a few career professionals, children, a handful of charity cases, and Marvin Pancoast. The one thing Vicki believed the patients shared in common was that most were seriously crazy—not mildly neurotic, but really fucking gone. She discovered many patients were in and out and back again, as soon as they discovered they simply couldn't cope. Those she met acted surprised that this was her first time at Thalians. Vicki found this unsettling, akin to a loss of virginity. Once you committed yourself, she was reminded, you were destined to return.

"My god," thought Vicki, "what have I done? I'm the straightest one here."

Overwhelmed at first by what she had voluntarily let herself in for, Vicki wanted to leave. But then she considered her available options in the outside world. She could return to Tara and Robert Schulman, or call Alfred and have him lease her one more house. The Princess by now would love to have her back. Or maybe she could even start dating. Vicki shook her head in exasperation. She was better off where she was.

The voyage to Hawaii had all but annihilated her sense of proportion, as well as her sanity. She had regressed terribly and her behavior was childish. She would sit in a ball, hunched over her knees, her legs drawn tightly against her chest and rock back and forth like a little girl, a veritable pendulum of emotional extremities. She stiffened when people drew near, and her speech impediment was more pronounced than it had been in years. She stuttered when forced into conversation. It frightened her when patients shouted and struggled, or when the doors slammed in the corridors.

Gradually, Vicki adjusted to life in the mental ward. She had her bad days and good days. On the good ones, she believed she had a chance to gain control of her life, to assume the responsibilities of adulthood as achieved through confidence and productivity. On the bad days, she believed she might never leave the mental ward, that she'd be trapped among the lunatics, with nowhere to go and nothing to do, lost among her personalities, those people inside her who guarded the secrets of the real Vicki Morgan.

"I am a mistress," she would declare at her therapy sessions. "And what is a mistress? Is she a high-class call girl? A second wife? A friend? For half my life I tried to define it. Movies, books, they've all had an influence in forming the image I live with. I tremble just hearing the word."

Vicki was told it was the stigma and not the role itself that plagued her. She was not ashamed of being in love with a married man, but ashamed of her image in a critical society. Since she was a child and her father began sending her checks in the mail, Vicki had always associated money with love. This, she was told, had justified his absence, while defining her status and value. This, she was told, had fostered her greatest dilemma, especially when standard portrayals of love and romance conflicted greatly with her experience and interpretation. Despite her hidden emotions and secret fantasies, she was haunted by the reality that men had tried to buy her.

Vicki had long since given up trying to reconcile the standard definition of romance with her own interpretation. That, she knew, was an exercise in futility. She considered love not as a linear emotion but that which can assume versatile forms and myriad dimensions. Love was more than the sentiments on greeting cards, the figures on a wedding cake, candlelight romance or tender affections. Love was spawned from desire and passion, the needs of two parties, integration and consensus. Love was volatile, yet delicate, forming different combinations, appearing in all shapes and sizes. Love was unattainable when pursued on someone else's terms.

"Part of your problem," Vicki was told, " is that you never finish anything. Not once in your life have you completed a project you started. Your occupational therapy is a perfect example. One minute you're working papier-mâché, the next you're making leather belts. And after awhile, you give that up and start drawing pictures.

"Vicki, you've never had direction, or focus. You've been too easily influenced by the men in your life."

"It doesn't start out that way," protested Vicki. "It just seems to happen."

"I can see it here," said the therapist. "Nearly all of the men are attracted to you—not just the patients, but the orderlies and doctors as well. They fall for you, and you either don't seem to care or you're hardly aware of it. Jealousies abound in here, Vicki. You're the object of competition."

"That's why I'm here," she admitted. "That's what's driving me crazy."

To add to the pressures of adjustment, Alfred was calling her with distressing regularity. He claimed to be her father and demanded she be paged, a frequent ritual provoking jealousy in some of the other patients. He was ebullient and raspy when he spoke to her, comparing her breakdown to his withdrawal from Percodan years ago. He was convinced that buying her a house would cure what ailed her.

"We'll buy one for you, just as soon as you get out," he repeated.

"Alfred, I can't be thinking of houses right now. And please don't tell them you're my father. They know my father's dead, Alfred. Besides, after all the therapy sessions, they know all about you. So please don't put me through these charades. Just tell them who you are."

Alfred had a talk with Dr. Monke and, with Vicki's approval, he was to be apprised of her daily condition. Ironically, Alfred was the only one who inquired about her progress on a regular basis. Bob had been exhausted by it all and basically left Vicki alone. Vicki's friends and family would phone occasionally, and a few stopped by to visit her. She didn't blame them for their paucity of visits, as she was often incoherent and subject to abruptly changing moods. There were times when she couldn't talk and times when she wouldn't listen. Her nerves were so frayed that when her friends came by they sounded foolish and shallow.

In lieu of visits, Vicki was receiving flowers, voluminous arrangements that must have cost a ton. There were so many flowers that she distributed them to her fellow patients. The patients were grateful; they boasted about it and a new form of status was created inside the ward. It was a big thing, a badge of honor to be presented with flowers by Vicki. In return for her attention and generosity, the patients gave her drawings, paintings, and crafts they had made during therapy sessions. Grown men, business professionals, blushed and giggled when she kissed them on the cheek to demonstrate her appreciation. She would put their artworks on display, tacking them onto her bedroom walls until her tiny quarters resembled a bulletin board in grade school.

As Vicki adjusted, she began to take over. Patients served her, did her bidding. When someone had a complaint, they lodged it with Vicki, who then sat down and hashed it out with the appropriate members of the staff. She'd comfort patients in times of crisis. She was their mother and she was their goddess. Inside the "loony bin," as she liked to call it, Vicki was a voice of authority.

As the months passed, Vicki grew increasingly comfortable with life in Thalians Clinic. She dated patients, those given special passes, sometimes for weekends but mostly for single evenings. She had her Mercedes parked in a nearby parking lot. She had additional clothing brought to her, until the closet was overflowing, and she stacked her Laszlo beauty supplies neatly on shelves in her bathroom. Her Louis Vuitton steamer trunk was set at the foot of the bed. She even went on group excursions. But when it came to determining future trips, Vicki did her best to influence majority rule. At all costs she wanted to avoid her old stomping grounds, for fear she'd be spotted among the busload of imbalanced personalities.

Marvin Pancoast had also been checked into Thalians. He had tried to hang himself after leaving his job at the Rogers and Cowan Public Relations Agency. For Marvin, it was one of a number of unsuccessful attempts, most of which had been committed in public. He liked the attention, it seemed. He enjoyed being servile, being dominated and humiliated and physically and mentally treated poorly.

Marvin was gay, but incapable it seemed of maintaining a steady relationship. Instead, his sex life was ephemeral; he got his thrills by living in jeopardy, thriving on quickies in parked cars and public restrooms.

Whatever caused Marvin to be servile, he soon discovered he had come to the right place. Vicki was more than willing to allow Marvin to fix her tea and do her chores. She let him massage her feet, using skin cream and dampened towels. Marvin idolized Vicki and was grateful to be at her side. For Vicki, he was someone to talk to, someone who would show proper adulation as he listened to her stories. And in turn, when he had a problem and needed a mother's comfort, a shoulder to cry on, he always went to Vicki Morgan.

"Vicki, you're too aware of Marvin's condition to not know what you're doing," she was told by the doctors who were concerned with the relationship's inherent liabilities. Marvin had not been responding well to therapy, but had been relying on Vicki instead, seeking her approval, boasting of his love for her.

"He's here to overcome his problem," warned the doctors, "and you make it worse by making him your servant."

"I'm a patient," snapped Vicki. "I'm supposed to be nuts, remember?"

"Vicki, it's potentially dangerous. Marvin hates his mother, he dreams of killing her. And, in his mind, you're becoming his mother."

The benefits of therapy included a better understanding of her relationship with Alfred Bloomingdale. With guidance from her doctor, Vicki purged herself of intransigent anxieties. A mistress, she was told, like a wife, a mother or a girlfriend was a social condition with its advantages and disadvantages, and was an honorable role in many societies. She was told not to punish herself for being a mistress, and not to view herself as a social pariah, but as a woman deeply involved with the man she loved. At first, such an overview was difficult for her to accept, after all those years of guilt and frustration. It was true that she had found her life amusing, but she also hated herself as well. Now, through intensive therapy, she was becoming painfully aware of the destruction brought on by that self-hatred. She spent many nights crying herself to sleep. Eventually, without the aid of barbiturates, she was getting no sleep at all.

Vicki began to look forward to Alfred's visits. She was relaxing more, enjoying his conversation. Alfred was trying to be more expressive, more open about his life with its triumphs and disappointments. It was ironic, after all the years they had spent together living the good life and seeing the world, that they were sharing their most sensitive intimacies in the hospitality room at a mental clinic. Perhaps it was because there were no social obligations and no business distractions that they were able to communicate more openly, talking comfortably for hours like rational human beings. Here, Alfred applied no sexual pressures, and she didn't spite him by playing her games. Alfred was there because he cared. It was that simple. And he was the only one there. He was flustered and bewildered, but nearly every day he came to visit her. Vicki felt closer to him than she ever had. This alone had made committing herself worthwhile, just to spend the time with him.

But not everything he said to her was cause for a sentimental journey. He retained certain beliefs that were less endearing, including his admission that, although he had agreed not to include her in his sexual scenarios, he could never cease his own endeavors. Be it her threats or psychiatric help, it wouldn't do any good. He couldn't help himself, and he didn't want to.

"What I'm going to say to you may sound strange," Alfred blurted one Sunday afternoon. He was laughing and chuckling, but Vicki knew he wasn't kidding. "When you're in here, at least I know where you are. I know you're safe, and I can always reach you. I don't have to worry so much."

"You sonofabitch," chided Vicki. "The doors are locked and you know I'm not going anywhere. You can call me or visit whenever you please. Right, Alfred?"

He roared with laughter, delighted by the look on her face. After all the years, he still liked to tease her, to see her pissed off. Suddenly, he was serious again. His eyes were wide, his face laced with tension as he took hold and squeezed her hand.

"I don't think I have much time left," he whispered. His deep voice was hoarse and very subdued. "I haven't been feeling well. I've been getting pains in my stomach."

She didn't know what to say to him. It was not like him to talk this way. The subject of death, when it came up at all, was never taken seriously. When he spoke of his mortality, Vicki would assure him that he would live forever. Or she would tell him she'd be dead before he would.

"I'm sure it's nothing," she tried to persuade him. "I just can't see you getting sick, Alfred."

"We'll see," he concluded. "But that's why I want you close to me. In case it is something...and it's the end of me."

Up until the day she was ready to leave the Thalians Mental Health Center, Vicki had no idea where she was going to live. Dr. Monke had advised both Alfred Bloomingdale and Robert Schulman that Vicki needed from four to six months of peace and tranquility. She had to establish a better foundation to learn to do things for herself and gain a sense of direction. Everyone agreed they would do whatever was necessary.

Alfred offered to find her a house and furnish a nurse in addition to servants. That was how well he comprehended the doctor's recommendations that she live a simple life. Bob Schulman offered her residence at Tara for six months, until the lease expired. He was planning to move into something more to his taste. However, he was busy and he didn't know when that would be.

Vicki thought she would share an apartment with Marvin Pancoast, but the doctors rejected that idea due to the potential for violence and conflict. Vicki argued, but to no avail. If she was to leave Thalians, then she had to find a different solution.

"I know one thing's for sure," Vicki declared. "I'm not staying here anymore. Alfred wants this and Bob wants that. Meanwhile, I'm stuck in here with no place to go. To hell with it! I'll check into the L'Ermitage. With what it costs for a suite there, somebody better do something."

So Vicki checked into L'Ermitage and called room service as soon as she entered her room. It was time for a celebration. She called Polly, a hairdresser she'd met one night while out on a pass from Thalians, and invited her up for caviar and Dom Perignon champagne. And that was it, the total congregation, the entire greeting party, after spending five months in a mental ward. The following morning, Alfred Bloomingdale came to visit when he was able to sneak out of his house.

Common ground was finally established between Alfred and Bob...they both wanted her to move out of L'Ermitage Hotel. She took a suite in Le Parc Hotel in West Hollywood and remained there for over a month. Polly, the hairdresser, who had been utterly impressed by Vicki's lifestyle, visited frequently, hanging out for days. Marvin Pancoast stopped by with regularity, as did Vicki's friend Janis, who introduced her to Mary Sangre.

It was almost Christmas of 1979, and Vicki was still at Le Parc Hotel. Alfred, for the holidays, gave her a few thousand dollars with which to buy gifts. Most of the money Vicki spent on Todd, who was staying with Bob. On Christmas Day she drove up to Tara and visited with her son. That evening she returned to her hotel suite, in keeping with the agreement she'd made with Bob. She got drunk that night and stayed up until dawn, crying, wondering what would become of her. The foundation, the new cycle of life that Dr. Monke had spoken of was slipping out of reach.

Bob Schulman offered to try and reconcile their marriage, but Vicki rejected the idea. So Bob took another house and let Vicki move into Tara until the lease was up. Polly, the hairdresser, joined her there, as did Janis and Mary Sangre, with whom Vicki had begun an affair. It was a spontaneous romance, convenient and safe, with Vicki typically using sex as a hedge against abandonment and loneliness. She had learned much from the men in her life, regarding the utility of cash and favors. Much of the money Vicki received from Alfred each month was given to Mary. She borrowed Vicki's clothes and started driving a Porsche.

Ensconced in Tara, Vicki would get high and stay in bed, chain smoking cigarettes, sometimes until dawn, listening for traffic accidents, which occurred with alarming regularity. A sharp and precarious deadman's curve encircled Tara's perimeters, as Benedict Canyon snaked upward to Mulholland, at the crest of the Hollywood Hills. About once a week she would hear the screeching tires, the shattering glass as another vehicle spun off the road and smashed into the rocky and tree-laden embankment. Initially, Vicki would dash outside, looking to help the victims. She'd find them stunned and injured, their vehicles a twisted mess of steel. Some survived the crash, while others didn't. Some were grateful, while others seemed angry that she had bothered to interfere. After awhile, Vicki stopped running outside to offer her assistance, remaining instead in her bedroom, where she would summon an ambulance, then return to her thoughts. It was better that way. She would live without their gratitude.

Vicki wanted little to do with men in her life, any men, no matter how promising they seemed. It was wise, she believed, to keep them at a safe and reasonable distance, relieved of their pressures and questions. It was months before she agreed to see Alfred Bloomingdale, and then only after he had persisted by calling her a dozen times a day. She met him for lunch, and he was the perfect gentleman, declaring his love, lamenting his past mistakes.

"I'm gonna make it up to you," he promised. "This time, we'll be sure to buy a house."

"Alfred, you gotta be kidding me," came Vicki's sardonic response. She was incredulous, smiling as she regarded the look on his face. Slowly, she shook her head and tried to keep from laughing, so as not to insult him by doubting his sincerity. "You really gotta be kidding me," she added, propping herself on her elbows as she leaned across the table. She thought of all the years she had spent looking at houses, roaming the hills, the canyons, the flats, and the beaches. After ten years of it, she was on a first-name basis with every major realtor on the west side of town. House hunting had exhausted her, made her crazy. She was always at the mercy of Alfred's moods, his financial condition. It made her ambivalent, to say nothing of what it had done to the realtors. One minute she was buying, the next she was not.

"Vic...I'm serious," Alfred protested. "You should have a house of your own."

"You know...I'm not so sure anymore. Maybe it's been the source of my troubles. I always thought a house would give me security, but now I don't think it would. The more I've tried to set down roots, the more rootless I've become. I don't think I'm supposed to be that comfortable."

Alfred gently stroked her hand and spoke softly as he tried to reassure her. "I want to do it. I want it for you. Besides," he started to laugh, "you could've built a fortune in equity with all the rent I've paid over the years. I know it's not your fault, but it's something to consider."

"Why bother? We can't do a thing about it now. So you want me to shop for houses, huh?"

"Darling, you know I do."

One thing about house hunting, it was a damned good reason for Vicki to get out of bed each morning, something she had been finding increasingly difficult to do as the days wore on. But this way she would rise early, shower, and put in time with her makeup and hair. She always felt better when she was attractively dressed, although during the past year she had been neglecting herself. Her nerves were frayed and she had circles under her eyes. She had lost weight, gained weight, drank, snorted coke, took valiums and downers. She had married one man and then run away. To change her luck she took up with the princess and had been forced to escape from the woman's domination. She had suffered a breakdown, partially out of guilt concerning her ongoing affair with Alfred Bloomingdale. She had desired him, but tried to duck it, in order to please her family and friends who were down on Alfred. Now her friends and family hardly spoke to her, but Bloomingdale was still by her side. It was all so strange and the truth so elusive. Since time began, people have tried to find love. Vicki found it and was pressured to reject it. Why? She knew why. Because she was his mistress instead of his wife. A wife can be involved in a loveless setup, a social arrangement, and this was fine by society's standards. But when you're the mistress and you're in love with the man, connected to his dreams and ambitions...well...look out, honey, or they'll turn you inside out. Vicki could never get over it.

To keep her occupied, Alfred got Vicki a non-paying job as a mailing-list checker at the Los Angeles office of the Republican campaign headquarters. Through Alfred she met various political figures, including Edwin Meese and George Bush, along with the behind-the-scenes personalities who were responsible for the fund raising and general operation of the campaign machinery. Certain men, with Alfred's permission, if not encouragement, escorted her to fund-raising banquets and other party functions.

"I have to go with Betsy," Alfred stated. "But this way, you can be there too."

One man who served as Vicki's escort was Nascib La Houd, a former mayor of Beruit, Lebanon. Nascib was a personal friend of Alfred's who had a special affection for Vicki. Later the two would become romantically involved. Whether Alfred knew it or not is hard to determine. But if he did, there was a reason he chose to ignore it.

Vicki told me she had wondered why Nascib was present at these different campaign functions, and she had asked Alfred about him.

"What's he doing here?" she asked. "He almost seems out of place."

"No," Vicki claimed Alfred had responded. "He has major connections with the oil money. Be nice to him, Vic. He's a good friend of ours."

Dressed in her pumps and conservative dresses, in her favored colors of black and tan, Vicki started looking for houses again. She was almost twenty-nine now, no longer girlish, but still very beautiful despite the ravages of life in the war zone. She enjoyed the cruising, if for nothing else but the air and solitude. Houses, she found, had gone way up in price, and there were fewer on the market than there were prior to her nervous breakdown. Most of what she inspected weren't worth half the asking price, thanks to the big boom in California real estate. It would take more time than she had expected if she was to be satisfied.

Meanwhile, the months had gone by, and pretty soon the lease would be up at Tara. She started looking for rentals, and finally leased a house at 1611 Tower Grove Drive, a quiet cul-de-sac up on the rim of Benedict Canyon. She had room for the dogs, a view of the city, and privacy. When she told Alfred about it, he was pleased that she finally settled on something. By now, he was once again having problems with his cash flow, and a rental, instead of a big down payment, gave him an extra breath.

Still, Alfred wanted to see Vicki happy. "Do what you want with it," he instructed. "Buy what you need to feel comfortable. Furnish it, paint it... whatever you want to do. Then you can afford to take your time and buy the house you really want to live in."

Vicki took him at face value. She had twin ivory custom sofas and matching chairs made for the living room. She ordered thick, gray woolen carpets, glass tables and tall, white tulip floor lamps, and an expensive stereo system with speakers running into every room. She spent thousands for security gates and burglar alarms. She bought pots and pans, two refrigerators, black-lacquer bedroom furniture, and an ash-colored tweed, custom foam bed and frame, with five-hundred-dollar Pratesi linens covering the mattress. By the time she was finished, she had transformed the rented house into an acceptable domicile, all for $40,000.

She moved in with her son Todd and Mary Sangre. Although the friendship remained, with its interdependencies, the romance between the two women was rapidly on the wane. Vicki was bored and Mary was restless. By their nature they were loners who would be assuming the habits of spinsterhood if they weren't careful. Mary decided she would visit friends in Europe the summer of '81, which was rapidly approaching. Vicki would continue lying out by the pool. But when she told Alfred that Mary was leaving, he did his best to discourage her. Vicki wondered why.

"I've been having terrible pains in my stomach," Alfred explained. He was nervous, dreading having to tell her as much as the illness itself.

"What was the matter with Sammy Colt? Remember? He had pains in his stomach, but he's almost over it now."

"I've talked to Sammy. Vic, it's different."

Vicki was frightened, her eyes were tearing and her hands were shaking. She tried to convince him all would be well. "Alfred, you need to see a doctor. Get it taken care of."

"I will, as soon as I return from London. I promised Betsy

I'd escort her to the Royal Wedding. Already got my bowler hat and tails," he said, referring to the marriage of Prince Charles and Princess Diana.

"Alfred, see a doctor before you go away."

"Naw, I'd rather wait until after."

"Why?"

Alfred rubbed his mouth with the back of his hand and glanced around her living room. He hesitated, sighed and finally came out with it. "I think I have cancer again," he said, looking her straight in the eyes.

# 22

ALFRED'S ILLNESS WAS diagnosed as cancer of the esophagus, and he was admitted to UCLA Medical Center at the end of August 1981 for what would be the first in a series of critical operations. A team of surgeons removed a third of his stomach and more than half of his esophagus. He spent two nights and three days in intensive care before he was returned to his private room. The second night in intensive care, he was rushed back into surgery for a ruptured ulcer. He contracted pneumonia, decreasing his chances of pulling through. A priest was summoned to give him last rites, but Alfred fooled him and lived. He would survive the subsequent nine months, playing brinksmanship with death. Illnesses plagued him and complications exacerbated his suffering. Alfred was dying; it was only a matter of time.

Betsy Bloomingdale tried her best to keep it quiet. When friends asked, Betsy told them that Alfred would soon be well. She, like Vicki, didn't want to believe it was the last roundup, that he was knocking on heaven's door. In the company of her husband, Betsy was cheerful, trying to take his mind off his pain by keeping him up on the latest gossip, relating her tales of the banquets and parties, asserting he'd soon be well enough to attend. After each operation, she moved her husband into a different room, claiming she was superstitious. Whether they loved each other, or hated each other, it must have been difficult for her to see him fading away. So she kept her visits brief, and started travelling, preferring to take her mind off the imminent death of her husband.

While Betsy visited Alfred, somewhere in the hospital Vicki Morgan was hiding out, waiting for her to leave. Vicki wore a nurse's uniform to keep from being recognized, pulling her hair back into a ponytail and wearing boxy, crêpe-soled shoes. Almost every day she was there at Alfred's bedside, assisting the nurses, changing his bedsheet and washing him down with sponges. She seldom slept anymore, and when she did it was with the aid of sleeping pills. Without them, she'd lay awake at night, crying, praying for his recovery.

But Alfred knew better. A month after his first operation, it was discovered he had a ruptured spleen. He was in constant agony and beginning to lose control. He could feel what remained of his former self draining from his body. The doctors, however, believed the ruptured spleen, given the spreading cancer, was comparatively minor, and, as is their common practice, didn't want to operate for fear of complications. In time, perhaps it would heal.

It was the end of September, and Vicki was attending an open house given by Todd's high school when she called the hospital to receive her daily update concerning Alfred's progress. Alfred was not in his room. Panicked, she telephoned Mary Sangre, who picked her up and drove her to the hospital, where they discovered Alfred had suffered a relapse and once again had contracted respiratory pneumonia. He had undergone surgery and been moved back into the ICU. Vicki and Mary remained overnight at the hospital, sleeping on sofas in the visiting area. In the morning she was permitted to see Alfred, despite the rules that normally limit visits with a patient in ICU to family members only.

Alone in the Intensive Care Unit, Vicki approached the bed, calling softly to Alfred. He didn't respond to her whispers, so Vicki drew nearer, only to recoil in horror from the vision before her. What was laying in bed was not Alfred anymore, but his decaying vestige. He was old and weary, his face all rutted and gray. Tubes were everywhere, connected to his body and running to the machines responsible for monitoring his life. There were tears in his eyes, the agony of expectation apparent on his face. Alfred had realized his time had come, and since his death was imminent, he didn't want to suffer.

"Vic," he cried, sobbing uncontrollably as she knelt at his side, placing her cheek against his. "Vic, I just want to die. I can't stand it anymore. I just want to die."

Vicki refused to accept the fact that he was dying and remained at his side, diligently working to help him, hoping to boost his spirits. Of the different tasks she had assumed from the nurses, one of them was rubbing a special cream on his back in order to prevent severe rashes and bed sores. While doing so one day, she discovered a lump rising from under his shoulder blade. Vicki was frightened and summoned the doctors who soon diagnosed the initial signs of edema, the internal poisoning that was spreading throughout his system. Within a couple of days, huge blisters appeared on his back and his chest, while swelling his scrotum to hideous proportions. His infected testicles were the size of a couple of oranges. Alfred was again rushed into surgery, and his scrotum was lanced and drained of the poisonous fluids. While in surgery, his blood pressure dropped to critical levels, endangering his kidneys.

Before Alfred's illness had forced him into the hospital, he and Betsy had been scheduled to give a dinner banquet at the Bel Air Country Club in honor of Edwin Meese. Needless to say, the show went on. While Alfred lay in intensive care with his attendant nurse and Vicki Morgan at his bedside, Betsy hosted the banquet with her inimitable aplomb.

"It's hard to believe he's hosting a banquet tonight," quipped the duty nurse who had spotted the announcement in the *L.A. Times*. She shook her head and stared at Alfred, noting the machines to which his body was connected. Alfred's mouth was wide open, there were tubes up his nose, his eyes were dark and hollow, his face gaunt. He was in so much pain they had been giving him shots of morphine. The nurse clucked and turned to Vicki. "The man's at death's door. I would've never thought it possible."

Despite her grief, Vicki smiled at the nurse, acknowledging that yes, indeed, it all was pretty absurd. While Betsy, his wife, attended banquets and parties, Vicki, the mistress, attended to Alfred. She wondered what Betsy would do if she learned that Vicki was there at Alfred's bedside, watching him drift away, losing touch with reality, having succumbed to what doctors describe as ICU psychosis, the affliction suffered by normally active patients who have been bedridden for periods longer than they could stand. She pondered Betsy's reaction if, like Vicki, she had seen her husband flail wildly about, punching at machines, ripping the tubes and needles out of his skin, grabbing at nurses, shoving, clawing at them until they were forced to restrain him by tying down his arms. And then Vicki began to cry. The vigil of watching Alfred suffer was starting to destroy her. She was exhausted and traumatized, unable to function or think about anything else. Her delicate chemistry was reaching a serious imbalance. Her anxieties were causing her hair to turn gray. She was being victimized by the experience, yet she remained instead of bailing out.

The new year began, and Alfred's kidneys were failing him. Abruptly, for reasons unknown to his doctors, they restored themselves and started functioning again after a week on the kidney dialysis machine. However, he had lost his hearing, a frequent consequence of severe kidney malfunction, which left Alfred feeling helpless and disoriented. In addition, his deafness forced Vicki to communicate everything in writing; she jotted down sentences on paper from the note pads she now carried with her. It was a disconcerting process, painfully slow for two active people who were so used to speeding unhindered through their lives and times. Out of sheer frustration, Alfred would break down and cry.

"I don't want to die here," he'd implore. "Just let me die at home."

Before he could be discharged from the hospital, Alfred was again rushed into surgery. Blood was pouring from literally every orifice in his body, and he was given massive transfusions that barely compensated for his blood loss. The emergency operation lasted for hours, until a surgical laser was successfully employed to stop the hemorrhaging from his stomach. Once again he was placed in the Intensive Care Unit. After several days he was finally returned to his private room—a different one, since Betsy, who was said to be superstitious, insisted it be changed after each crisis.

"Does she keep changing rooms because of me?" Vicki wondered, as she stood at Alfred's bedside and wiped the perspiration from his brow.

Alfred hesitated and thought for a long time before he finally replied. "No, it's not because of you. She's trying to keep them from getting to me. I think they're trying to kill me."

Vicki trembled and started crying. Because of his semi-coherent condition, she remained dubious, but his words had an impact nevertheless. "Alfred, what are you saying?" she scribbled in a shaking hand.

Again Alfred paused before responding. "All that bleeding the doctors couldn't make sense of. Rat poison makes you bleed from every part of your body."

In the end, Vicki dismissed it by chalking it off as a manifestation of his ICU psychosis, and not really anything more. It was difficult enough for her to acknowledge that he was dying of natural causes. She could never believe that someone was trying to murder him.

Two days later the bleeding started all over again, and

Alfred was rushed back into surgery. The doctors didn't think he'd make it. They were wrong.

A month later, and nine months after he had first entered the hospital, Alfred Bloomingdale was discharged from the UCLA Medical Center. As a result of his series of multiple ailments, he was psychotic, deaf, and reduced to almost half of his original weight. And although Vicki Morgan had stayed by his side, it was Betsy Bloomingdale who took him home. He spent all but the last three weeks of his life tucked away in his separate bedroom in a rented hospital bed. A private-duty nurse was with him constantly, as there were three of them working eight-hour shifts, twenty-four hours a day. Vicki got to know them all quite well, but it was Jan, the male nurse from Holland, to whom she was the closest. Jan had been inspired by Vicki's concern for Alfred's well being, and he did his best to keep her posted on the state of his health. Jan arranged for Vicki to visit Alfred, when Betsy, who was travelling frequently, was gone from the house. Except for his brother, and a couple of others here and there, she was his only visitor.

Vicki would sit in a chair at Alfred's bedside and pass scribbled notes to him. She also brought the letters she had written at home, which attempted to explain her despair and frustration. She was annoyed that Betsy had received support and encouragement from his friends, while Vicki was simply ignored. She was angry that Alfred had not spoken up for her, had not praised her out in the open, where she believed it really counted.

"It's a terrible thing to sit and watch you waste away," she wrote. "It's awful. I don't think you understand the toll it's taken on me."

"Vic, I love you," he said. "You don't know what you mean to me. The only reason I care about living is because of you. Otherwise, I could go right now. It wouldn't matter. It would only relieve the pain."

Vicki shook her head in exasperation. He didn't understand. She didn't wish to be harsh with him, but her resentment was building, ready to burst inside her, not from the months, but from the years of self-doubt and unrest, the years she spent waiting. "Alfred," she began, "I know you love me, and I know it's not just talk that you care. But I'm the one being left alone like this. In the hospital I had to dress in a nurse's uniform. Here I have to sneak in to see you. You know why? Because I'm the hired help."

"Vic, please don't say things like that."

"Say it?" she hollered. "I have to write it down on a goddamned piece of paper!"

Jan interrupted them before Alfred could properly respond to Vicki's charges. Perhaps he had an answer, or he might have been relieved by Jan's intrusion.

"Betsy's coming home tonight," Jan reminded them. "It's time for Vicki to leave."

Alfred reached for her hand, but Vicki snatched it away, whirled, and raced for the door. She was sobbing and didn't want Alfred to see her like that. "Alfred, I love you," she called over her shoulder, forgetting he couldn't hear her, never turning around. "I'll always love you."

With that she departed, as Jan followed behind her, trying to calm her down. "He loves you Vicki," he assured her. "He worships the ground you walk on. He thinks of you and he wells up and starts crying. 'Jan,' he says to me, 'one day she won't be able to come anymore, and I'll never see her again.'"

The last time Vicki saw Alfred was the day she had arranged for Jan to bring Alfred to her house for lunch. Some of Alfred's friends were also invited. This was to be a very special meal, including all of Alfred's favorite dishes from the restaurants he preferred. Vicki spent more than a thousand dollars, although she didn't pay for the food. Duke's, the Palm, and the Polo Lounge had presented her with complimentary servings in tribute to Alfred Bloomingdale. The money went for elaborate floral arrangements, silver shells for the seafood entrées, crystal glasses and virtually every accessory from the best of *Town & Country.* It was a "Betsy table," as Vicki called it.

Alfred was all smiles and feeling proud when he cast his eyes on the table. "Fabulous, darling. Just fabulous," he said before sitting down in his favorite chair. Jan, the male nurse, quickly stuffed cushions behind Alfred's back, in order to prop him up. He was slumping more and he tired easily. He looked to his friends, who smiled and tried to joke with him, forgetting he was deaf.

"Write it down," Vicki implored, handing out pencils and tablets. "Please remember! Alfred can't hear you."

Despite Vicki's efforts, it remained an awkward situation. Alfred's friends had trouble relating to him. Perhaps they saw in him the vision of their future, when, in due course, they too would be subjected to enfeebling ailments, causing pain, humility and subsequent alienation. And when they saw he needed assistance in feeding himself, it was about all they could stand. They were confused and embarrassed, eager to beat a hasty retreat. Alfred was mortified as he observed the telling signs of his friends' anxieties. He stammered and began losing control of his thoughts.

To make matters worse, Jan had bad news for Vicki. "She knows you've been at the house," he said, referring to Betsy. "The houseboy told Robert, and he told his sister. It was Lisa who told her mom."

"Does Alfred know?"

Jan shook his head. "I figured it was up to you to tell him."

"Thanks. You were right. I should be the one."

Vicki sat alone with Alfred and carefully wrote it all out for him. "It won't be taken lightly," she had written. "You can't be afraid. You have to be stronger than ever. It'll go hard on you, if she's been told. And you know you're not well."

Alfred read the note carefully and then struggled to his feet. "Jan, I gotta go," he said, before turning to Vicki. He bent over and kissed her, tenderly stroked her cheek. She looked into his eyes and saw he was too weary to be frightened.

"Don't worry," he said. "I'll handle it, like I always do."

Vicki watched Alfred hobble from her house, knowing she would never see him again. Sure enough, Betsy hired guards to prevent Vicki from visiting her lover. With the lawyer and accountant standing beside her, Betsy persuaded Alfred to transfer power of attorney, giving her total control of the Bloomingdale fortune. According to Vicki, Betsy dismissed the nurses, locked the door to the bedroom and, alone with her husband, persisted for nearly six hours, demanding Vicki's name. A failing Alfred resisted her for as long as possible, but finally gave it up.

Soon after, Betsy cut off Vicki's check, setting in motion one of the largest scandals reflected on any American administration. Because these two women, who had shared the same man for the past twelve years, couldn't resolve it amenably, or at least, discreetly, Alfred Bloomingdale, a member of Reagan's kitchen cabinet and an appointee to the Foreign Intelligence Advisory Board, and his wife, Betsy, best friend to Nancy Reagan, and one of society's most notable hostesses, would soon have their names plastered all over the world, right along with Vicki Morgan. Alfred Bloomingdale died in shame, Betsy was ruined and Vicki was left penniless. If it did anyone good, it sure beats the hell out of me.

# 23

IT WAS THE English playwright William Congreve who wrote, "Heaven has no rage...nor hell a fury like a woman scorned." He certainly knew his stuff. First it was Betsy, who in June, having discovered the sums of money Alfred had given Vicki over the years, acted with what appeared to be total disregard for possible consequences. She seized control of all holdings and cut off the checks to Vicki. Then it was Vicki's turn. When three weeks had passed and no checks had come, Vicki determined she would have to sue the dying Alfred Bloomingdale to obtain satisfaction. She, like Betsy, believed she was in the right, having continually received Alfred's word that he would "always take care of her." In addition, back in February, only five months earlier, Alfred had drawn up a pair of contracts, one which promised Vicki $10,000 a month for two full years, beginning March 1, 1982. The second agreement provided Vicki with half of Alfred's million dollar interest in Showbiz Pizza, a nationally expanding franchise chain, provided, of course, he finalized his investment.

Vicki had few friends to whom she could turn for legal advice. There was her friend and lawyer, Michael Dave, but she was reluctant to go to him. There were Sally, Janis, and Rebecca, ex-husbands, lovers and her mother, Constance Laney. In essence, after years of living the high life, of hobnobbing with celebrities and rulers of the world, Vicki was close to no one whose opinion she trusted when it came to recommending a capable attorney. Vicki wanted someone formidable, someone with pizazz. She would probably have been wiser to have used discretion and retained a conservative individual, one from a prestigious law office, known for its dignity and clout. But Vicki was impatient; she needed money and wanted revenge. Not only had Betsy cut her off, but many of Alfred's friends had as well, now that he was clearly dying. She selected Marvin Mitchelson, largely because of his celebrity, the result of his winning the precedent setting Marvin *vs.* Marvin palimony suit, in which actor Lee Marvin was ordered by the court to compensate financially and share community property with Michelle Triola Marvin, his unmarried live-in. It all sounded swell to Vicki. Mitchelson, as promoted by the media, appeared as the woman's champion, a redoubtable seeker of justice.

On July 8, 1982, Vicki filed a $5 million lawsuit against Alfred Bloomingdale. Later it was doubled to $10 million when Betsy Bloomingdale was included in the legal action. The suit, prepared by Marvin Mitchelson, claimed Vicki had agreed to relinquish all other ambitions to serve as Alfred's confidante, travelling companion, and business partner. In the three-hundred-and-twenty-page deposition given August 13, which she never believed would be made public, Vicki related the details of her relationship with Alfred Bloomingdale, including specifics regarding his sexual proclivities. She spoke of his multiple-hooker sessions, his passion for sado-masochistic practices, his love for her and his repeated promises to support her for life. It was a mistake, a strategy designed by Marvin Mitchelson that backfired and blew up in their faces. Instead of being intimidated, as the plaintiffs had calculated, Betsy steadfastly refused to settle out of court and instead authorized her attorney, Hillel Chodos, to make public Vicki's highly controversial deposition.

Predictably, the media had a field day. Vicki and Alfred

and the details of the more sordid aspects of their twelve-year relationship were broadcast throughout the world. Responsible newspapers and magazines joined with the rag sheets and gossip-mongers in describing the more titillating details. It was a fun story, a regular circus. Vicki was besieged by clamoring hordes of paparazzi. They swarmed all over her house, taking pictures through the windows and calling out from the streets. And while the distinguished cognoscenti of New York and Beverly Hills traded anecdotes and rumors, Vicki, aghast at what had happened, retreated and stayed out of sight.

She had never thought it would all lead to this. She, like Mitchelson, had believed Betsy would capitulate. Back then, on the day her story had first hit the papers and before the media had obtained her private listing, Vicki had sat alone by the phone waiting to hear from what remained of her friends. No one called. Just like that, the telephone was silent. Vicki stared hard and began to wonder what was happening. One hour passed, then another, until fear and rage began to dominate her emotions. The deadly silence was more terrifying than any thundering shock wave. Vicki slowly began to realize the party was finally over.

"Oh my god!" she cried, as rage overwhelmed her. Nausea pervaded the hollow pit of her stomach, tears filled her eyes, and she began to tremble. She raced through the house, overturning tables, smashing lamps and dishes, then collapsed into bed, where she remained for days and weeks at a stretch, consuming barbiturates and tranquilizers.

But then the phone started ringing...only it wasn't friends, but newscasters and journalists, demanding exclusive interviews, wanting to know under what sign she was born. But despite the extensive and potentially lucrative offers, Vicki kept silent, refusing to add to the travesty by exploiting herself in the media. She believed granting interviews and appearing on television would only subject her to a gauntlet of indignities. She was already near the

261

breaking point...further humiliation she simply couldn't bear.

To make matters worse, Alfred died without her knowledge. On August 2, 1982, just three weeks after Vicki sued him, Alfred was rushed to St. John's Hospital in Santa Monica, where he had presided as chairman of the board. To avoid publicity, and perhaps for other reasons unknown to me, he was admitted under an assumed name, and that's how he died on Friday, August 20, alone, wasted, and forced to pretend he was somebody else. Less than sixteen hours later, Alfred Bloomingdale, a converted Catholic, was laid to rest in Holy Cross Cemetery in a secret service attended only by his immediate family. His death wasn't announced until that following Monday. It was only then that his brother, his friends, and Vicki Morgan learned that Alfred had passed away.

Approximately two weeks later, at the request of Hillel Chodos, attorney for the Bloomingdale estate, the case came before Superior Court Judge Christian E. Markey for summary judgement. Unfortunately for Vicki, the judge didn't see it her way. Ruling her relationship with Alfred Bloomingdale was "no more than that of a wealthy, older, married paramour and a young, well-paid mistress...and ...was explicitly founded on meretricious (paid) sexual service...adulterous, immoral and bordering on the illegal." Markey rejected the bulk of the suit, claiming also that since the couple never lived together, the Marvin *vs.* Marvin palimony case was not an applicable precedent. Only the portions involving the two written contracts listed in Vicki's suit were left intact. A year and a half after Vicki's murder they would be decided in her favor.

But when September ended in 1982, Vicki Morgan found herself in desperate straits. Her case had been lost and her money was gone. She had been branded, stranded, and eaten alive by the media. She was shocked and confused and flirted with suicide. But lurking inside, at the heart of her being, was a need for vindication. She would see it to the end, she determined. She would go down fighting, having mustered the few remaining shreds of arrogance and geniune anger for the one final assault. She would write a book and tell it all.

Even this was easier said than done, as Vicki and friends solicited the cream of literary agents; they rushed at her and then ran away after a couple of meetings. No reasons were ever given—none that made sense, anyway, since it was unanimously agreed that her book was indeed commercial. Vicki was frightened by the back-off, but all the more determined. She would eschew the big guns and do it herself. She would sit down with a writer.

Weeks passed and no writers appeared with whom she was satisfied. Some of her friends insisted she collaborate with a woman. A woman, they believed, would be more sympathetic and better able to integrate the crucial elements of Vicki's story. But after conducting several interviews, Vicki didn't find this to necessarily be the case. As many women as men had wanted to be overtly exploitational, churning out in a couple of months tawdry fluff that soon would be forgotten. And many writers of both sexes offered to serve as ghostwriters, a suggestion that Vicki deplored.

"If you're gonna write this book," she told them, "then you'd better have the balls to stand up to it. It's the only indication that you'll do the best work."

Finally, Vicki turned to Michael Gruskoff, who provided her with the names of several writers. Vicki met separately with each of them. She talked and listened and put them through her numbers. But as it was fated, I would write her story.

Now, here we were, nine months later, caught up in a love affair as we tried to write the book. And with the passage of time, her story wasn't simplified, but appeared

263

increasingly complex as perceptions and histories were intertwined with fantasies and facts. To unravel it all was a massive task, painful for Vicki and chaotic for me. The harder we tried to straighten it out, the more difficult it became. If it wasn't domestic or financial distractions hindering our progress, then our romance would get in the way. The intimacy that had brought us together was starting to break us apart.

Vicki's money was all but gone, adding to the anxiety and the pressure. Although I had picked up the groceries every now and then, we had agreed at the beginning that it would be inappropriate for her to take money from me. Even when I offered, she had steadfastly refused it.

"Thank you, but it's a matter of pride," she laughed. "I need to change my habits. I'd rather take it from strangers, or those who owe me, rather than take it from you. Besides, it's not like you're rolling in cash."

"No, it's not like that at all. But you're almost out of money."

"Marvin Pancoast wants to move in with me," she explained." You remember...faggot Marvin...who used to work at the William Morris Agency. He'll do most of the chores and share the expenses. He isn't working and needs a place to stay."

"Why? What's he doing?"

"He just got out of the nut house and is collecting disability. Marvin always tries to kill himself whenever he loses a job."

Marvin had been coming around for several weeks now, initially in the late afternoon, gradually extending his visits to the mornings and evenings and eventually staying the night. Meanwhile, Vicki had failed to mention her doctor's warnings that Marvin could harm her. She preferred ignoring this danger to rejecting Marvin's services. Later this would prove to be a fatal mistake.

"Try to be nice to Marvin," Vicki exhorted. "You scared him last time. That's why he's not been around."

"I don't remember scaring him," I argued.

"It doesn't take much," she smiled. "Marvin's in La-La Land. He's dingy. You can't believe a thing he tells you, so be nice, but pay him no mind, if you know what I mean. He can't be taken seriously."

Later, I would wish I had spoken more with Marvin Pancoast. I now believe he knew a great deal about Vicki's past, especially concerning her relationship with Alfred, much more than she had wanted him to reveal. And Marvin never appeared to be as daffy or as stupid as Vicki, and later, Marvin's longtime associate, Arthur Barens, would depict him. But knowing me, it's likely Vicki realized a slip from Marvin's mouth would start me thinking, asking more questions. Time and again throughout the last couple months of her life, Vicki would urge me to disregard him, not to talk to him or encourage him to talk to me. If Vicki felt better having Marvin around, then I wouldn't oppose it. This way she'd have her obsequious, *yenta* sidekick and Marvin would have a purpose in life.

What I saw was a terribly strange relationship, joint portrayals of master and slave. Vicki ordered him about like a dog, and willingly Marvin obeyed her. It was hard to watch sometimes. Whining, slump-shouldered, tall, and slender, he walked around with a stiff-gaited shuffle, deriving pleasure from Vicki's abuse. He ran errands, did the laundry, the cooking, the cleaning, and a variety of chores. For tension release, Marvin took off into the late night for anonymous back-alley sessions that regularly occurred in the driveway behind an adult bookstore. Dutifully, he'd return to Vicki's, unless she told him not to. But either way, when morning came, he'd be walking the dog. He always offered and never argued. For a low-budget operation, servants like this were hard to find, and Vicki, who throughout the years had gotten used to being waited upon, couldn't resist such a bargain.

In addition, Marvin upped his value by obtaining from his doctor a Valium prescription, supplementing Vicki's rationed supply. He served as Vicki's chauffeur, and as we began to argue and I grew intolerant of all the distractions, the stalls and the fits of depression, it was Marvin who would soothe her by listening to her reminiscences. They would talk about the good old days, waxing nostalgic about Vicki and Alfred, cutting up on anecdotes, recalling their stay in the bug house. And when Vicki learned she would soon be evicted from her North Hollywood condominium, it was Marvin, harmless and self-effacing, who drove her around in search of another house. To bolster her spirits, he seriously offered to marry her.

"Marvin wants to marry me," Vicki had called to tell me. She was amused, giggling over the telephone. She was seeking my reaction. "He says he'll do it so Todd and I can be listed on his health insurance. Can you picture me as Mrs. Marvin Pancoast?"

"I can picture you as anything. Dress him in white and you wear the tux. The media will love it when they see your new bride."

"Do you think I should do it?"

"Do what?"

"Marry him!"

"Vicki, what in the hell do you want me to say?"

"Is it worth it for the health insurance?"

"You've gotta be out of your mind."

When Vicki turned down Marvin's marriage proposal things slowly began to change. Marvin was no longer as obsequious or diffident. Whatever he had in mind, he cared less and less about disguising himself and playing the role of Uriah Heep, the Dickens' character whose ambitions and ruthlessness were concealed by false humility. Marvin still obeyed Vicki's commands, but tension was building inside him. Traces of anger were revealed now and then. He started to lose his patience.

With eviction day approaching, Marvin and Vicki went looking for houses. They would drive for hours, perusing the classifieds, searching in vain for a rental Vicki would live in. Vicki hated the whole idea of stepping down to lesser digs, not to mention the actual task of moving. At times she wanted to leave everything behind—taking only the bare necessities—and stay with friends, sleeping on sofas or wherever she could. Divesting herself of her material possessions was more appealing to her than retaining souvenirs from a bygone era. She needed no reminders. She wanted to start anew.

But Marvin didn't see it that way. He was joined by her mother in claiming Vicki was being much too critical and unrealistic, in view of her modest budget. He lectured her about discipline and responsibility, believing that he, Marvin, was not merely a servant, but was there to change things, to provide guidance and a sense of direction. He was critical of her habits, as if Vicki's behavior was suddenly all new to him. He attempted to discipline Todd, once a stylish young preppie, but now, through a dramatic metamorphosis, a radical punker. Todd wore his hair in a Mohawk, wore bondage pants, combat boots, and leathers. He was acting tough while searching for order and purpose. It all had been so strange for him—his mother's sudden exposure and the subsequent lies she had told him. He was in no mood for Marvin and his authoritative postures.

"Go fuck yourself," he said, threatening violence if Marvin persisted.

Instead of taking it literally, Marvin whined and complained to Vicki, who was still treating him like a eunuch, emerging naked from the shower where Marvin stood ready with a nice clean towel.

It was becoming too much for me, all the conflicts and distractions. I was restless and annoyed. But I was never so outraged as the night when Marvin, serving as Vicki's liaison, called me at home to negotiate the evening's agenda. I was fit to be tied.

"Who said you could call me?" I demanded.

"Vicki said I should talk to you."

"Where is she? I want to talk to her."

"She's busy," he nervously answered.

"Look, asshole, you don't ever serve as the go-between! Do you understand me? If Vicki wants to know something, then she talks to me. Don't ever do this again."

As the days passed it was becoming clearer to me that he and Vicki were discussing more than superficial topics. Despite her claims that Marvin was an imbecile living in a fantasy world, Vicki was confiding in him, talking scams. Nonsensical ideas, such as feeding bits to the ragsheets, were discussed as ways to make money. The wilder ideas I passed off as their way of killing time. However, it was clear to me that Marvin was making his move.

"Has Marvin ever been with a woman?" I asked while returning with her from lunch one afternoon. Vicki, who was struggling with her house key, hesitated at first, collecting her thoughts by feigning preoccupation with trying to unlock the condo's front door.

"What makes you ask?" she inquired.

"Marvin's making a run at you. I think it's his bid to try to go straight."

Vicki, sighing, turned around to face me. "Gordon, look ...he's been trying now for thirty years. And for thirty more he'll hope and dream about sleeping with women. But in the end...he'll still be a faggot."

With that said, Vicki pushed open the door and stepped inside without turning around to look in my direction. I stared, wondering why she had been so abrupt and answered so tersely. Her remarks about Marvin were funny and probably the truth, but I couldn't determine Vicki's reasons for avoiding the issue. Something was up, I told myself. I would watch and wait and listen more closely.

# 24

MOVING DAY WAS only a couple of weeks away, and Vicki and Marvin still hadn't found a place. Disgusted and morose, a listless Vicki spent much of her time in bed while Constance Laney and assorted volunteers did most of the packing. Mrs. Laney complained bitterly, saying it was time for Vicki to take responsibility for herself. The free ride was over. It was time to get a job. Of course, Vicki was in no mood to hear all this, and the fights would start, the battles would rage, as they had for so many years, until Mrs. Laney would depart in a huff, swearing she'd never return. But she did return, usually a few days later, to resume the packing and the bickering.

While Vicki and Mother were fighting among the ruins, Marvin Pancoast was seldom around the house. He'd leave in the morning and return in the late afternoon, performing his chores before taking off for the evening at about the time I'd arrive at Vicki's. Sometimes he'd return before morning, but often he wouldn't.

I sensed that Marvin was avoiding me, and although I didn't care, I was curious, since on a few occasions he had mumbled something about visiting a friend of his at Cedars Sinai Hospital. His friend supposedly was dying of cancer. Months later, I would learn that this man, who was Marvin's Alcoholics Anonymous sponsor, was in fact under treatment for an ailing liver, not cancer, and has since returned to work in his flower shop.

In any event, despite what he claimed, I couldn't picture Marvin spending every day and part of his nights at the hospital.

"Did I scare him away again?" I asked, unable to imagine how that was possible.

"No, I did," Vicki admitted. Exhaling a long, steady stream of cigarette smoke, she sighed and gathered her thoughts. "I told him we were sleeping together," she sighed.

"What prompted it?"

"He was pressing me. I told you he's asked me before. But I always denied it. This time he started in about my sexual needs, asking me how they were being satisfied. I mean, he goes off into this whole big thing about it, telling me that if I wanted, he had someone to service me. I told him my needs were already being taken care of, thank you..."

"Who did he offer? Himself?"

"No," she answered, smiling, shaking her head then taking another drag on her cigarette. "His friend, the attorney. I've told you. He offered to take care of me if I let him handle my case. This was back in September, after I fired Mitchelson. He'd put me up in a condo, lease a Mercedes...money...the whole routine."

"You didn't want it?"

Vicki shrugged and made a face. "Obviously not. I'm not that kind of girl," she added, lightening the mood. She was laughing, pausing to consider. "I don't know," she went on, turning serious again. "He was kinda slick and slimy. After suffering with Mitchelson, I was looking for someone conservative and dignified, like I should've done in the first place. I didn't think this one was any improvement.

"Anyway, that's who Marvin suggested. I said, no thanks. Then he asked me if I was sleeping with you. I warned him not to tell anyone, otherwise I'd kill him."

"I don't care if Marvin knows or not," I said, alarmed by Vicki's reaction.

"I do," she declared. "He has a big mouth. Marvin's gotten around this town, you know. He's made the circuit, the wealthier gays with kinky side trips. Producers, actors ...agents. Some famous people have had their way with Marvin Pancoast. He gets them to help him, but then he screws it up. He likes to impress them. I told you, he's a regular gossip. I know what he's told me about others. Plenty. I can't imagine what he's said about me. You get my drift?"

I was angry that Vicki had held this back from me. After all the lecture sessions warning her against getting involved with the wrong kind of people, those who would exploit or abuse her, largely by betraying her confidences, now I learn that Marvin, the same Marvin who drove her around and talked to her constantly, was now making sure he was absent whenever I was around.

"Vicki, what's going on around here?" I demanded. My eyes were wide, glazed, boring into hers. "What's happening that I'm not supposed to know about?"

"What do you mean?" she asked, turning away from me.

"You know what I mean. Between the dirty deals and the laundered money, you know too much. Things you haven't told me...so tell me now...what the fuck are you up to?"

"I'm not up to anything," she responded. Suddenly she was angry and scowling. I could see her body fill with tension, her eyes widening as she vainly attempted to stare me down. "What are you worried about?"

"I don't need any trouble."

"It's really no concern of yours. You're married. One day you'll leave me and I'll be alone again. It's no good. You really don't care about me. Even Michael Dave tells me the lawsuit will have to wait. He can't take a deposition from Betsy until he gets back from his pilgrimage to India."

"His what?"

Vicki got to her feet and poured herself another measure of wine. I stood up from the table and followed her as she wandered into the dining area.

"Every summer they visit their guru."

"Look, August first is when our contract expires. It's not too far away."

"So?"

"We haven't been working. I keep asking you to read what I've written, but lately you've been putting it off. I want to go over the outline, but you can't be bothered. We sit down to talk about things and you go on about Todd, his friends, and their basic teenage troubles. Everyone's running out on you and your life is totally shit. Fine! But what's gonna happen when the contract expires?"

"Then we'll have to renew it. Won't we?"

Instead of being reassured, I was suspicious. She had failed to turn around and look me in the eye, preferring to keep her head down, her back to me. Her voice was unusually low and measured. I had struck something. Fear—but not your ordinary, every day variety. This was fear in the realm of greater consequence. Only I wasn't sure what had brought it on.

"If you have something to tell me, then why don't you say it now?"

"Why don't you trust me?" Vicki retorted. "There's nothing going on."

"I can feel it."

"No, you're wrong. I hate it when you question me like this. What makes you do it?"

I shrugged. "Self-preservation."

Something was the matter. Despite everything she said, I refused to believe her, trusting my instincts more than Vicki's denials. She was an unconvincing liar, tentative, nervous, and easily read. Unable to lie or drive me off with her histrionics, she resorted to aloofness and tacit formalities. It was strange. Our conversations were restrained, our thoughts punctuated by increasing periods of silence. Distrust and hostility pervaded the atmosphere. Occasionally the mood would shift and we'd be affectionate and attentive. Try as we might, those moods refused to linger, and in the end, only served as a brief respite before the final destruction.

War broke out one July evening, provoked by a minor conflict that had escalated out of control. I was sitting at the dining room table, reading and doodling, when a nervous and pacing Vicki suddenly dashed over, snatched the pen out my hand and closed the books and papers. I said nothing at first, just stared at her in amazement. Not since I was in fifth grade had anyone made a move like that.

"It's unhealthy for you," she said, referring to my doodles. Although they were abstract and somewhat grotesque, they were more humorous than shocking, hardly worth the commotion. But Vicki was very upset, shaking and angry. "You shouldn't draw those ugly creatures."

"Oh, fuck this," I shouted, getting to my feet. It was almost two in the morning and I wanted to leave. I was angry, suspicious and in need of a break.

"Gordon," Vicki called. "I'm sorry."

I sighed and began to slow down. "It's not that," I explained, gesturing toward the dining room table. "It's the way you've been acting. It's everything. You're starting to make me sick."

"I love you," she called as I opened the screen door and started to leave. She wasn't trying to persuade me to stay, but she didn't want to see me go. She had spoken in that sing-song tenor, that special inflection which insinuates sacrifice and the pain of bidding farewell. She was camouflaging her motivations for no apparent reason. Perhaps that's what angered me the most. It wasn't like her. If anything, Vicki was excessive when it came to speaking her mind.

"Don't give me that," I argued. "For weeks now you've been walking around with your head up your ass. You don't want to work, you don't want to talk. . . ."

"And I really don't want to fight, either," she interjected.

"Then what are you doing? I mean, this is all too much. I'm tired of it. It's bullshit, if you ask me."

"Then go, Gordon. I don't care anymore. About any of it. You don't understand. . .you couldn't possibly."

"It's all too much for you, right?"

"See? Your attitude. You really don't care about me."

With that said, Vicki turned and headed for the kitchen. Angry, wanting answers, and cursing stupidly, I followed behind her. "You better talk to me," I warned her.

Vicki ignored it, opened the refrigerator and extracted the magnum bottle of wine, which by now she had almost finished. That was all I needed. I snatched it away and shoved her into the kitchen cabinets. My sudden gesture had frightened her and she didn't move. My fingers were around her collarbone, my hand was pressed against her chest.

"Now you'd better tell me what's happening."

"Just get off of me," she hollered. "Leave me alone."

I did, reluctantly, after a series of verbal exchanges didn't yield a decent explanation. But soon the argument started up again. Vicki slammed down her wine glass, shattering it on the kitchen floor, causing Katie, her Doberman, much consternation. Naturally, the dog had to be trotting across the linoleum at precisely that moment in time. Shards of glass were getting underfoot, cutting her paws. Vicki went storming back into the dining room, while I cooled my temper by pausing to sweep up the glass. I returned to the dining room, hoping Vicki was calmer. She wasn't.

"Get out of here," she ordered. "I'm going upstairs."

As she got to her feet I grabbed her by the upper arms. Angrily I forced her back down in the chair. "You just sit right the fuck down, and tell me why you've been acting like this. It's not fair. There's something going on and you'd better tell me what it is."

"I told you, I don't want to speak to you. Don't call me! I don't want to write the book with you. We're no longer working partners."

"If this is what's been on your mind, then why didn't you just come right out and tell me? Instead of being up front about it, you gotta raise a shit storm. Typical Vicki!"

"Just leave me alone. I can't stand this! I never want to speak to you again."

"You're sure about that?" I asked, as Vicki stood and walked by me, climbing the stairs to her bedroom.

"Get out of my life, and stay out," she hissed at me, while crouched at the top of the stairs.

"You've got it!" came my final declaration as I turned and stepped into the night. I was distraught and exhausted, but was also filled with a sense of relief. The battle was over. The war had been lost.

I knew I would never call her. Usually, I would be the first to apologize, good old magnanimous me, but with Vicki, in this case, it would signify weakness, and I'd be treated with scorn. Besides, I was tired, and as one day and then the weekend came and went, I had resolved it was all for the best. I had just about convinced myself, when on the following Tuesday I got a call from Vicki. She greeted me warmly. She was charming and calm, articulate and sober.

"I think we should talk," she proposed. "At least we should settle our business."

"There's nothing to settle," I told her.

"What about the book?"

"Fuck the book. I really don't want to talk to you."

"Why?" she asked.

I called her names, told her she wasn't serious, was drinking too much, and wasting away in her misery. But Vicki wasn't about to get angry. Her unusual self-control made me suspicious. No matter what I said, or how I said it, Vicki kept her cool; normally she'd be off in a rage.

"Alright," I relented. "If you want to talk, then I'll see you tonight around seven-thirty. But only if there are no distractions. No kids running through, no phones. And get that asshole out of there. You want to talk, then we'll talk alone."

Little did I know that I had almost set myself up as the fall guy, had her murder occurred as I believe it was planned. For Vicki had cleared the house, and she waited alone for me to arrive. She was clear-eyed and sober when she greeted me at the door. She had set her hair and made up her face, something she hadn't done in weeks. She wore a designer's hand-painted tee-shirt and a pressed pair of jeans. There was a gleam in her eye and a trace of a smile on her mouth. A patterned silk scarf was tied around her throat.

"Todd's away for the night," she told me when she greeted me at the door. "And Marvin's out for at least a couple of hours."

In Vicki's condo we had rarely used the living room. But on this night we did. The sofas, the chairs, our formal manner of sitting, the polite exchanges, the feeling out, it all took us back to our first meeting some nine months prior, when we had started out at opposite sides of the room. However, I wasn't conscious of this, never gave it a thought, but maybe Vicki had, since she took the chair and gestured that I take the sofa.

"Well. . . I'm here. What did you want to talk about?"

"I wanted to know what it would take for you to organize and arrange the information so someone else can write the book." She was whimsical as she discussed her proposition, as if it were a joke to her, a means of breaking the ice. It almost felt like someone had put her up to it and Vicki, for reasons unknown, had agreed to go along with the program.

"Who's been talking you into this?" I wondered, having

reacted to her tone of voice. "Whoever it is, tell him to kiss my ass. I'm tired of being helpful."

"Right away you have to get angry," Vicki retorted. "I'm trying to be fair with you. And I don't want to go through it all over again, the story of my life. You've gotten enough of it to help someone with the organization."

"You fired me, remember? Let's keep it that way. You go back to the starting line and I'll go take a hike."

"I can't go through it again. Not alone, with a stranger, having to explain.... That's what I thought you could do. Explain me, and what I'm looking to do."

"Sorry. I couldn't do you justice."

She got angry. "Why can't you just make a list for me ...people, dates, places. You've got it down somewhere. And I'd pay you. It's better than ending up with nothing."

"How much?"

"Maybe something like fifty thousand."

I laughed at her. After listening to her go on about her struggle for pocket money, the casual mentioning of fifty grand appeared to be rather bizarre. "You have the money?" I tested. Admittedly, I wouldn't have been surprised if Vicki said she had.

"No. Not now. You'd get it when I sell the book." She paused to think. "Maybe before. First I have to make a call."

"Let's discuss it when you get the money. Besides, that's not what I came here to talk about. You've got   a lotta nerve to aggravate me like you have, with all the accusations, the simple-minded tests. Maybe others thought it was cute. I don't. So grow up already! And stop playing games."

"Don't even talk to me about playing games," argued Vicki. "Why didn't you call me? That was the least you could do."

"You said you didn't ever want to speak to me. You told me not to call. So I didn't. I never would've called you. Don't you understand?"

"The least you could do was apologize. Here," she said,

pulling the scarf away from her neck. "Look what you did to me. I'm black and blue. So are my arms, where you grabbed me."

"I'm sorry for that. I really am."

"You push me around. You don't even call."

"Hey, Vicki...? I said I was sorry. I am sorry, so let's just cool the dramatics. Okay?"

We were off and running, getting down to what really had ailed us. To our mutual relief, business was the last thing on our minds. We were hurt and bewildered. We wanted to talk about us. What happened? What had come between us? These were the things that mattered. A friendship like ours was too hard to find for us not to respect it. We had come too far and shared too much to defile the experience with name-calling and irrationality. When tempers flared we cooled it down, since anger that night was a useless emotion. For this was a night of quiet affection, of high regard for our mutual rapport. If we were unable to get back together, then we could finally depart as friends.

"What do you see in me?" she wondered. "Why do you think I'm stupid?"

"I don't think you're stupid. Erratic, maybe, but hardly stupid. You've got a lot to offer. Where you've been. What you've seen. Christ, I've learned a lot from you. Good, bad, it doesn't matter. You have insights and talents, the skills of persuasion. But it's wasted, because you don't even know what you have. Vicki, if you only knew what you could really have done...you have so much potential, but you never understood it. You sold yourself short for trinkets and beads. It bothers me to no end. I get sick from it. I see you going under. It's like you're stuck in the quicksand and I'm holding on. I don't want to let go, but I can't let you drag me in with you. I love you. And I'm one of the few who even gives a damn. But with all this fear and depression, you're driving me out of my mind."

I was telling the truth, and she knew it. I saw it in her

face, the school girl's posture, the folded hands in her lap. Tearfully, silently, she listened as I lectured her.

"You should latch onto someone with money," I told her, wanting to see her reaction. "Go out and get married. In the long run, you'll be better off."

"I can't," she admitted. "I can't pretend anymore. Men see through it. They know I'm faking, that I don't want to be there. They can tell by the way I smile. My heart's not in it. Not even for the money."

"Why not?" I asked.

She looked at me with widening eyes. "I don't want to get into it," she muttered before she turned away.

"Because of me," I prodded.

"I told you I'd rather not say."

I let it drop rather than press it. We had talked for a couple of hours, and I had said what was on my mind. I stood up and prepared to leave, taking Vicki by surprise. She remained seated, looking askance in horrified silence as I collected my bag and my jacket. I looked at her, not knowing what to say or do.

"What about the book?" she asked. "We didn't finish our business."

"I'll let you know," I shrugged. "After I give it some thought."

She nodded, looked away from me, then turned to stare in my eyes. "Do you have to go?" she asked.

I stood over her, shaking my head in disbelief. "What am I gonna do with you?" I asked.

"I don't know," she whispered, standing, slipping her arms around my neck. She kissed me and started crying as she pressed her face to my chest. I lifted her chin and stared into her eyes. I knew I wouldn't be leaving her, not this night at least. It figured...here we go again.

Shortly after, Marvin Pancoast returned from his evening tour. He had stayed away an extra hour, generously allowing us three hours to finish our business. He figured I would be long gone, and was astonished to find I was still in the house. Marvin was enraged, nearly speechless. His face was red and scowling, his fists clenched, his body stiff. All those days of feigning subservience, awaiting his pay off, which he obviously thought was now at hand, had exhausted Marvin's patience. He was unable to conceal his hostility the moment he realized the best of his efforts had ultimately been in vain.

Vicki had betrayed him. He believed that. I could see it in his eyes. He had a scheme, half-baked at best, and it certainly didn't include me. I sensed the tension building in Vicki, who was suddenly very quiet. She nodded at Marvin as he stalked off into the kitchen. After getting something to drink, he climbed the stairs and flopped into Todd's vacant bedroom, which was directly overhead.

"What's the matter?" I asked Vicki.

"Nothing," was all she would say.

Joe T., a very dear friend of mine, had expected me at his house nearly two hours earlier. I had called once from Vicki's and postponed it. Only now, as I glanced at my watch, did I realize that I was running so late. Rather than call again, I figured I'd take the five-minute drive and speak with him in person. He wanted to know how things were turning out with Vicki. Having explained all this to Vicki, I departed, claiming I'd be back shortly. Vicki, I'm sure, related this to Marvin. With hindsight, I believe it's the only reason she didn't die that Tuesday night, because, had she died that evening, following our argument that previous week, with no one but Marvin aware we had at least reconciled our differences, then the blame for the murder would've fallen on me. Except for Marvin, I was the last one who would have been seen at her house. Moreover, I had demanded that she be alone when I came by to speak with her. No interruptions, and no distractions. That's what I had told her.

But I did come back, shortly after midnight, and stayed

up talking with Vicki until dawn. Marvin, meanwhile, paced overhead until two o'clock in the morning. This for Marvin was not customary behavior. He was never one for restless pacing, preferring instead to settle quietly, unobtrusively, losing himself in his thoughts. The sound of his footsteps was continuous and distracting, and the carpet did little to muffle them.

"What's with him?" I asked. "Why is he so restless?"

"Who knows?" was Vicki's answer, as she did her best to shrug it off.

Just before two A.M. Marvin made a telephone call. I had glanced in the direction of the downstairs telephone, a rotary line with several buttons, and noticed that one of the lights was on, signifying the phone was in use. He soon hung up, the light went out, and shortly after, Marvin was quiet. The pacing had stopped.

"Do you still intend to take a place with Marvin?" I asked.

"I don't know," she answered. "I'm not sure what I want to do."

"You don't have much time," I said. "Moving day's the day after tomorrow. Have you called a mover?"

She shook her head. "No. Not yet."

"Then what have you been doing? I'm sure since I've been gone you've been getting plenty of rest."

Her eyes widened, filled with anxiety, her head cocked to the side. "Like hell, I have. Like I told you, I went to an Alcoholics Anonymous meeting. Marvin took me to the one in Beverly Hills. Anyway, I realized I didn't need it, that I could clean up my act without it. It freaked me out...those confessions. I wasn't about to stand up and tell my troubles to the world, thank you. So I came back here and started to think about you. Marvin came home and I told him to leave me alone for awhile, to give me an hour. When he got back, I had him drive me past your house."

"About what time?"

"Maybe one-thirty," she said. "I was afraid you'd see us. Your car was parked outside."

Vicki suddenly changed her line of thought. "Why do I make you feel embarrassed?" she asked. It was a concern that had obviously been plaguing her.

"Vicki, that's silly. You don't embarrass me."

"Then why don't we ever go anywhere?"

"What are you talking about? We go to the movies, we go out to eat. You're the one who's afraid to be seen."

She nodded. "But you never tell your friends about me."

I couldn't believe it. "Vicki, you told me not to say anything. You made me promise up one side and down the other. Now you're saying the opposite."

Vicki sighed and shook her head. "After all I've been through, that doesn't matter anymore. I'd put it up on a billboard, on one of those things that gets pulled behind a plane."

"Great. So this is what's been bothering you?"

She nodded. "It's a lot of it. Yes."

# 25

AROUND SEVEN-THIRTY the following morning Marvin stirred in the upstairs bedroom. Dressed in his undershorts and tee-shirt covered by a plaid flannel bathrobe, he slowly descended the staircase, rubbing the sleep from his eyes. His face was creased from where the wrinkled sheets had left their impression. Although he was barely conscious, he was in a decidedly better mood.

"Were you two up all night?" he wondered, brightening our day with a knowing smile.

"Marvin, see if there's any coffee," Vicki commanded. "And check the freezer for bagels."

Dutifully, Marvin did what Vicki asked, reporting they were all out of coffee and bagels. "Only tea," he remarked.

"Then why don't you go to the store?" asked Vicki.

"It's all right," I interjected, slightly disturbed by the interchange between master and slave. "Let's just make the tea and have some regular toast."

"He can go," Vicki assured me.

Marvin was quick to agree. Self-sacrificing, his high-pitched voice echoing Vicki's sentiments, he volunteered for the job. It's all right," he said. "You two have been up all night. I've had a full night's sleep."

He got dressed and soon returned to the room. As always, I went to give him money, but Marvin politely refused. "We still have money," he motioned to Vicki.

"Here," she said, removing a ten-dollar bill from her jeans.

I watched attentively, noted the vibes as Marvin stood over Vicki and accepted the money. A non-verbal interchange was going on between them. She was uncomfortable and he, despite his willingness, appeared to be annoyed. Why were they making such a big deal about paying for the coffee and bagels?

"Marvin, would you please call my mother and tell her not to come 'til a little later? I have to get some sleep."

Marvin refused. "Vicki," he whined, "it's time you grew up. Tell her yourself. Be responsible."

So while Marvin ran his errand, Vicki called her mother and explained that she'd been up all night and had to get some rest. As it turned out, Mrs. Laney hadn't planned on coming until later that afternoon. Vicki was relieved as she hung up the phone.

"She's bringing Sharon, her friend, to help with the packing. But they won't be here until later."

After we ate, we went upstairs and went to bed for several hours. As usual, I was the first to awaken. It was after one o'clock, and I could hear voices and movement downstairs. I got dressed and prodded Vicki. "Your mother's here," I announced. "I think you'd better get up."

With that I was out of bed and down the stairs, where I found Mom and Marvin Pancoast chatting it up in the kitchen. Sharon Porto, Connie's friend, was busy packing in the garage. Having said hello to Mrs. Laney, I poured myself coffee and sat at the table. Marvin was washing dishes, standing over the sink.

"The All-Star game is on tonight," he announced, referring to the baseball classic. And then he expounded on his love for the Dodgers, complaining that Vicki was responsible for his missing the televised games.

"The All-Star game?" I repeated, ignoring what I'd

considered his typically catty nonsense. "That's great. I'll probably stay home and watch it."

I doubted there was anything I could have said that would have pleased him more. He paused from his dishwashing and stared up at the ceiling. A huge, shit-eating grin was spread across his face. I thought it was strange that he should react like that. In the months and years to come I would remember that moment, picture that smile and wish that I'd been more in tune to Marvin's intentions. It was the giveaway and I didn't catch it. Sometime after midnight, Vicki would be dead.

But that afternoon I warned her about Marvin, sensing something, but nothing so drastic as what was to come. "Take it easy on Marvin," I urged her while we were driving around looking at condos. "You're pushing him around too much. His feelings are hurt. He's acting strange."

Vicki mumbled something, but otherwise, she didn't seem to care. She brushed it off with a wave of her hand. "Don't worry," she said. "Marvin gets like that at times."

I dropped off Vicki outside her house around four-thirty, promising to call her sometime after the game. I didn't get around to it until about twenty after ten that evening.

"I thought you weren't gonna call me," she said. She was glad to hear from me. She was up, enthused.

"What time are the movers coming?"

"Around seven," she replied. "I won't wake you. I'll call you later instead, after we get organized."

"Are you taking that condo in Burbank?"

Vicki was laughing. "I'm not really sure. By the morning I'll know, after Marvin gets his money from his grandmother. He's supposed to leave around six A.M."

"Four," Marvin corrected. He had been laying beside her, watching television while we talked, which Vicki sometimes allowed him to do.

"Four," laughed Vicki. "Not six. Anyway, I won't disturb you. I'll call you later on."

She was off the phone, only to call back an hour later. She was pleasant, but seemed a little nervous. I chalked it up to her moving the following day.

"What are you doing?" she asked, her voice filled with innuendo. It was her way of asking me if she could change my mind and persuade me to come over.

"I'm exhausted," I said. "I thought you'd be sleeping."

"No, I'm too restless. Incidentally, Marvin wants me to buy out his Mustang when the lease expires. You know, the car I smashed up."

"Are you gonna do it?"

"I don't know. What do you think?"

"What for?"

Marvin was laying nearby, interjecting. I could hear him whining in the background. "Vicki," he pleaded, "If you don't buy my car my mother will kill me."

"Another country heard from," I quipped.

"Marvin, please don't annoy me," snapped Vicki. "You're not coming by?" she asked, returning her attention to me.

"I can't. Besides, it'll be a long day tomorrow. Get some sleep."

It would be the last thing I would ever say to Vicki Morgan. At six-forty-five the following morning, exactly a year to the day after she had first filed suit against Alfred Bloomingdale, the telephone rang. It was Constance Laney, distraught but still in control.

"Gordon, it's Vicki's mother. I'm afraid Vicki's not here anymore. Marvin apparently killed her last night with a baseball bat. The Montclair police were just here. I'm supposed to go to Los Angeles to identify the body."

# 26

IN THE DAYS that followed Vicki's death, grief and recollection were by necessity constrained to fleeting indulgences, superseded by the eerie reminder that I was possibly in danger. With the defense against personal harm as my first priority, Marcia, Casey, and I moved out of our house and stayed with my friend, Joe T. Despite the risk of danger and involvement to himself, his wife, and newborn child, he put us up in his guest house. Joe's house was actually a compound with an iron fence serving as its perimeter. If its walls protected us from nothing else, they guaranteed our privacy. Here, we were out of the reach of the media, the strange calls and the reporters cruising my street. After the bomb dropped regarding the "Vicki Morgan Sex Tapes," my house was deluged for days on end, with newspeople banging on the door as the telephone rang incessantly, driving our poor dog insane.

Joe would sit up through the night with me, listening to my thoughts and assisting me with my strategy. In the wake of Vicki's death, I was shocked, suspicious, and angry. However, I can't say I was all that surprised. From day one, Vicki and I had discussed the possibility that either she or both of us could be killed. Although it seemed unlikely, the thought never left our minds. And now, as I retraced the events leading up to her murder, I began to see more clearly how much of a threat there had always been. Following her murder I learned much about Vicki and Alfred from friends of mine, and the different contacts with whom meetings were arranged. Slowly, gradually, the picture was coming together. Alfred, I knew was rich and powerful, though initially I had assumed he was more of a namesake figurehead than a dangerous operator. But, in fact, I discovered he rode the range across some pretty volatile territory. I learned of his ties in business and politics, and connections in the underworld. I was told he had previously been blackmailed, that he was complex and vindictive and, in the years before he had served in the kitchen cabinet, he had gotten into legal trouble for extortion schemes and blackmail attempts of his own. No one could talk much about it, and no one really had all the facts, but too much was said in too many places for me to ignore the persistent accusations. Vicki, who had been a part of it all, apparently had left a few things out of her story.

Wonderful, I thought, as I chased around the city during midnight forays, intending to learn as much as I could. I was scared and angry, and I wanted to know who to look out for in the event that, despite his confession, it wasn't Marvin alone who had wielded the bat. That he was involved in her murder, I never doubted, having seen him build up to it in the weeks before her death. His general demeanor, his changing behavior, the smile that afternoon when I told him I wouldn't be there that evening, convinced me that he'd been involved in a plan that resulted in her murder. But Marvin alone? Had he been the one to have struck her so precisely, cracking her six times on the right side of the skull?

He had claimed she was drunk, or had been sleeping, and yet her hands were mashed, fingers were broken, one in each hand and there were contusions on her forearm which she had obviously raised trying to protect herself. In other words, despite her attempts to resist him, servile, obsequious Marvin kept right on slugging. He claimed that afterward he had left the house and driven his car to the local Big Boy for a late-night hamburger, but when he found it closed he went across the street to the North Hollywood police station, announced he had killed someone and then took a seat and waited patiently until a police officer heard his confession. There was no blood on his clothes, and his statement was short, sweet and to the point, which was uncustomary for Marvin Pancoast. He sold it as a mercy killing, claiming she was broke, depressed, and tired of living. But also, during his confession, a vitriolic Marvin maintained he had killed her in reaction to the terrible way she had treated him.

"I was tired of her Queen-of-Sheba attitude," he said, calling himself "her little slave." "I just wanted her to go to sleep."

The police, headed by Detective Sergeant William Welsh, apparently were convinced on the spot that Marvin had acted alone, for there is no record of anyone asking if Marvin had an accomplice. The police were so certain Marvin acted alone that, in contrast to their usual practice, after a cursory investigation and the removal of the body, they didn't bother to seal the house. Members of her family and a couple of friends were permitted to empty the condo of Vicki's possessions, taking with them, in addition to everything else, the bloodied bed on which she'd died. To top it off, forensic testing would later reveal there were no fingerprints on the murder weapon. Except for his confession, there was no evidence that Marvin Pancoast killed Vicki Morgan.

To make it worse, on July 11, the day of Vicki's funeral and four days after her murder, Robert K. Steinberg, a Los Angeles attorney, announced to the world that a mystery woman entered his office and plucked from her Gucci pocketbook three different video tapes depicting Vicki Morgan, Alfred Bloomingdale, a United States congressman, four high Reagan administration appointees, and three or four other women in hot pursuit of carnal knowledge. This magnanimous and civic-minded attorney declared he would destroy the tapes the following day unless they were formally requested by the President or his representative. Fat chance!

So the following day, Steinberg, who apparently had had quite enough of the limelight, with the media stampede in his office and with the press surrounding his house, beat a hasty retreat. He claimed he had left his tapes in a gym bag in his office overnight, and that someone had crept in and stolen them. Speculated Robert Steinberg, it must've been Larry Flynt.

"It's in my opinion that Mr. Flynt, or his agents, did steal them from my office," Steinberg claimed.

Flynt, the publisher of *Hustler* magazine, denied he stole anything, but did say that Steinberg had offered to sell him the tapes for $1 million in cash. Flynt then went on to aggrandize his newly gained celebrity by clowning around with both the media and the judicial system until he was found in contempt of court, fined, and thrown into jail. Months would pass before he'd reemerge from captivity.

Meanwhile, I watched it all on television. Several times a day there was an updated news brief—in-depth reports on every channel. From the moment Robert Steinberg sounded the clarion call, the media swarmed like bees in heat, searching for these alleged depictions of an active government sex scandal. No stone was unturned as the press interviewed anyone who even whispered they knew something about the tapes. Claiming such knowledge gave obscure people the chance to be on television, fulfilling their lifelong dream. All kinds of people suddenly claimed to know Vicki Morgan. Everybody, from Valley girls to a black psychic from Watts, got a chance to tell their story. And the press was spending all kinds of money to add fuel to the fire. Abruptly, with one woman's premature death, political competence was no longer judged by issues and actions, but by the collective belief that senior officials were lascivious dunces who were screwing around on the taxpayer's money. It was ludicrous to me that, without any basis of factual knowledge, on solely the word of one puzzled lawyer, the media would so readily and so irresponsibly pursue such an asinine story.

But they did. And I sat and watched it, thinking that one of life's tragic episodes was slipping from my grasp of reality, infringing on my privacy and mutating into a dark comedy of misguided myth and illusion. If the public wanted to believe there were video sex tapes, then, even if they had to embellish and decorate a rumor, the electronic procurers were there at your service.

Not since the War of Jenkins' Ear have things been so blown out of proportion. While the press got high on the prospect of scandal, Vicki's family, friends, ex-husbands, and lovers held a funeral service at Forest Lawn Cemetery in Burbank. Vicki and I were the only ones who didn't make it. Mine was a simple explanation. I couldn't bear the thought of standing around while these people acted sanctimoniously. However, Vicki was absent because someone screwed up the paperwork, and her body wasn't released from the morgue in time for the funeral. So, they made do with a photograph of Vicki, the one her mother liked the best. Michael Dave gave the eulogy. A few days after the funeral service, Vicki's body was cremated.

The night of the funeral service, a wake was held at Art and Sally Talbert's house, a million-dollar Normandy-style estate in the Canyon Country, a lonely, rustic suburb north of Los Angeles. The day before, I had called Sally Talbert, who had invited me to the funeral, and told her I wished to attend the wake. I didn't want anyone to know I was coming, having detected the first rumblings of the acrimonious scapegoating that would later thunder all around me. My intentions were simple. I was not attending to commiserate with the others, but to speak with Michael Dave in private. Since it was he who seemed in charge of things, and he was given updated information by homicide detective William Welsh, Dave's old high school buddy, I figured it was wise that we finally meet with each other, exchange our views and share what we knew about the murder.

Since the Talbert's house was off the freeway and down miles of darkened, empty highway, my friend Gavin came along for the ride. Not only did he provide additional security, but my instincts told me I'd better have a friend to serve as a witness.

"Wait 'til you see this," I cautioned, as we crossed the grounds and approached the house.

From all appearances, most at the wake believed in the celebration of life, as opposed to the normally muted grieving one finds on these occasions. With the exception of Constance Laney, sister Barbara, Sally Talbert, Robert Schulman, and perhaps a few others, Vicki's friends were extremely convivial, talking loudly and seeming to enjoy themselves. I'm sure there was a great deal more genuine pain and bereavement than what I saw upstairs in the Talberts' bedroom, where some had gathered, and downstairs in the living room. But what would the others do if they had music to dance to? I wondered as I heard them complain of the rigorous efforts they had spent in emptying Vicki's condo and the money spent for the funeral. Most important, everyone pondered how much money could be made from a movie and a book.

Mary Sangre and her actress friend Joanna apparently thought so. According to Sally Talbert, while I was upstairs talking to Michael Dave, they were downstairs pressing Mrs. Laney to give all rights to them. Meanwhile, I sat upstairs with Gavin and a bottle of cognac and waited for Michael Dave to finish with his tour of the mourners so we could have our talk. I wasn't thinking about books and movies. I didn't care that I'd been fired, or that nearly everyone in the funeral party resented me for getting involved with Vicki, learning their secrets while, in their minds, leading her astray. I was thinking too much about Vicki, the horror of it all, the suddenness. I was sick inside and missing her, searching through my memory, not for sentimental keepsakes, but for clues to the actual cause of her murder. In minute detail I retraced the previous events, the things she said, the abstract intimations and expressions, her behavior, even her most simple gestures. I remembered Marvin's comments, the awkward moment when she gave him money for bagels and coffee, and the Malibu lights that lined the sidewalk and how they'd been broken repeatedly for weeks before her death. When I had asked who was doing it, the only answer I received was, "The kids." I considered the way Vicki had ignored my warnings to cool it with Marvin. I remembered her allusions to a troubled weekend, and I wondered what events took place on the days when I wasn't around. I wondered what had gone wrong at the AA meeting and what had spooked her and caused her to flee. I tried to picture Marvin beating her to death; I tried to imagine him plotting, directing, and doing it all on his own. I considered the alleged sex tapes and reflected on Vicki's occasional comments, the things at which she might have hinted. And I thought about her dying at such a young age, alone and so cruelly.

Months later I would learn from different sources that Vicki, who up until now had shown little concern for her safety, had expressed to her sister and several friends, fears that she would be murdered. As to why she never divulged her fears to me, I can only speculate. Perhaps she remembered my earlier warning about involving me in anything stupid. Or it might've been that she wanted to protect me from possible repercussions.

But back then, I was also concerned about my personal safety, since I was the one who had been sitting and listening to her for the previous nine months. Obviously, out of instinct, and from the fragments of possibilities that I had logically assembled, I wasn't staking my life on the fact that wimpy Marvin Pancoast had for the first time in his life, without management, acted solely on his own. Of the fact that he was involved in her murder, there was no doubt in my mind. But Marvin alone? Really? Marvin alone? If it really was the case, then he was a living testimonial to this world of contradictions.

Michael Dave didn't have much to say. He seemed unconcerned with any imminent danger or with the way the investigation was being handled. What he did say was that there might be some validity to the video sex tapes since he was aware of one particular tape that existed in private.

"A very reliable source," Dave stated, "approached me, somewhat embarrassed, and told me of a sex tape involving Vicki, himself, and one other guy. A producer. A very big one. He used to work at Paramount. He said the tape has existed for a number of years."

"You're sure about this?" I asked, after Dave, who was being rather dramatic, staged reluctance before revealing the name of the gentleman in question who had formed the ménage à trois.

"I don't think the person who told me about it would have any reason to lie."

"What about the political sex tapes? Do you think they're real or not?"

"Vicki could've done it," Dave answered, "during one of her self-destructive periods."

I left soon after, but not before meeting with Todd, Vicki's son, who had been wandering alone on the grounds. Despite his punk attire and his tough-boy countenance, Todd was an intelligent, sensitive kid. Even then, after his mother's death, he remained calm and analytical despite the painful turmoil he obviously felt inside.

"Do you think it was Marvin?" he asked in all sincerity, becoming the only one who did.

"I'm not sure what it's all about," I said. "I believe it's Marvin, but whether he acted alone or not, I really can't say.

But I'll do my best to find out. I'll do everything I can. You do know, I loved your mother very much."

He nodded. "Can I call you?" he asked.

"Sure. I want you to."

Less than two weeks later, Todd and his steady girlfriend ran away and sought refuge in my house. Dutifully, after discussing it with Todd, I called Constance Laney, with whom I was then on speaking terms. I had listened to her questions and lamentations during her genuine time of grief, while doing my best to offer proper consolation. I knew that, despite their frequent battles, Vicki's rebelliousness, and the chaos of her early childhood, Constance Laney had a sincere but paradoxical love for Vicki, her youngest daughter.

Having informed Constance that Todd had showed up on my doorstep, she gave her permission for him to spend the night. We talked for hours, during which time he registered his disapproval of the attitudes with which he was surrounded. He was critical of Michael Dave, noting the pompousness and self-righteous attitude in dealing with the entire matter. He despised Montclair, and hated living with his grandmother.

"Can I come live with you?" he asked when he felt the time was right.

"No," I had to tell him, although I hated to, since I realized I might be condemning him to the same cycle of frustration his mother had suffered while growing up in provincial Montclair. Now it would begin again, and there was nothing I could do about it, since Todd was underage and I was under the gun. I could sense the adversity building all around me. If I wasn't careful, I'd be ass-deep in trouble. I had learned from former landlords that alleged private detectives, the kind that left no business cards, were checking me out. And it was at this point that Robert Wiener, a newsman from CNN, came to my house. Armed with theories provided by Arthur Barens, Marvin's defense attorney, he speculated that I was perhaps some kind of secret agent who was assigned to milk Vicki for her information and then arrange for her execution. Crap like this was very Kafkaesque, but I had to deal with it nevertheless. It disrupted my solitude, as I mourned the loss of a friend.

However, and perhaps with a twist of irony, the real gentlemen who arrived on the scene turned out to be the investigating detectives from the District Attorney's office, as well as Stanley M. Weisberg, the deputy district attorney who had been assigned to the Vicki Morgan murder trial.

Herschel Aron and Joe D'Virgilio were veteran officers, intelligent and well-mannered. Aron, who was on either side of fifty, had grayish white hair, which he generally complemented by choosing blues and grays in which to dress. D'Virgilio was the larger of the two men, with swarthy good looks and conservative dress. These were no children who came to the door that September 15, more than two months after the murder. Nor were they thoughtless, impersonal, hard-bitten veterans. They were tactful and sensitive, especially when discussing the more delicate, personal matters. I knew legally, since they didn't have a subpoena, I could ask them to leave or let them stay and talk to me. I decided to let them stay. I only wondered what had taken them so long.

"I want to assure you that we don't consider you a suspect," noted Aron, after we had sat down in my study. "However, we may want you as a witness when the case finally comes to trial," he added.

"Christ," I thought to myself two hours later, after they had gone, but not before assuring me that I would most certainly be subpoenaed as a witness. They had to be kidding. Though I anticipated it, this was one role in life I had never foreseen. I gave them a statement, but I would have preferred to stay out of the limelight and discreetly provide information. Who needed to submit to all that public scrutiny? It was a disturbing projection, to picture myself taking the stand, being subjected to Arthur Barens doing his Perry Mason act before the hungry television cameras. Barens reportedly had never before defended anyone in a murder trial, but with a case as potentially significant as this, perhaps he figured it was time he started. Clearly, from my reviewing the media coverage, I determined Barens relished his new-found celebrity, which was giving him the opportunity to sell himself to a city of prospective clients. I could see him now, this purported defender of justice, strutting around in his custom-tailored suits, his ego pumped up with delusions of self-importance.

After an additional meeting with Aron and D'Virgilio, and one with Stanley Weisberg, I became aware of the particular importance of my testimony. Marvin, as represented by his attorneys, had retracted his confession and was now pleading "not guilty and not guilty by reason of insanity," a rather perplexing plea. Because I had been the last one to talk to Vicki, and because it was I who had heard Marvin on the telephone, therefore placing him in the condo within the relative time of her murder, my testimony would be critical. With it, the prosecution would have an easier time ensuring that Marvin's confession would be admissible as evidence. Without his confession, there was no chance Marvin would be convicted.

And, if that was not enough to prime my civic duty, whether I liked it or not, it was clear I had no choice. Aron, while stopping by one day, assured me that "this is something that won't just go away." Speculations of friends who thought they were bluffing, proved inaccurate as the subpoena was served, and I was once again reminded of my judicial responsibility. Due to legal postponements of the starting date of the trial, I was under subpoena for approximately seven months. The idea of it, more than the reality, was bothersome and distracting.

But Stanley Weisberg, after a brief period in which we

were in conflict, displayed astuteness and sensitivity during my interview sessions and I began to feel more confidant about his ability to obtain a conviction against Marvin Pancoast. Weisberg was forty years old, slender and bespectacled, with large dark eyes and small-boned features. He had been with the district attorney's office for fifteen years. He dressed conservatively in off-the-rack outfits. In counterpoint to the showman's bombast displayed by the wealthy Arthur Barens, Weisberg was owlish, direct, and soft-spoken, making his points and then moving on. His style was that of subtlety, in contrast to Barens's obvious tactics. From the outset, I believed he would win. To assist his efforts, I did my best to recall all potentially salient facts. I offered my perceptions of Marvin Pancoast, since I was the only one who actually knew him and had any idea what had taken place on those days before the murder.

"Do you think you can get him convicted of murder one?" I asked Weisberg just before the trial got underway.

"I'm not sure," he shrugged. After thinking about it, he added, "I hope so."

In addition to Barens, Charles T. ("Ted") Matthews was retained to defend Marvin Pancoast. Matthews had once been with the district attorney's office—"for a short while," I had been assured by an uncomfortable Hershel Aron. Matthews was an obese and balding man, with glasses fronting his large rounded face. He wore ill-fitting, blue suits with brown socks and shoes that begged for a polishing. He spoke in a fluid, deep voice that would have served him well as a local radio announcer. He, at least, had some experience with murder trials, although one could hardly compare him to Clarence Darrow. Matthews would give the play-by-play, while Barens provided the color.

It has never been disclosed what Marvin's mother, who for fifteen years had managed some of Barens' real estate holdings, shelled out for this judicial tag team, but some maintain it was more than $100,000. For this she had my respect and sympathy. She maintained herself stoically throughout the trial while media persons and spectators alike hissed in derisive response to Barens's and Matthews's attempts at legal strategy.

Barens—who back in July 1983 had maintained he was not particularly interested in the sex tapes and then remarked to Robert Steinberg, "I didn't see how they would be relevant"—now reversed his position. As the trial began in the Van Nuys Superior Courtroom, almost a year later, in June 1984, he claimed the sex tapes were extremely relevant in proving the innocence of Marvin Pancoast and that he, Arthur Barens, would prove their existence during the defense phase of the trial. Melodramatically, Barens, the supposed "brains" of the outfit, undertook a massive fishing expedition.

"We have information that the tapes exist and that the government has them," Barens declared. He subpoenaed Edwin Meese, then nominee for attorney general, as well as members of the FBI, the CIA, the Los Angeles Police Department, the Rancho La Costa Country Club, and the Westwood Marquis Hotel. He also subpoenaed me and Marcia, my wife, who would eventually testify that I was home with her the night of the murder. God, how I hated dragging her into this mess. Not many would have been so supportive.

As to the confession, according to Barens, that "was the product of a crazy man and that confession can't be believed. He gave a version of her death that combined some fact with fantasy. Every probable fact, when contrasted with the murder scene, is wrong. If Marvin said it was raining outside," Barens would later comment, "I would go to the window and look."

What Barens never did explain were the reasons that this same crazy man should be accorded credibility regarding his claims that he had seen the video tapes and had spoken about them with Vicki. What he also didn't explain was how Marvin—who, Barens admitted, had spent the night at Vicki's condo and who Barens had placed in the same bed with the victim—had failed to awaken as Vicki was beaten to death. And what also wasn't discussed was Barens's own fifteen year relationship with Marvin Pancoast. This, among other facts, I had learned from Jonathan Beaty, of *Time* magazine after our paths had crossed during his investigation. A sickening feeling came over the four of us; Jonathan, his wife Linda, Marcia, and myself realized one night at dinner that it was Arthur Barens who for many years had exercised an extraordinary amount of control over Marvin. Ambitious Arthur... the very same man who, Vicki claimed, had approached her through Pancoast back in September 1982, and whom she had turned down. It certainly was food for thought.

Barens and Matthews did succeed in depicting their client as a totally repulsive individual, whose psychological profile included Marvin's extremely masochistic homosexual activities, his anger for women, and his need to be degraded. In addition, Barens and Matthews cited Vicki's possession of the video sex tapes, whose existence they never did prove. Furthermore, they claimed she was planning to use them for blackmail and erroneously maintained that, for months and not just weeks before her death, she was living in constant fear. And when that didn't appear to be working, "Slick Art" and his corpulent sidekick did their best to cast me as the murder suspect. Over and over they described me as desperate, strung out on drugs, and prone to bribes and suggestions from a mysterious secret agency that wished to do in Vicki.

In their closing argument, it was suggested that I hypnotized Marvin Pancoast into confessing to the murder. Matthews explained to the jury that I had accompanied the actual killer to Vicki's condo and kept the dog in control as the agent dispatched her, all while Marvin snoozed peacefully at her side.

"I suggest," said Matthews, "that Gordon Basichis called the house, woke Marvin up, and said, 'Marvin, you killed Vicki. It's your fault. You did it. You're responsible.'"

Wow, what powers I had that I was never aware of. To hypnotize over the telephone...that trick, along with the defense's closing argument had to be one for the *Guinness Book of Records* and *Ripley's Believe It or Not.*

"That," exclaimed prosecutor Stanley Weisberg, "is a whopping good story. He [Matthews] said nothing based on fact, but it's still a good story.

"He [Pancoast] had reached the point where he couldn't take it anymore," countered Weisberg. "Viciously, and with planning, premeditation, and after lying in wait, he struck Vicki Morgan again and again until she was dead."

On June 11, 1984, the trial began. Three weeks later, it was over. On July 5, just two days shy of a year since Vicki's murder, the ten-woman, two-man jury, which Barens and Matthews had believed would be sympathetic to Marvin's tragic plight, deliberated just four and a half hours before returning with a verdict of guilty in the first degree. Two weeks after that, the same jury decided Pancoast was legally sane at the time he murdered Vicki Morgan.

On September 14, Marvin Pancoast was sentenced by Judge David Horowitz to twenty-six years to life in prison. He's now at San Quentin serving his time, although attorney Charles T. Matthews has filed an appeal.

I believe he has about as much chance of winning the appeal as I have of flying to the moon on angel's wings.

IT'S BEEN NEARLY two years since Vicki's death and close to three years since the day I first met her. During all that time I have been committed to telling this story. For, despite the nine months we had spent together, when Vicki died I still didn't know all the facts. I doubt if I ever will, since so much of her life ran deep and wide, permeating treacherous landscapes. It is the way with such stories; they are never fully completed, they mingle with others, in this case my own, and the conclusions drawn will always be slightly flawed.

However, what does come to pass is a greater under-standing of the dynamics of power, romance, and human motivation. Like one who has gazed into a crystal ball, I have seen in myself both the reality and the illusion. I have suffered the anguish of loss and the discomfort of public exposure. But I have also been enlightened, and I have grown stronger from the experience. Most past mistakes I believe I'll avoid in the future, while a few, I'm sure, I'll probably make again. Such is life and such am I, imperfect but always the tenacious romantic.

Vicki is dead. As I said at the beginning, she lived way past her years and died before her time. There is nothing that can be done for her, except to remember her as a remarkable woman, who was unique and complex, with some extraordinary qualities blended in with foolishness and destructive characteristics. She was both good and bad, as most of us are—only she was more extreme. Never was she the two-dimensional *femme fatale* that the media had erroneously projected. To think that way, to judge her in such a manner, denies what truly exists and prevents an expanded perspective.

Much can be learned from unusual people, outsiders who sometimes make it. Whether they are successful or not and live to a ripe old age, or are overwhelmed early by their inherent, tragic flaws, their stories remain with the living, as examples of right and wrong. And it is through such understanding that we, in the end, can endure.